DIRECTING
ACTORS

To
Evelyn M. Weston
1924-1994

DIRECTING ACTORS

CREATING MEMORABLE PERFORMANCES FOR FILM AND TELEVISION

JUDITH WESTON

Published by Michael Wiese Productions
12400 Ventura Blvd. #1111
Studio City, CA 91604
tel. 818.379.8799
fax 818.986.3408
mw@mwp.com
www.mwp.com

Cover Design: Art Hotel, Los Angeles
Book Layout: CopyWrite Media Design
Editor: Bernice Balfour

Printed by McNaughton & Gunn, Inc., Saline, Michigan
Manufactured in the United States of America

Note: The information presented in this book is for education purposes only. The authors are not giving business or financial advice. Readers should consult their lawyers, accountants, and financial advisors on their budgets. The publisher is not liable for how readers may choose to use this information.

When You Comin' Back, Red Ryder? Copyright 1974 by Mark Medoff

Caution: The reprinting of *When You Comin' Back, Red Ryder?* included in this volume is reprinted by permission of the author and Dramatists Play Service, Inc. The amateur performances rights in this play are controlled exclusively by Dramatists Play Service, Inc., 440 Park Avenue South, New York, NY 10016. No amateur production of the play may be given without obtaining in advance, the written permission of the Dramatists Play Service, Inc., and paying the requisite fee. Inquiries regarding all other rights should be addressed to Gilbert Parker, c/o William Morris Agency, Inc., 1325 Avenue of the Americas, New York, NY 10019.

Library of Congress Cataloging-in-Publication Data
Weston, Judith
        Directing Actors: creating memorable performances for film & television / Judith
Weston
        p. cm.
    ISBN 10 0-941188-24-8
    ISBN 13 978-0-941188-24-1
        1. Motion pictures--Production and direction. 2. Television--Production and direction.
I. Title
PN1995.9.P7W45   1996
791.43'0233--dc20   96-25539
                                                           CIP

Books from
MICHAEL WIESE PRODUCTIONS

Directing Actors
Persistence of Vision
The Digital Videomaker's Guide
Shaking the Money Tree
Film Directing: Shot by Shot
Film Directing: Cinematic Motion
Fade In: The Screenwriting Process
The Writer's Journey
Producer to Producer
Film & Video Financing
Film & Video Marketing
Film & Video Budgets
The Independent Film & Videomaker's Guide

DIRECTING ACTORS:
CREATING MEMORABLE PERFORMANCES
FOR FILM AND TELEVISION
BY JUDITH WESTON

TABLE OF CONTENTS

ACKNOWLEDGMENTS

This book would not exist without some five hundred or so directors who have taken the Acting for Directors course and the Script Analysis and Rehearsal Techniques workshops. It takes courage for a director to study acting, to allow himself or herself to be on the other side, to partake in the vulnerable condition of the actor. I am always moved that students put themselves in my care and allow themselves to go places and do things they may have never done before. Even when I was completely unknown as a teacher, they were trusting and eager to learn. They constantly pushed me to define everything and to create tools that would be specifically useful for directors. They have truly taught the teacher at least as much as I taught them. I love and thank each one of them individually.

All the wonderful actors I have worked with as colleagues or taught as students have contributed mightily to this book as well, as have all the students in my Acting for Non-Actors classes, especially the first one.

I want to thank the teachers from whom I studied acting and directing: Jean Shelton, Wendell Phillips, Robert Goldsby, Angela Paton, Gerald Hiken, Lillian Loran, Jack Garfein, Harold Clurman, Stella Adler, Paul Richards, Jose Quintero. Especially Jean Shelton, my first teacher, the one who made me fall in love with acting. Her fierce insistence on the truth of the moment, her interdiction of "pedestrian" choices, her love of good writing, her passion for acting and for actors, imprinted me forever. She made me understand that finding and illuminating the truest truth in a moment on stage or film was a calling of the highest nobility — that it was worth doing, that it increased the value of life on our planet. And she encouraged me to believe that I might have something to offer the world as an actor, director, and teacher.

Soon after I started teaching Acting for Directors, students began encouraging me to write a book. Frank Beacham was the first with this idea. A number of students — including Paivi Hartzell, Cathy Fitzpatrick, Esther Ingendahl, Joe Syracuse, Lesley Robson-Foster and Peter Entell — shared with me their workshop notes as support and assistance toward the notion of a book based on my workshops for directors.

Frank also introduced me to David Lyman; this began a long and fruitful association with the Rockport Maine Film and Television Workshops. In Rockport I met Claude (Pico) Berkowitch and Bertrand Theubet, who brought my workshops to Europe, and pushed me to bring my coaching for directors to the "second level" with workshops in Script Analysis and Rehearsal Techniques.

But none of this was anything like a book until Michael Wiese came along, and I thank him from the bottom of my heart for everything — for being the genuine article, for trusting his intuition, for believing in me, and especially for his patience and support when the writing took a little longer than we thought it would. Ken Lee, of Michael's office, was a constant source of assistance, enthusiasm, and tact.

I received tireless, generous, insightful, invaluable feedback from those people who read all or part of the book in manuscript: Amy Klitsner, Irene Oppenheim, Claudia Luther, Polly Platt, Pico Berkowitch, Bruce Muller, Leslee Dennis, Wendy Phillips, Joy Stilley, and John Hoskins. Lisa Addario and Joe Syracuse also gave me crucial notes on the manuscript and helped in about a hundred other ways as well, as did Sharon Rosner. John Heller made a tape of one of my workshops, which was incredibly useful.

Finally, I am grateful to Dr. Carol S. Stoll, my family, all my friends, and most especially my champion, the source of my happiness and light of my life, my husband, John Hoskins.

INTRODUCTION

DIRECTORS IN JEOPARDY

"I knew exactly what I wanted, but I couldn't verbalize it clearly." "I thought I was describing it exactly as I wanted it, and the actor said, 'Yes, I understand,' and then he didn't do anything like what we'd talked about. So I just kept repeating the direction and the performance got worse and worse." "The actor was a star and she wouldn't rehearse, wouldn't take direction. She did it her way and that was that." "How do I establish credibility with the actors on the first day of rehearsal?" "Sometimes I can tell that something is untruthful or not working, but then I don't know what to do." "How much should I tell them? How much should they tell me?" "Sometimes under the pressure of being on the set, it's hard to see the performance — I can't see what's happening in front of me." "The production and financing problems took up so much of my energy that, once I got to the set, I was exhausted, I had no energy for the moment." "On a television series, the regulars already know their characters, they won't take direction." "How do I keep performance consistent, get them there and keep them there?" "I think I talk too much. It's easy for me to direct someone right out of the role, tell them too much." "I think I overdirect." "How do you rehearse? When do you say what?" "I need to know how to give the actor an on-the-spot solution, the one word that brings his performance to life." "Where is the button you press to achieve results fast?" "What do you do when you give a direction that worked in rehearsal and now that it's time to shoot the scene, the performance doesn't work anymore?" "The actors loved me and I felt very comfortable on the set, but when I got to the editing room it was all crap." "I think I overrehearsed." "When we don't have time, where should we put the main energy?" "I didn't want it to go that way, but I had no choice."

Directors want short answers to these questions, but in order to learn to direct the short way, you first need to learn how to do it the long way, then practice a lot until you can do it faster. Arriving at simple solutions takes a lot of work. If you happened to do it well the first time and thereafter you struggle, it may mean you had no craft, only beginner's luck. Or it may mean that you are in the grip of the learning curve — which is always two steps forward, one step back (unless it is one step forward, two steps back!).

There really aren't shortcuts. There isn't any kind of blueprint for working with actors that you can decide on ahead of time, and say, "I'm going to do exactly this and exactly that and it's all going to work." But there are principles, there is a craft, there is a lot of exhilarating, arduous preparation — and then you get to jump off a cliff without any expectations about whether it's going to work or not, ready to be in the moment when you get the actors there, ready to throw out every scrap of your preparation if you need to.

ACTORS: THE MYSTERIOUS "OTHER"

Directing film or television is a high-stakes occupation. It captures your full attention at every moment, calling on you to commit every resource and stretch yourself to the limit; it's the white-water rafting of entertainment jobs. But for many directors, the excitement they feel about a new project tightens into anxiety when it comes to working with actors.

The entertainment industry is conflicted in its attitude toward actors — actors are both fawned over, and looked down upon. Actors are an irrational and baffling "other." Many directors come from a technical background and know very little about how actors work. Directors who have come up from the production side of film may even have a prejudice against actors. There is often a feeling on film and television sets that, compared to the expertise and long hours required of the crew members, what actors do is not really work. After all, anybody who can walk and talk at the same time could do it, right?

Writers who turn to directing often become troubled and impatient with actors because the lines when spoken don't come out exactly as the writer imagined they would. Directors who are highly gifted visually and completely at ease with the camera are sometimes uncomfortable with dialogue, and hence with actors. And I am sorry to say that it is my observation that students can graduate even from prestigious film schools, knowing nothing about techniques of directing actors.

Indeed, most people seem to believe that directing actors can't be taught, that it's a matter of instinct and intuition, that you either have it or you don't. I find that many directors I meet, including talented and successful ones, are practically rudderless when it comes to directing actors, and worse, embarrassed about asking for help.

Most directors know that they could benefit from better communication with actors. The horror stories of breakdowns in communication between actors and directors are legion. It's easy to see how this can happen when inexperienced directors are paired with experienced, high-profile actors. I heard one story of a major star with a tough-guy image who, every time the director took him aside, would look up and say, loud enough for the crew to hear, "You want me to suck what?" Now maybe the veteran actor was trying to relax the young director by teasing him out of some of his earnestness — or maybe he was crudely letting the poor fellow know how stupid he thought the director's input was.

It's not unusual for actors to be dismayed at how little directors know about them. First-time directors typically put a lot of care into getting the most production value for the money they have available, but very little care and preparation into guiding the performances; as a result, the worst thing about low-budget films is usually the acting. And communication problems are not limited to low-paid, inexperienced directors. Sometimes well-known actors and directors are disappointed when they finally work together. Why? Because, with the exception of the handful of filmmakers with a background in theater or live television, who have had rehearsal experience, most do not have a reliable technique for working with actors.

3

THE CRAFT OF DIRECTING

Directing actors can be taught as a craft. It does not need to be mystified. Over the years that I have been teaching my courses in acting, script analysis and rehearsal techniques for directors, I have evolved a set of principles and an assortment of tools which are the subject of this book. These principles and tools are simple, not in the sense of simple = stupid, but in the sense of simple = basic. They are not esoteric or fuzzy-headed; they are objective and usable. If you wish you can think of them as a set of rules — they are that followable. They are not meant to be a cookbook, however; they are meant to open up for you your own priceless intuition.

There is no cookbook. You've got to completely let go of doing things "right." This is hard for a lot of people; it seems to go against all of our education. Although I've been teaching mainly in Los Angeles, I've also taught throughout the country as well as abroad, and have found that children everywhere basically are taught to please the teacher, do well on tests, and impress their classmates.

I want to change your minds around a bit. When I teach my class I take the students through a series of exercises, first with a monologue and then with scenes, and I ask them to be patient with me, to go with me, even if something seems a little strange. Because with each exercise we isolate some element of acting technique and examine its usefulness for directors, one at a time. Sometimes people get worried. They're looking for results, they're looking for performance, they're looking for the way to do it right, to not make a mistake.

You have chosen a profession where mistakes are not always bad. For brain surgeons or airplane pilots, mistakes are nearly always a bad thing. But for those of us lucky enough, foolish enough, to follow our dreams into the entertainment industry, a mistake can be a blessing in disguise; it can jolt our attention away from preconceived ideas and into the present; it can open us to a new creative path. Sometimes a mistake is our subconscious speaking, and we ought to listen to it. If anything, an artist needs to get kind of excited by mistakes.

You *will* make mistakes. We are mistake-making creatures; we were built that way. What you as a director, the person in charge, must learn how to do is to bring creativity and a positive approach to mistakes, your own and others'.

Artists tend by nature to be dark, worried, superstitious creatures. This is not bad. It makes you perfectionist, it makes you care. Moreover, the ability to see the darker side of life is an asset not just for directing dramatic and tragic movies, but also for directing comedy, since comedy often has pain inside it. But a director who is negative or who projects his own insecurities onto his actors is very bad news. I often tell my students that whatever problems their actors present them with — whether the actor is objecting to a line of dialogue or a piece of staging or the color of a wig or is forgetting his lines or hates her costar — they should say to themselves, "I'm glad this happened!" And mean it!

I offer you the exhilarating prospect of never again saying these four words: "I had no choice." Our jobs in the entertainment industry *always* allow us creative choice. If you want a rehearsal period, you *can* find the time and money for it; you might have to give something up for it, you might have to sacrifice a special effect or an expensive location, but you have a choice. If the producer of your feature film tells you she can't get the money for the project unless you accept a certain actor in the lead role — perhaps an actor you think is wrong for the part — you must make the *choice* to work with that actor or give yourself permission to walk off the project. Not that I encourage you to renege on your promises or give your word frivolously, but tackling disappointments with the sensibility that you are sticking with it *out of choice* gives you your freedom. And without freedom there can be no creativity.

Some students tell me that the ideas and techniques I put forward seem at first radical and destabilizing. One young writer said she found the things I was saying "counter-intuitive." At first I was surprised, but then I realized that many people mistake opinion for intuition. Opinions are easy to have; they require no reflection. Sometimes people think intuition is the first idea that comes to you, that intuition requires no reflection. This is not the case. In order to access your intuition, you need to get below your preconceived ideas and access your deepest resources. You need to recognize and reject pedestrian and obvious and clichéd choices.

I don't intend to dampen or make you distrust your intuition. You can't be a good director without good instincts. There is no recipe I can give you that will guarantee you'll have a good movie. Every rule I will give you can be broken, and should be broken if breaking it makes the movie better. Technique is not an end in itself. The purpose of technique is to prepare the ground for inspiration.

Everybody knows what to do when inspired! That's true by definition. But you can't *decide* to be inspired. And if you *try* to be inspired, the strain of the effort only creates tension, taking you farther and farther away from the effortlessness that characterizes inspiration.

Technique does two wonderful things: it gives you something to fall back on, something to do while you are waiting for inspiration; and it aerates your brain, makes you think, makes you choose — and then you are ready for inspiration, should inspiration decide to strike. When you are *working well*, you are in the safest place for trusting your instincts.

When you are not working well, you may confuse intuition with assumptions, you may mistake prejudice for vision. So I invite you to break habit; I invite you to question conventional wisdom, to get beyond your prejudices and assumptions, to go below the surface, and awaken your intuition at a new, deeper level. In other words, learn the rules. Then forget them.

This takes work, probably more work than you realized was involved in directing. But I'm going to take you through it, step by step. Once you get on the inside, you will feel liberated. And if you are among the happy few who already have a directing technique that works, then you already know how important it is to keep learning and growing; for you, the proposals and exercises of this book are intended to challenge, refresh, and stretch your skills and imagination.

Just one warning: I'm not going to teach you how to be "commercial." Trying to be commercial is just an excuse for not doing the hard work of being original. No one knows what's commercial anyway, not until the weekend box office figures are printed in the newspaper on Monday morning. In this business, people who claim they can assure you commercial success are not to be trusted.

THE ACTOR-DIRECTOR RELATIONSHIP

The very best actors make it look easy. Their technique is invisible, they seem to "become" the character, they seem to speak and move out of the character's impulses and needs, their feelings well up strong and apparently unbidden. They don't look rehearsed, they seem to be speaking their own words, they seem to be improvising. To the general public it probably looks as though the actor must be just like the character and must not have had to do any work to play the role. To people knowledgeable about the demands of performing, such a seamless portrayal is a touch of the divine, a miracle.

Rigorous technique and careful detail go into such performances. One of the things this book will do is to investigate the actor's world, his tools, resources, and training.

Sometimes directors ask me why I want them to know so much about actors. Is the director supposed to monitor the actor in each and every choice? Is the director supposed to guide the actor through Method "emotional memory" exercises? If the actor is having problems, should the director give acting lessons on the set? How much responsibility does the director have for the performances?

Acting and directing are two very different jobs. It is exactly because I think the director and the actor each should be — must be — free to do his own work that I believe directors should know more about actors and acting. This is why even actors themselves don't automatically know how to direct other actors. They are two separate skills.

Here is the crux of this sometimes painful, often frustrating but potentially exhilarating relationship: the director is the viewer and the actor is the viewed. The actor is exposed, vulnerable. The success of his contribution hinges on his ability and willingness to allow himself to be viewed without being able to view himself. This means he must surrender completely to feelings, impulses, and simple choices without knowing whether they are working or not. If he watches himself, the relationship of viewer/viewed is broken and the magic is lost. He depends on the director to stand in for the audience and to tell him whether his efforts succeed; he cannot evaluate his own performance. His central paradox is that this dependence frees him.

You are the one who gets to say, who has to say, "Yes, that's okay. Print," or "No, let's take it again." It's a giant responsibility. It's hard for a director who has never acted to understand its magnitude. You are the protector; only you can say whether the work is good enough. You must make sure the work is good and that the actor looks good, and so you have to know what is good work and what isn't.

Sometimes very intelligent actors hold back until they decide if they can trust your taste, intelligence, and knowledge. If the actor determines that the director can't tell good work from bad or doesn't understand the script or doesn't know how to tell a story with a camera, the actor retreats from the actor-director relationship and starts to monitor his own performance. He watches himself, he directs himself.

This is not good. Because if he is doing someone else's job as well as his own, he can't surrender his full attention to his own job. This is especially poignant because his own job precisely is to surrender, to live truthfully moment by moment in a structure of created circumstances; and the act of self-monitoring distorts what is monitored. If he watches himself, it shows. Experienced actors working with a bad director are aware of the dilemma and make a choice, either to follow poor direction or to direct themselves. Inexperienced actors subjected to poor direction often flounder.

If you understand the script, know how to tell a story filmically, can tell good acting from bad, and the actor is floundering anyway, it's not actually your job to make the acting better. It's the actor's job to find his performance and to adjust it if you ask him and to make those adjustments believably.

But if you are the viewer and they are the viewed, shouldn't you be able to tell actors when their performance is not good enough? And if you saw them floundering, if you saw them having trouble getting where they need to go, and if you knew how to help them — wouldn't that be great? You could help each other. For example, blocking (i.e., staging the physical movements of the actors) is part of the director's job but a lot of times the actors will help you with blocking. They'll say, "I have an impulse to move over there on that line," and you'll say, "Wow, that solves all kinds of problems."

The director's main responsibility — and prerogative — is telling the story. This means finding a structure to the script and setting up the events so that they are at once surprising and inevitable. You give the actor direction in order that the actor's actions and interactions illuminate and create those events. The actor has a responsibility — and prerogative — to create truthful behavior while following direction and fulfilling the requirements of the script. Actor and director must respect each other's creative territory.

On a practical level this could mean that an actor agrees that your direction is logical and apt, and wants to please you, yet cannot find a way to execute it and still be truthful to her impulses and understandings. This is because we are not dealing with chemistry formulas here; we are dealing with human beings.

At this point the actor and director can clash — or they can collaborate. I don't like to use the word "compromise" because that suggests that both of you are settling for something less than what you desire and believe in. It's more like a synthesis. Actor and director are thesis and antithesis; each prepares, each brings to the table his best understanding of the script and his own sovereign imagination; they face each other and give each other everything. Then something new comes out of that, ideas for the characterization that are perhaps better than either one of you thought of separately. The happiest response an actor can make to one of your directorial suggestions is, "That gives me an idea for something to work on."

This is the good stuff. Unlocking the subworld of the script, making discoveries, going places. Actor and director can do this work together, in rehearsal, or separately, and surprise each other; they can keep secrets from the other actors, even from each other; they can establish a level of communication at which only a word need be spoken. You may come up with the insight that turns a competent performance into an indelible one — you may be present and midwifing the creation of a character who continues to live in the audience's mind long after the movie is over. This can be addictive, working with talented actors on a high level of creativity, sparking and challenging each other's ideas and imaginations.

The level of trust required for this work is breathtaking. Jessica Lange, in a <u>Los Angeles Times</u> interview: "Actors are always at the mercy of the integrity of the director. It's a leap of faith, and sometimes you leap into the abyss and it doesn't pay off." Or Donald Sutherland, also in the <u>Times</u>, on the actor-director relationship: "I've often described [it] as sexual. I'm his concubine."

Actors refuse direction at their peril; they are throwing away the potential for an unself-conscious performance. And directors, once they cast an actor, should surrender the role to that actor; you must cease judging; it's time to engage. Sometimes you have to adjust or even let go of your ideas about the character if they finally don't sit truthfully on the actor. Always you must let actors know that whatever level of risk you are asking of them, you are willing to take yourself. People who are fearful of intimacy and confrontation should probably not become directors.

WHAT DO ACTORS WANT?

Here are the things that actors need from a director.

First, knowing when to say "Print." They want you to know when to say "Print" and not give up until you get there, and that is to say when the performance has life, and when what the actor is doing tells the story. To a really good actor, the worst sin a director can commit is to be satisfied with less than the very best the actor has to offer.

Equally important, the actors must have confidence that you understand the script, and that the characters and the events that befall them spring to life in your imagination. In other words, they must feel that your ideas are intelligent and imaginative and that you know what the movie is about.

Then, your understanding must be communicated: they need clear, brief, playable direction. If any. Perhaps it would be more accurate to say that they *don't* want vague, confusing direction. Actors are usually better off left on their own than trying to follow confusing direction. In any case, they need freedom and permission to explore the implications of your direction and to make it their own.

Last but best, they want to be pushed, to grow and to learn. A director with actual insight is a bonus, it's icing on the cake; actors don't expect it, but they love it. The highest praise an actor can give a director is to say, "I learned from working with her," or "He got me to do things I didn't know I could do."

WHAT IS IN THIS BOOK

Understanding the script and giving actors playable direction and freedom to explore and permission to make your direction their own are the main concerns of this book; I plan to give you simple, effective tools that you can use immediately. It isn't a question of merely memorizing a jargon. The techniques and principles I will outline have to do with understanding human behavior and applying that understanding to scripts and rehearsal situations. They are all geared toward making your direction briefer and more loaded.

For directors with extensive technical background, setting aside decisions about F-stops and special effects and dipping into these areas can be intimidating. It is easy to find yourself setting aside time for script analysis and ending up staring at the page with nothing coming to you. My techniques will give you some simple, practical alternatives to procrastination and despair. I even have charts that you can fill out if you find them helpful, but the purpose of this work is not to fill out charts. There is no cookbook. We are looking at ways to trigger your understanding, insight and ideas; to awaken your powers of suggestibility and invention.

Knowing when to say "Print" is something I don't think you can learn from any book, but this book will give you some food for thought, and ideas for what to look for as you practice and study and make mistakes and develop this skill.

Of course actors also need you to know where to put the camera and how to tell a story filmically. Where to put the camera is not dealt with in this book at all; I am going to assume that you already have some knowledge of the technical side of filmmaking.

Scaling the heights of the actor-director relationship, learning how to collaborate and challenge each other and grow together — that is, becoming an "actor's director" — will mean taking everything you learn from me and from all your other teachers and from everything you know about life, and making it your own and believing in your gift and giving your actors everything you have to give, with love, with passion, with humility — and then, having some talent and some good luck.

You don't have a choice about how much talent you are born with — that's already been taken care of. You do have a choice about whether or not to develop the talent you have.

RESULT DIRECTION AND QUICK FIXES

The biggest complaint I hear from actors is that directors don't know what they want. I expect this to come as a surprise to many of you, because I think most directors think they have a very clear picture in their minds of exactly how they want the movie to look and sound.

The problem is directors who don't know how to prepare.

Most people while reading a script watch a miniature movie version of it projected on the inside of their foreheads. They see with their mind's eye the face of the character (usually that of a particular A-list actor), they hear in their heads the lines read with a certain inflection, they project specific facial expressions and movements. No matter how many times they read the script, they see the same expressions, inflections, and movements. They call this their "vision" of the script, and they consider the time spent in such fantasy their "creative preparation." Then they get down to the "real work" of making budgets and deciding on lenses.

Why is this so bad? Because it limits you to the images of the script that fit onto a flat, four-cornered movie screen. It's like insisting that the earth is flat and that people (characters) who walk off the edge just disappear. It causes you to look at a line and say to yourself, "How can this be made dramatic?" or "How can this be made funny?" rather than "What clues does this give me to what the movie is about and what the characters are doing to solve their predicaments?" It causes you to make your artistic choices based on what you know about other movies rather than on what you know

13

about life. It denies any life to the characters beyond the four edges of the script's pages.

It also leads to directing the actors with what is known as "result" direction. Many directors have heard of result direction and been terrorized by warnings of its evils, but are not really sure what it is.

Result-oriented direction attempts to shape the actor's performance by describing the result you are after, i.e., how you want it to end up looking or sounding. The close kin to result direction is *general* direction. The preferable alternative to result direction or general direction is *specific, playable* direction. These terms are slippery. They are difficult to define. I remember that when I was first studying acting, it was years before I really understood what was so bad about being "general." And the problems of definition are compounded because within the acting and directing communities, the terms are sometimes used differently. Perhaps the gamest way to tackle the issue is to start by giving examples.

Okay. Here are ten examples of result direction:

1) "Can you make it more quirky?"

Telling the actor what *effect* you want him to have on the audience is a perfect example of directing by describing a *result*. Instructions of this ilk — such as "This scene should be funny," or "I need you to be more dangerous," or "Can you give him an epic quality?" — make an actor's heart sink. The director wants him to do something different from what he is doing — what can it be? From this point the actor-director relationship dissolves into a guessing game, because the direction is so vague. The actor tries something — is this it? Usually it never is, because the actor has begun to watch himself, to worry about how he is doing, and what the performance looks like. It is death to an actor's gifts to put his concentration on the effect he is having on the audience.

Describing to the actors the "mood" of a scene or the movie falls into this category; e.g., sultry, distant, electric, etc. Paradoxically, actors who try to play a mood can end up evoking exactly the opposite of what the director was hoping for: efforts to "look" serious often produce an unintentionally comical effect; efforts to "be" light and frothy can prove heavy-handed. This is because the attention is wrongly placed; the actors' eagerness to please you by coming up with the desired effect has caused them to concentrate on the effort itself; consequently the *effort itself* is the effect that finally reads.

If you want the actors' help in evoking a particular mood, you might try instead an imaginative **adjustment.** An adjustment can be an "as if." For example, if you wanted a "chilly" atmosphere in a family dinner scene, you might ask the actors to play the scene "as if" the first person who makes a mistake in table manners will be sentenced to a prison term.

Sometimes very experienced actors have worked out sets of prearranged adjustments that they can produce at will. They have a facility for coming up with a precise mood or some other result on demand. Directors are relieved — the actor has "nailed it." But such facility can come to substitute for a genuine, moment-by-moment connection to the material and the other actors. Actors call this "pulling out the old bag of tricks." An extreme example of an actor overusing her bag of tricks might be an actor typecast as a stock character old maid in movies of the thirties and forties playing every role pursing her lips as if she is constantly sucking on a lemon. If we want a performance of freshness, surprise, and insight, we want to ask the actors for more than what is facile for them.

2) "Can you take it down?" Or, "Can you give it more energy?"

These are the commonest requests actors get from directors. What's wrong with these directions is that they are vague or *general.* "Take it down" may mean that the actor is overacting, not listening to the other actors, or should make another choice. "More energy" could mean that the acting is flat, without inner life, or the actor is not listening or needs a different choice. But who knows? It's too vague — too general — to be sure what the director is objecting to.

And actors, when responding to these directions, can fall into bad traps. Asking for "more energy" can cause them simply to add emphasis to the uninteresting choice they have already made. "Take it down" may be interpreted as a request to flatten their affect or say the line in a monotone, and dampen their expressive fires. How can that be a good thing for an actor to do?

3) "Don't say, '*You* always do that.' It should be, 'You always *do* that.'"

This is called giving the actor a line reading, that is, telling the actor what inflection to give to a line. For the line "You always do that," there are at least four different line readings, because there are four different words you can inflect: "*You* always do that," "You *always* do that," "You always *do* that," or "You always do *that*." And the different readings make the line mean different things.

What's wrong with giving line readings? Well, one problem is that the actor might obey you, and repeat back the line with the new inflection but without any life behind it. Of course it is their job to give it life, but sometimes the line reading makes no sense to the actor; if he asks you what it means, you want to be able to do more to clarify the direction than just repeat the line reading over and over.

The *meaning* of the line, not the inflection, or result, is what the director should be communicating to the actor. It is the actor's prerogative to create the delivery that conveys the meaning that the director wants. The worst problem with giving line readings is that they may signify that the director doesn't really know what the line means, or what the **intention** of the character is, or what the scene is about.

4) "I think [the character] is disappointed."

Telling the actor what feeling the character should be having, or what state of mind to be in — for example, angry, disappointed, worried, annoyed, excited, in love, frightened, resentful, disapproving — is a very usual way that direction is given. It may seem radical of me to tell you not to do it.

But it is not actually a playable direction.

As soon as an actor *tries* to have a feeling, or produces a feeling on demand, he looks like an actor, not a real person. People in real life often find our feelings are *obstacles* to what we want to accomplish; we would prefer *not* to feel nervous at an important meeting, not to feel upset when an ex-lover and new spouse appear unexpectedly at a party, not to feel angry and disappointed with our loved ones. An actor caught trying to have a feeling is not believable. Watching an actor crank up his feelings is stressful to the audience and distracts them from the story.

A playable choice must be *choosable*, and *we can't choose our feelings.* This idea is sometimes very hard for people to take in, but I want you to think about it: *We don't get to decide how to feel.* For some reason we humans don't much like this about ourselves. Bad actors, as well as much of the general population, go to great lengths to make the world believe they feel something that they don't actually feel, but most of the time no one is fooled. Of course feelings can be hidden or repressed, but we can't selectively shut down just one feeling; when one feeling is held back, all feeling gets shut down. Clearly, this is not a desirable condition for an actor. Actors need to have their feelings available to them.

Emotion and impulse are the very province of the actor. The ability to be emotionally free and available to many subtleties of feeling is central to her talent. But feelings are pesky critters, cropping up inconveniently, and then disappearing just when you want them. And the thing both terrible and wonderful about feelings is that they change. You have seen it in real life; a person can be crying one minute and laughing the next. In fact the more you let yourself feel whatever you are actually feeling, the more available you are to a new feeling. This goes double for actors.

The director is in a position to do violence to the actor's delicate emotional mechanisms. It can have a shrinking effect on actors to tell them their emotions are wrong, as in "Don't play it so angry." When actors try to have "less" feeling, for example in response to the direction "Don't play it so angry," they may simply shut down or become cautious. When they try to have "more" feeling, as in response to a direction to "be more nervous," the temptation is to push, to overact. *Whenever* they try to have feelings because they think the character should have them, or because the director tells them that the character should have them, there is a danger of their acting becoming indulgent and actorish. At the very least a smidgen of self-consciousness is bound to creep into the performance. They may not believe it themselves — they may even ask you what emotion you want them to have — but as soon as you start envisioning the characters in terms of what emotion they should be having, you are losing the chance for a genuinely exciting emotional event to take place.

The character's emotional life is not off-limits to the director. The emotional events of the script and each character's participation in them are very much within the province of the director. It will be a major purpose of this book to suggest ways to approach that emotional life that are not so result-oriented as telling the actor what feeling to have.

5) "When she tells you that she doesn't have the money, you get angry."

This is an extension of telling the actor what emotion to have — telling her what reaction to have. Again, the notion that one can decide on, aim for, and deliver a particular reaction simply because one wishes to do so is at variance with our life experience. In real life we may wish we could plan our reactions — we may wish we could react calmly to bad news, or laugh merrily when a client or boss tells an unfunny joke — but it is the very nature of such occurrences that they take us by surprise, however gracefully or subtly we may manage to deal with them.

In a script these little or big surprises are the emotional **transitions** of the movie. For an actor, the character's transitions — her reactions to the emotional **events** — are the trickiest part of acting. It is the place where the acting is most likely to go sour and start to look like acting — when the transitions are labored, or forced, anticipated, telegraphed, indicated — or flat, not there. It gives a performance the texture of real life when the reactions are spontaneous and idiosyncratic. Whenever we (the audience) catch the actors working on their next reaction, it takes us out of the story.

Getting to the emotional transitions of a role cleanly, economically, believably and fully is the actor's most difficult task. In a movie, the characters don't know what is going to happen to them, so they don't know what they are going to do or say when it does. The actors, of course, do know. When the director, out of his prearranged idea of what the scene is supposed to look like, tells the actor to react this way or that on a certain line so it can look like the movie he has running in his head, the actor is being asked for a result at the very moment that connection to a *process* instead of a result would be the most valuable for her.

6) "When the scene starts he is worried because she is late. He is relieved when she arrives, but then disappointed because she hasn't got the money, and then he becomes suspicious that she might be holding out on him."

This is what I call a fully loaded *emotional map*, outlining all the feelings and reactions you have decided the character is supposed to have in the scene.

Mapping the emotional terrain of a character is my own term for what is sometimes called explaining the character or psychologizing the character. Emotional mapping, or explaining the character's psychology, commonly passes for an understanding of what the script is about.

At first glance, emotional maps look innocuous enough. You may be asking yourself, what could be wrong with this? How else would you describe a character's behavior? Everybody talks about characters this way, don't they?

In fact, people in real life talk about each other like this too. It's called gossip. Now gossip in real life can be harmless and fun, but it is not productive, and it can be harmful. Gossiping about characters — i.e., mapping their emotional terrain, or explaining their psychology — is likewise, at best, an uncreative waste of time.

Emotional mapping causes so many problems! First of all, it is tedious and long–winded. Directors need always to be concerned with ways to save time. Actors respond best to direction that is simple and to the point. I want you to learn briefer, more muscular ways to evoke characterizations than the convolutions of emotional maps.

Emotional mapping is almost always a superficial analysis of the script, usually no more than a regurgitation of the plot or dialogue. When actors try to follow an emotional map, the performance degenerates into an emotional connect-the-dots drawing, contrived, predictable. It can't flow, because it has no **through-line**.

The through-line is the way that actors believably connect to the character's emotional reality. One of these keys actors use to connect to their character's through-line is a sense of **objective**, or **simple intention**. I will be talking lots more about intention and objective, or **need**, later. But briefly, an objective is what the character *wants* from the other character, and the intention is what he is *doing* to get it.

Rather than drawing an emotional map, a director can better serve the actor by discussing the character's intention or objective. I'd love to give you an example of how this works, but because this is a book, let's pretend that the imaginary emotional map I outlined in the heading of this section ("he is worried because she is late," etc.) is a real scene and think about some possible objectives that might make it work. (All we can do here is come up with *candidates* for appropriate choices of objectives. We can't decide which ones will work unless we try them out with actors.)

At the moment, we don't have a script, or even a set of facts, from which to make a proper scene analysis, so I'm going to refer you to a list in the Appendix called Sample Simple Objectives. Let's take two possible interpretations of the imaginary scene. In the first interpretation, let's say the woman is not to blame for the missing money and the man is taking out his frustrations on her. Using that interpretation, the female could have the objective "to get him to put his arms around her," and the male "to get her to hit him." In a second interpretation, the man wants to trust her but she doesn't care much about him, and perhaps has betrayed him. In this scenario, the female could want "to make him cry," and the male "to get her to take care of him."

The purpose of this simplistic example is only to begin discussion about the difference between direction that is *experiential*, such as an understanding of what the character needs or wants, versus direction that is result-oriented and intellectual, such as emotional maps. If the actor's transitions become rooted in intellectualization rather than experience, she starts to telegraph them, or push; the work becomes forced or mechanical. The actor falls into what is called "indicating," that is, *showing* the audience the character's inner life rather than living it. A director who is interested in having good acting in his movie will do everything he can to prevent this.

7) "This is how I see the character..."

Talking about the character in terms of "what the character is like" is unproductive. This kind of direction is both result-oriented and general.

In the same way that we don't get to decide how to feel, we don't get to decide how or what to be. Just think of New Year's resolutions: sometimes people make a resolution that they are going to become "a nicer person," or "more decisive." It never works, does it?

21

If you have ever studied communication skills, you already know how ineffective it is to criticize someone's character; in other words to tell someone, "You're a bad person." It is more helpful (and indeed more accurate) to say, "You did a bad thing." You are giving them the opportunity to change.

Although people cannot change who they are, they can change what they do; they can pay attention to detail. To use our New Year's resolution example, a person could resolve to write more thank–you notes, and at the end of the year he might feel like a "nicer" person. Our indecisive person might need to do some research into decision-making skills. The good self-help books are very task-oriented. The ones that do nothing but exhort the reader to have more self-esteem are worse than useless; they add strain and self-doubt to the reader's burdens.

Likewise for an actor, trying to be "what the character is like" usually produces stress and self-doubt. Acting becomes an obligation, a burden. The character becomes some sort of Platonic ideal, a "character in the sky" that the actor feels she must live up to or become. I don't even like the term "in character" because it sounds static.

The actor and director need to break down their ideas about the character into a series of playable tasks. This takes insight and knowledge of human behavior, and it takes time. It is the actor's job to translate the director's result-oriented direction into playable tasks. But if actors keep getting result direction thrown at them just before the camera is about to roll, there may not be time to make it playable. So it helps a lot if the director gives direction in playable terms.

8) "Can you play him aggressive, but pleasant?"

You could call this the fine wine direction — "This character is frightened, but determined." "She is in love with him, but doesn't want to hurt her sister." "He is defensive yet vulnerable." "She is catatonic, yet curious."

Directors think that by giving a direction like this they are calling attention to the complexity of the character, but in reality they are asking for something completely confusing and unplayable.

People are surely complex, but they are not actually able to do two things at once. They may *say* one thing while *doing* another. Or they may rapidly alternate what they are doing from one thing to another. But that's not the same thing as being "cautious yet cheerful" at the same time.

An actor can't play two things at once. The two things cancel each other out. Or the actor ends up faking one or both of them. Now, of course there isn't only one way of creating complexity in a character — after all, it's complex. We'll investigate this issue more fully in Chapters on Actor's Choices and Script Analysis.

9) "He's a punk." Or, "She's self-destructive." Or, "He's a nebbish." Or, "She's a castrator." Or, "He's stupid."

These are negative **judgments** on the character. Judgment is the most dangerous consequence of deciding "what the character is like."

If the actor is not on the character's side, who will be? No one is born bad. Characters get to be who they are because of the needs they have, the things that happen to them, and the choices they make. The writer, the director, and the actor together create a character who, like all of us, has both good and bad sides; they approach the character *experientially*, placing him in a situation, allowing him to have needs and make choices — and not judging him. The *audience* gets to make the judgments, to decide who is weak, strong, ambitious, lazy, etc.

This idea is central to the artist-audience relationship. And it applies to all genres of movies. Suspense is delicious to an audience. The basic posture of the audience is *what happens next?* This is true even if we know that the hero is going to win, or the lovers are going to get together — even if the movie is a "character piece" and all its events are private and emotional. When the actor judges a character and telegraphs to the audience, "I'm the good guy," "I'm the loser," or "I'm the villain," he is playing a caricature — who can care what happens to him? When the director directs by telling the actors: "You are the hero," and "You are the villain," he is setting up a situation in which there can be no suspense, in which the actors will be showing us the end of the movie at the beginning. This is boring. The audience wants to participate in the emotional events of the movie, to feel something happen to the characters right in front of them. This is more likely to happen if there is in the characters some complexity and ambiguity.

But, you may say, what about comedy? fantasy? action-adventure? — where there is fun in the stereotypes and in the certainty that the hero will prevail. Well, this is exactly why people say that comedy is harder to do than drama, because you must have the style, energy, and special skills needed for the particular genre, while maintaining the integrity of the characterization. Even if you are directing physical comedy or live-action characters based on cartoon figures, it is just as important to find a central humanity to the character as when you are directing naturalistic drama. The performances of Michelle Pfeiffer as Catwoman in "Batman Returns" and of Claus Maria Brandauer as the villain of "Never Say Never Again" show that it is possible to meet the demands of a genre movie without caricature.

And of course serious drama loses any opportunity for insight or revelation when good and evil are portrayed without ambiguity. Villains portrayed as recognizably human are far more frightening than cardboard cutouts. Heroes whom we see making choices and coping with problems are more appealing than formula heroes. This accounts for the success of the movie "The Unforgiven": Gene Hackman plays the cruel sheriff as a regular guy who is doing his job; Clint Eastwood portrays the hero as a man with many misgivings about the rightness of his actions.

It is very disappointing for a good actor to work with a director who judges the characters. It may cause an instant loss of faith in the director or, at the least, a slow erosion of any chance to collaborate and create. The director, in his preparation, should approach each character as if he were going to play that character himself; he allows himself to believe in each character's reality. When he speaks to each actor, he takes the side of that character; he allows each actor to prepare a fully realized character, allows the characters to honestly conflict with each other, and trusts the script.

10) "Let's give [this character] a hostile edge."

I'm talking here about attitude, deciding the attitude, talking about the character in terms of his attitude. People often think that deciding the character's attitude is the way to develop the relationships of the script; for example, deciding the character has a wary attitude toward his brother, a tender attitude toward his sister, a hostile attitude toward his father, etc. This is vague and general. Characters and relationships created this way tend to be generic and formulaic.

The very grave danger in asking actors for an attitude is that in attempting to do as you ask they may start "playing attitude." By "playing attitude" I mean the difference between *doing* something and *showing* something. Playing attitude is playing *at* the character. Playing attitude is analogous to talking *at* someone rather than talking *to* someone. When actors play attitude they are posturing, they are showing us their performance.

They are not **listening** to each other. Nothing makes a performance look more amateurish than a failure to listen and engage with the other actors. The first thing a director should learn, and the first-last-and-always thing he should look for from his actors, is whether they are listening; that is, whether they are genuinely affecting each other **in the moment**, or whether they are just saying lines *at* each other, overlaying their words and movements with a predetermined, canned attitude or unction.

People confuse attitude with "edge." Edge has become a catch-all phrase. My impression is that most often when people talk about "edge," they are referring to something exciting and unpredictable.

The way to create an exciting and unpredictable performance is *not* by playing attitude, but by getting under the characters' skins and into their subworld, and by setting up an atmosphere of creative trust and freedom where the actors can engage and play off each other.

*   *   *

When you ask for a general result, the worst thing that can happen is that you might get what you have asked for: a generic brother-sister relationship, a clichéd villain, actors emoting, posturing, telegraphing the dramatic moments and forcing the humor, with no connection to the other actor or to the words or situation of the character.

Most of the time when directors give result direction or general direction, it means that the only ideas they have are clichés. They haven't gone beneath the most obvious, surface possibilities of the script. The choices themselves are pedestrian and uninspiring.

Whether your ideas are superficial or profound, if you frame them in terms of result, you need to understand that you are asking the actors first to figure out what you meant, and second to translate your wishes into something playable. If you are going to give result direction, it's very helpful at least to give the actor enough time to make the translation, perhaps to mention, "I know I'm asking for a result here and you're going to have to find something playable, something that works for you."

If, on the other hand, you want to save time on the set, it is vitally important that you spend time ahead of shooting to prepare and to know your script and characters inside and out, and to learn how to give direction in playable terms. It's not just a question of vocabulary, it's a different way to approach a created reality.

But I can give you a quick way to spot general, result direction in the way you talk to actors about their characters: train yourself to notice when you are using *adjectives* and *explanations*.

First, a quick grammar review. Adjectives are modifiers of nouns, and adverbs, their close kin, are modifiers of verbs. They describe the thing (noun) or activity (verb) itself. Examples of adjectives are: happy, sad, seductive, angry, beautiful, sweet, vicious, casual, bitter, abrasive. Examples of adverbs are: happily, sadly, seductively, angrily, beautifully, sweetly, viciously, casually, bitterly, abrasively.

Now, what's wrong with adjectives?

ADJECTIVES

Adjectives are static, they describe someone else's impression of the character. The essence of a person is not other people's descriptions of her. What other people see is only the tip of the iceberg. Many directors, because their script analysis has consisted of passively watching the movie in their head, have only such superficial descriptions of the characters available to them. In order to create an alive, believable characterization, the actor needs insight into how the character experiences life, in language that is experiential, not descriptive.

Adjectives are subjective, interpretive, and therefore not ideal communication tools. Using adjectives to describe a character may tell the actor more about your personality than about the character's. We know from real life that people's interpretations of behavior vary widely; for example, behavior that one person considers "friendly" may be seen as "sexual" or even "aggressive" by someone else. So you can see how communication can get all bollixed up if people rely on adjectives.

You can easily get off on the wrong foot with an actor by critiquing his performance using adjectives, for example by telling him, "No, not like that. Play it sexy." What if the actor thinks he already was playing it sexy? If so, he will have one of two reactions. Either he will start to doubt himself, thinking, "I'm not sexy enough for this role. The director doesn't think I'm sexy." Or he will make a mental note about you: "What's wrong with this guy? He doesn't know sexy when he sees it."

Adjectives are generalizations. They serve our social needs to summarize, to intellectualize emotion, to categorize experience. They are a shortcut, a social necessity, a step removed from primary experience. Primary experience is the experience of our five senses, what we see, hear, smell, taste, and touch. When we are in the middle of an earthquake we hear very specifically the sounds of breaking glass, car alarms; we feel the bed move under our bodies; our eyes strain in the pitch darkness to pick out shapes; we may suddenly drench in sweat — our sensory life is alive to detail. For about four months after the 1994 Los Angeles earthquake, Los Angelenos would describe their earthquake experiences to each other in great sensory detail. After about four months, it became socially gauche to go into such personal detail; so now when someone asks us about the earthquake we summarize the experience by calling it "scary" or "weird."

But the actor needs to access exactly such primary experience, so instructions that summarize or intellectualize primary experience lead the actor away from the tools of his trade.

It's a good idea to be suspicious of adjectives (and adverbs), and even to avoid them altogether. Likewise explanations. Explanations (emotional maps, psychologizing) have all the bad attributes of adjectives: glib, subjective, static, superficial, intellectualizing, and categorizing. And besides they are too logical, too dead-on. They are not creative. Lawyers and accountants should explain things; artists are here to suggest, illuminate, juxtapose, and let the audience draw their own conclusions.

*　　*　　*

Good direction, that is, playable direction, generates *behavior* in the actor, so it is active and dynamic rather than static, sensory rather than intellectual, and objective and specific rather than subjective and general. Instead of adjectives and explanations, I want to start you out with five powerful tools you can use to shape performances — *verbs*, *facts*, *images*, *events*, and *physical tasks*.

Now I call this chapter "Quick Fixes" because verbs, facts, images, events, and physical tasks are the quickest fixes I can think of, and also because I wanted you to read the chapter and I knew a chapter titled "Quick Fixes" would be the first thing you would read, no matter where I placed it in the book!

Verbs, facts, images, events, and physical tasks are more *playable* than adjectives and explanations because they are choosable and repeatable. They are more *specific* than adjectives and explanations. They work because they are active (verbs), objective (facts), sensory (images), dynamic (events), and kinetic (physical tasks).

I shouldn't give you the impression that result direction never works, because sometimes it does. But when it works it usually works just once. The actor "nails it" in rehearsal or on the first take, but then another take may be needed for some other reason, and the performance vanishes. Everyone involved is mystified and depressed.

Specific, playable choices can also stop working unexpectedly, *but they are less likely to.* And if they do stop working, the situation is less hopeless, because verbs, facts, images, events, and physical life, in addition to being good language for direction, are useful script analysis tools. They help your imagination kick in. They are keys to the characters' subworld. Once you are alive and active in the subworld of the script, you will have new ideas to replace the ones that don't work.

VERBS

Anyone who has taken a writing course has heard the teacher say that writers should whenever possible select verbs over adjectives and adverbs. Why shouldn't the same be true for directors? Actions speak louder than words. Verbs describe what someone is *doing*, so they are active rather than static; they describe experience rather than a conclusion about experience.

Not all verbs are helpful in this context. State-of-mind verbs, such as *to like, to resent, to fear*, are not necessarily any more helpful than adjectives. The helpful verbs I call "action verbs." An action verb is a transitive verb, a verb that takes an object, something you do to someone else. Typically, an action verb has both an emotional and a physical component.

For instance, *to believe* is a verb, but not an action verb, because what I believe is a description of my state of mind, not something I do to someone else; even "to believe in" someone, although there is an object, is still a state of mind, a condition; believing in someone is not something that I do to him, it's more how I feel about him. *To walk* also is a verb, but although it is an activity, in this definition it is not an "action verb," since it isn't something you do to someone else; it doesn't take an object. (I suppose a case could be made that "to walk [someone] through [a new task or exercise]" is an action verb.) The words *defensive* and *angry* are not verbs (they are adjectives).

To accuse is an example of an action verb. It takes an object; you accuse someone else of something, of lying, of underhanded behavior, whatever. It has an emotional component in that accusing is an emotional transaction between two people, rather than a physical one. So that "to strike" functions as an action verb in this context only if it is done with the voice and subtext, not if it is done physically. (Physically striking another person, in a theatrical context, is not an action verb; it is a piece of blocking or "business." Actually it's a stunt. Stunts must always be carefully choreographed and staged, whereas an action verb is something that when it works has great spontaneity.)

But the action verb "to accuse" does also have a physical component, in that it is something you do in the other person's presence. What if, during a conversation with B, A raises the accusation that C has stolen money from him? Although A is accusing C, since C is not present, we still have work to do to figure out A's action verb toward B, which will tell us what is the emotional transaction of the scene. Of course we know from life that sometimes when a person is mad at someone who is not present, he takes out his anger on the person who is present. So the action verb for A toward B might be "to accuse," but it also might be something else. *To convince, to beg, to complain, to punish, to tease, to soothe* — all are possible action verbs for this situation.

There are two lists in the Appendix, a Short List of Action Verbs and a list of More Action Verbs. Let's say you find yourself inclined to describe a character by saying he is "being defensive." See if you can translate that into a verb by consulting the Short List. Now you might say that the right verb is not on that list; you might find yourself inclined to say that the appropriate verb translation for "being defensive" is *to defend* or *to protect* or *to deflect*. These are verbs and they do take an object, so they are candidates. They are a little bit intellectualized, however, and not quite as muscular and immediate as the verbs on the Short List.

So I might suggest, in place of the direction to "be defensive," one of the following: *to complain, to belittle,* or *to warn.* You see, I am thinking about the defensive behaviors I have seen in life (including of course the ones I have committed myself). When people are feeling defensive it is usually because something is coming at them that they don't like, perhaps information they don't want to face. So they try to deflect attention from the information that is coming in. There are different ways they might accomplish this: they might *complain* about being picked on unfairly; they might *belittle* the source of the information; they might *warn* the person conveying the information not to persist. That's how I came up with those ideas, out of my imagination and my life experiences. Of course when we have the script and can make a proper script analysis (Chapter VII), we will be even better positioned to pick suitable candidates.

I certainly don't claim that the Short List (or even the longer list of More Action Verbs) comprises all of human behavior, but I have found it helpful to ask students, when they are learning to use more verbs, to start with the Short List and at least for a while restrict themselves to it. It's like a musician sticking to scales when she is first learning a new instrument.

Do you see how these verbs are specific? How in a situation where time is short, they could fix a performance? The great thing about verbs is that they focus the actors' attentions on their scene partner. This allows the actors to affect each other and thus to create the emotional events of the scene.

Verbs can be used as a quick fix, but they are also important to the basic understanding of a character. Verbs belong to the constellation of through-line, need, objective, intention and are a very useful way to structure a characterization as well as a way to structure a scene. I will be talking more about structure in later chapters. Here I want to give you a short list of ways that verbs can be alternatives to common result directions.

Use a verb instead of an emotion.

Although we can't decide how to feel, we can decide what to do. This makes the verb, something that we are doing, a playable *choice* and a playable direction. The action verbs describe an emotional transaction; when people *do* things to each other, something *happens*; hence action verbs create an emotional event. Using action verbs instead of adjectives is a way of approaching the emotional center of a scene in a way that is experiential and playable rather than descriptive and result-oriented.

What we do affects our feelings and can create feeling. In an exercise I use in my Acting for Directors classes I ask the students to practice action verbs from the Short List, using improv and gibberish. When, for instance, I have them play the action to accuse, if they do it honestly, they are often surprised to find themselves feeling something. It could be hurt, anger, self-righteousness — one can't always predict what the feeling will be.

The audience is not drawn to a story by what an actor is feeling, but rather by what the character *does* with the feeling, in other words, *what happens next*. The audience wants to feel things themselves! That's what they pay for! It's not what Jessica Lange is feeling in "Blue Sky" that makes her performance so thrilling; it's what she is doing. I had an acting teacher who used to exhort us: "You're actors, damn it — not feelers!"

How about remembering it this way: We can be put in jail for our actions, but not for our feelings, because what we feel is not our fault; we can't control it, whereas we can control what we do.

Use a verb instead of an attitude.

A critical point: When the actor is playing an attitude, his concentration is on himself; there is a tiny voice running in his mind, a subtext, thus: "Am I being sexy enough?" Or, "Is this enough anger?" When his concentration is on himself, his acting becomes self-conscious and stagy.

Superior actors will not be harmed by your using verbs instead of adjectives, and less experienced actors may very well be helped. An actor who is floundering may find the right track, and a scene come alive, right before your eyes! So instead of asking an actor to "play it sexy" (adjective), you might ask him "to flirt" with her (verb); instead of asking an actor to "be more angry" (adjective), you might suggest that she "accuse" or "punish" him (verbs). This shift in concentration allows and encourages the actors to **listen** and to **engage**. It also allows you the director to be more active in the collaboration. When you are active and alive in the process, you will be better able to bring the script to life and guide and shepherd your vision.

Use a verb instead of "take it down" or "give it more energy."

Actors actually hear directors saying things like, "Yes, you should be mean to him, but not that mean." Can you hear how hard it would be to interpret this direction? Verbs can help. You may notice, though, that it will take more thought on your part to articulate precisely what it is that you want using verbs instead of adjectives. The extra mental exertion is good for you! Directing is not supposed to be easy.

Now, do you want the actor to punish? to warn? to complain? Each of those verbs would give a different level of intensity to the line; *punish* might be the most intense, and *complain* the least intense. Again, you can't be sure until you try it. It's not a chemistry formula, where "x" milliliters of hydrochloric acid combined with "x" milliliters of bleach will always turn the litmus paper a certain color.

Asking an actor to *coax* rather than *demand* might be another way to getting them to "take it down." It can sap actors' energy to be constantly told to "take it down" instead of a more specific direction. It can make them feel that you don't care if they commit, that you don't want them to engage.

Sometimes, of course, "take it down" is exactly the right direction when it is given as a *permission* not to push or force, as in "It's okay to relax, to let it happen; let it all be there; you don't need to show us what you are feeling." And sometimes an actor is "hovering" over his performance and needs to let it go, in which case "Give it more energy" would be almost the right thing to say. My point is that these two phrases are overused and actors, when they hear them over and over in situations that are not at all alike, may start to feel that the director does not really know what he is talking about.

Use a verb instead of describing "what the character is like" or "how I see the character."

I had an acting teacher who used to say, "If a man is standing on his head in the middle of the road, nobody asks if he's the type!" Actually, this statement, which he repeated often, was a riddle to me; I pondered it without understanding for a long time. What I know now years later is that actors and directors waste a lot of energy and time gossiping about the characters, arguing over whether the character "would do" such and such a thing. If he does it, then he would do it! We are what we do.

Actors sometimes resist this idea. You'll hear them say: "My character would never manipulate — she's too nice." Or, "My character wouldn't flirt — he's uptight about his sexuality."

News flash: Uptight people flirt! Nice people manipulate! Proud people beg! Shy people brag! People are complex. In real life we do lots of things that are inexplicable to others and to ourselves.

Actors and directors who get bogged down in "what the character is like" miss entirely what a tangle of opposites humans really are. Indeed, actors and directors who get bogged down in explanations have a terrible time when they want to describe a complex character. They psychologize the character to death, piling convolution upon convolution.

What makes a character complex is that he does different things at different times. Gene Hackman is a master at this, changing intentions (verbs) in the wink of an eye. He can charm, challenge, whine, demand, seduce — not all at once but in very quick succession. This makes his characters complex and unpredictable.

Don't waste time wrestling over what the character's personality is; just do it.

Use a verb instead of a judgment.

Instead of denouncing a character as manipulative, give some thought to the specific behavior of a manipulative person. Perhaps she cajoles, begs, goads, and finally punishes (for example, Bette Davis in — well, in a lot of her movies, but let's say opposite one of her worthiest adversaries, Claude Rains, in "Deception").

Use a verb instead of a line reading.

Harold Clurman, in his book <u>On Directing</u>, describes this technique. What I have called giving a line reading, he calls "demonstrating" for the actor, and he disarmingly admits to demonstrating "more than I believe fitting or desirable." Of course this happens to all directors, and Clurman even treats us to a private conversation he had on this subject with Constantin Stanislavsky himself. But Clurman is careful to point out that when he demonstrates a line to an actor, it's not because he wants the actor to say the line with the inflection he gave it, but that he wants to communicate to the actor a sense of the **intention** of the speech.

An *intention* is another term for what I have called an action verb. Now, coming up on the spot with the appropriate action verb when you are in the thick of rehearsal or shooting is not always possible. There are good directors who are not verbally quick. Sometimes a line reading is finally the only way you can convey the meaning of the line. Line readings are not actually so very bad as long as you do understand what the line means, i.e., what intention it carries.

Although I believe that adding more verbs and weeding out adjectives from your vocabulary will help you articulate your ideas, I don't want you just to get slick at translating adjectives and line readings into verbs. The important thing here is not that you are required to come up with and articulate the correct action verb for every intention that you want the actor to express, but that you can give more specific, more followable direction when you understand that what you are looking for is not really an inflection but the intention of the line.

FACTS

Directors and actors all too often underestimate the power of facts. They have a tendency to want to embellish them with explanations. Explanations weaken facts because explanations are subjective, interpretative; facts are objective. The power of an explanation rests with the persuasive abilities of the explainer. Facts speak for themselves, and often they are more eloquent than explanations.

There are two kinds of facts that are useful to directors and actors: facts that are in the script, that is, factual backstory and the events of the script; and facts that are not in the script, that is, imaginative backstory choices.

Determining the facts that are in a script is an important focus of Script Analysis. Script Analysis is something that many directors fear and avoid. But script facts of all kinds — backstory facts that are stated in the script, backstory facts and events that can be deduced from the script, and imaginative backstory choices that develop the skeleton of backstory facts into a rich, created universe — can be truly magical.

Use facts instead of psychologizing.

Saying that a character "can't express his feelings" is an example of a psychological explanation. Even if it is true (and to me the phrase is glib and lacks the ring of truth), it is not playable. A more helpful place to start our explorations into this character would be to note as a *fact*, "He doesn't express his feelings."

She wrote a letter to her mother every day of her honeymoon. That's an example of a fact. Doesn't that fact evoke her nature more vividly than the psychological description that "she is very attached to her mother"? Even a full explanation of the origins of this attachment would just get long-winded and intellectual. The honeymoon letters, unadorned, are more eloquent.

Don't embellish the facts with explanations.

I was working with two acting students on a scene from the movie "When Harry Met Sally"; Sally and her friend Marie are discussing Marie's married boyfriend. I asked the actress playing Sally what she thought were the facts of the scene. She said, "Sally's best friend is dating a married man, *and she disapproves.*" (I have added italics to the unnecessary embellishment.) Every woman I know, if her best girl-friend was dating a married man, would have some reaction, without needing to be instructed to have one. *Adding the embellishment waters down the direction.* The situation itself is more vivid and evocative than its embellishment. Directors often think they are sharpening the focus by adding the explanation of the character's state of mind, but actually they are blurring it.

Use facts instead of "what the character is like."

In one of my courses at the Rockport Maine Film and Television Workshops, I decided to screen for the class the movie "On the

Waterfront." In the class discussion the next day, we were going over the events of the movie in order to determine the spine of the character Edie (Eva Marie Saint). We were listing some facts of Edie's background, e.g., that she has been kept from the world of the docks by her father, who used his savings to send her to Catholic schools.

There is a scene about half way through the movie in which Edie comes up to Terry's pigeon cote on the roof and they have a conversation; the scene ends in a kiss and a fade-out. I mentioned to the class that one of the facts we had to look at concerning Edie is that she has sex with Terry when she actually has only known him a short time. Students took issue with me. Several insisted that the scene in question had not ended in sex, because Edie was "not like that," that a girl "like Edie" in middle-class America in the 1950s "wouldn't do that."

But look at the evidence. The next scene after the fade-out has Terry coming to talk to the priest. The priest mentions that Edie has an appointment with him and is on her way. Here is the fact we should look at: *the next day they are both coming to talk to the priest!* This is evidence that something happened on the roof that was troubling. If we look back at the scene and decide that nothing troubling happened in the scene, then something troubling must have happened after the scene ended. At this point we look at Edie, educated by nuns, sheltered by a doting father, and realize that a girl with that background might, the morning after her first sexual experience, make an appointment to meet with her confessor.

There is evidence, later in the movie, that I think closes the book on this bit of detective work. When Terry breaks down her door to see her, she is in her slip. She screams at him to get out, but never tries to cover herself. Since she does not seem to fear the loss of Terry's respect, what does that suggest has already been lost? Of course having Edie wear a slip in that scene may not have been in the original script; it may have been a directorial choice. This is in fact how directorial choices are made; they are based on evidence and deduction.

Facts are a potent weapon in script analysis. The great thing about facts is that, as the saying goes, you can't argue with 'em. If you have a disagreement with an actor, go over the facts of the scene together. You may be able to find out how the actor arrived at his choice, and then be able to discuss the problem more fruitfully.

Use facts instead of a judgment.

Instead of describing a character as "a bitch," you might invent a backstory fact, say that "she poured paint on the windshield of her ex-lover's car." Instead of saying, "He's a likable guy," you might say, "After he asks a question, he listens to the answer," or "He looks you right in the eye," since those are factual statements of behavior that many people find likable. It takes more thought, more imagination, to think up facts that describe a character.

Use facts instead of attitudes.

People see the line "I already told you that," and they immediately hear in their mind an attitude and tone of exasperation. You shouldn't jump to that conclusion. What you should get from that line is factual information: there has been a previous conversation between these two characters. Period.

From there, you may ask questions: How many previous conversations? What was actually said? Under what conditions? Did character B, who was told the information and yet is asking about it again, not believe character A? Or not listen? Was she distracted by some other secret concern? Facts and questions will begin to create a set of **given circumstances** that generate behavior that implies a point of view. Fresher, more vivid performances will result.

Coming up with facts can lead us into interesting areas. Once you decide that the line "I already told you that" doesn't connote any particular attitude, but only means that a previous conversation has taken place, then you start to have some curiosity about this previous conversation. It dawns on you, from your own experience and understanding of life, that people don't always remember a previous conversation accurately; the speaker may think he spoke on this particular subject, but really only skirted the issue, expecting a hint to be understood as a request. You start to come up with ideas that may lead to insight.

Once you've described a character by saying, "She poured paint on the windshield of her ex-lover's car," instead of "She's a bitch," your statement opens the door to some questions. Could she have had a good reason for pouring the paint? Maybe she's not a bitch at all! At least that's what you want the actor playing her to feel. The audience can decide for themselves.

Imaginative backstory facts are sometimes called **adjustments**. An imaginative adjustment can be used to add a layer or a twist to the inner life and imagined given circumstances of the character. In this case it might be phrased as a "what if?" Let's take as an example a scene in which an employee is told by his boss that he has been terminated. Let's say that the boss only appears in this scene. You could add texture to a sketchy characterization of the boss by asking the question, "What if her own father had been fired from his job when she was a child?"

IMAGES

By images, I don't mean only visual images, but the experiences of all our five senses, what we see, hear, smell, taste, and touch. Images (as well as facts) are the tools of the storyteller. A successful storyteller is one who can make images come alive, who by adding sensory detail can make us feel as if we are actually there where the story is happening.

The director's image, the picture he wants to convey to the audience, while an important part of filmmaking, is not useful to the actor because it is a result. If you want a certain shot to convey to the audience an image of, say, loneliness, telling the actor this will not be helpful, because you would be asking for a result. It would be more helpful to put the character in a situation (a set of facts) that might produce the behavior you want to photograph.

The kinds of images that speak to the actor are 1) the images of the text, that is, the images created by the words of the script, and 2) the images that the actor brings to the script, which become the images of the script's subworld.

To give you an example of images in the text, let's take this line (from Arthur Miller's "Death of a Salesman"): "To suffer fifty weeks of the year for the sake of a two-week vacation, when all you really desire is to be outdoors, with your shirt off." This line is full of images: "outdoors" is an image, with sensations that include sound and smell and tactile sensations as well as visual information; "shirt off" is an image with many associations; "two-week vacation" is an image with memories of many emotional colors for most people; even the two verbs "desire" and "suffer" carry images. In later chapters I'll talk more about how exploration of the images of the text can deepen and expand your understanding of the script.

Here are a few ways that directors can use images that spring from the character's subworld to open up and tap into the actor's emotional resources and help her connect her own imagination to the imagined world of the script.

Use images instead of asking for emotions.

Sensory memories are powerful evokers of emotion and subtext. The memory of the smell of baking bread can whisk us back to the kitchen of our youth; a phrase from an old song can return us to the delicate yearnings of a long-ago love; reading the news can make us weep or rage if we allow ourselves to see and touch the misery we are reading about.

Images can call forth expressive behavior from an actor and make his deep emotions available. For example, I was directing for a workshop a scene from "Orpheus Descending" by Tennessee Williams (made into the movie "The Fugitive Kind"). At the beginning of the scene Lady, who thinks she is alone, says, "I wish I was dead." Val, who has overheard her, steps out of the shadows and says, "No you don't, lady." After a few rehearsals I was not happy with what the actor was doing with this line; it kept sounding like a line in a play, rather than anything a person was actually saying to another person. When I mentioned to him that I thought the moment was not yet fulfilled, he began to speak the line with more emphasis, which only made things worse; he was adding a fake urgency to a moment for which he had not yet found an emotional reality. Finally I took him aside and, on an impulse, looked him in the eye and asked, "Have you ever seen a dead person?"

His eyes shifted, inward it seemed; he said quietly, "Yes." I said, "Let's run the scene." After that his delivery of the line was honest, direct, and emotionally full. We did not discuss it again, so I don't know what interior adjustment he made. But I know that for myself, the first time that I saw the dead body of a friend, a person still young — not all made up in a funeral casket, but lying on a gurney in an emergency ward — created an unforgettable image. Picturing it in my mind would make it easy for me to assure someone that it was a state that one does not really desire.

Use images instead of explanations.

Let's say you are directing a movie with a main character whose backstory is that at the age of four she was left with an unpleasant relative for six months during her mother's hospitalization for polio. You might find yourself wanting to explain to the actor the character in terms of the psychological effects of her abandonment — withdrawn, suspicious, self-destructive — whatever. But instead of spending hours psychologizing (intellectualizing) the character's deep emotions, you could invoke an image, perhaps that of the door closing on the child's father as he leaves her there, or the last light of his attempt at a smile.

Such images live with people (characters) the rest of their lives. Summoning the images associated with important events much more closely approximates the workings of these events on actual human psyches than explaining their effects. Access to such images is one of an actor's most important tools. Directors who can communicate with actors on the level of these images can get actors to do anything.

Use images as imaginative adjustments.

The term *adjustment* is used differently by different people. Sometimes it is misused. Sometimes it is confused with attitude; it's possible, even common, to hear a director telling an actor to use "a cheerful adjustment." But *cheerful* is an adjective, an attitude, not really a playable adjustment. What about this: "The adjustment is that you realize that she has betrayed you and you decide to kill her." This is definitely not a playable adjustment, but a disguised emotional map.

A way to use an adjustment if you want the actor to play the character with more "cheer" might be to suggest that she take the adjustment that everything the character opposite her is saying is really good news.

In addition to the "what if?" imaginative backstory adjustments described under "Facts" above, an adjustment can be a junior image, a brief metaphor, a quick fix. It often takes the form *as if*. For example, a love scene: you might ask the actors to play it *as if it is a business deal*. Or you might ask actors to play a business meeting *as if it is a children's play sword fight*. Or you might speak to the actors separately and ask one of them to make an adjustment *as if* the other character has bad breath. A quick imaginative adjustment of this type can bring spark to a scene that is playing too dead-on.

EVENTS

Every scene has a central event. The central event of a scene may be that one galaxy overthrows another galaxy's way of life, or it may be that one character makes another character blush. Creating the events of the script is the most important job of the director for two reasons:

1) Because the events of a script tell its story, and the director is a storyteller. The events must unfold emotionally and filmically so that they are at once surprising and inevitable, and so that the audience remains throughout the movie in that delicious state of anticipation of *what happens next.*

2) Because the events of the movie tell us what the movie is about, and the director is the shepherd and guardian of the movie's theme. Sidney Lumet says in his book <u>Making Movies</u> that what the movie is about — some people call this the movie's theme — is the central thing a director needs to feel and understand; *every* decision she makes about the film must be based on what the movie is about.

What I mean by "event" is not the same as plot or incident, but is more like an emotional event, such as a fight, a negotiation, a trick, a healing, a seduction. I will discuss event and theme further in the Script Analysis chapter, but for now I want to mention that talking about the event of a scene is a useful way of communicating with actors.

Telling the actors that the scene is about a fight between two people who used to love each other can help them rally the personal and imaginative resources they need to create the poignancy you are looking for in the scene, whereas telling them you want the scene to be poignant or giving them an emotional map will be subtly less exciting and less generative of good acting. It takes imagination and insight and thinking to change your perception of a scene from an adjective or an emotional map to a sense of event. Luckily the process itself is invigorating and stimulating.

Even when you know how to articulate the events, bringing them to full and vivid life is not necessarily easy. A director needs to be on the lookout for the fake confrontation, the clichéd apology, the "movie" love scene. We don't want to *indicate* the event; we want to make it happen in the here and now and let the audience in on it. I'll be talking more in the next chapter about ways to ask for, recognize, and encourage the honest, moment-by-moment acting that creates a genuine and dynamic sense of event.

PHYSICAL TASKS

The thrust of all these alternatives to result direction has been to look for ways to ask the actor to *do* something rather than to ask him to *be* something. Because then the actor can concentrate on what he is doing, and allow himself to *be* in the moment, so his behavior can be natural and spontaneous.

And the simplest thing you could ask an actor to do would be a physical task. When the actor or actors are concentrating on a physical problem or task, their concentration can give the scene a sense of its emotional problem. A physical task takes the actor's concentration off the lines, because he lets the lines *come out of* the physical task. Concentration on the lines — on remembering them or on delivering them the "right" way — makes a performance stiff, rehearsed-looking. Concentration on an imaginative task, such as a verb, fact, or image, takes the actor off the lines and into a created reality. The actor lets the lines *come out of* the imaginative task rather than out of a preconceived idea of how they should sound. But if the imaginative task gets too intellectualized or self-conscious, then a physical task may be useful.

I was told a story of one director of a major motion picture who was having trouble with a direction to an actor: She wanted him to play the scene less seductively. She kept telling him so, to no avail. The scene was stuck, too dead-on to the lines, emotionally stagnant in the actor's predetermined idea of how the line should be said. Finally (the scene took place in a kitchen) the director said, "Why don't you go to the refrigerator and look for a snack during this conversation. And let's let the refrigerator door be a little stuck." As soon as he had a physical problem — the stuck refrigerator door — to put his attention on, the words were freed from the actor's preconceived notion, and the scene played simply and naturally.

At this point I ought to talk about verbs again. Verbs are an emotional and imaginative extension of physical tasks. The more physical the verb is the better. If you want to punish someone, getting him to feel punished is a task, like making a sandwich or potting a plant, only it is a psychological task, not a physical one. A measure of how skilled an actor is is how effectively he can make that psychological leap so that an imaginative choice has a sense of *task*. Even if he is getting result direction, he automatically translates the result into a playable task; for example, if told to be angrier, he starts punishing the other character; if told to be sexier, he seduces the other actor. He works moment by moment, putting his concentration on the other actor. Afterward he feels tired, just like after a demanding physical task.

Whenever actors are struggling, it is helpful to make your direction as simple and as physical as possible. Having a very simple, physical thing to do brings down the level of stress so they can rally their concentration and confidence.

QUESTIONS, QUESTIONS, QUESTIONS

"Do you want it seductive? I can do seductive."

Directors are not the only ones who give actors result direction. Actors do it to themselves! Actors routinely come into casting sessions and immediately ask, "What's this character like?" In rehearsal or on the set you might give a solid, specific direction that with care and feeling creates the images and factual circumstances of the character's situation, only to have the actor respond, "You mean you want it more sarcastic?" or "You want me to pump it up?" He has fallen into "playing the result."

Don't be discouraged. Have faith. Don't allow your idea to be reduced to its lowest common denominator. Look for the experience, the process, rather than the result. When an actor asks you a question, even if he *asks* you for an adjective, answer with a fact, a verb, an image, an event, or a physical task.

Or a question. Preferably a question.

The very best way to direct is not by giving direction at all, but by asking questions. All the devices I have been discussing — verbs, facts, images, events, physical tasks — function best in the form of questions to the actor: "Do you think these characters have ever pulled off a robbery before?" "Do you think he wants to pick a fight or is he hoping she will stay calm?" "What if the character is lying when she says this line?" "What if she just received a crank phone call?" "What does the image 'cherry orchard' conjure up for you?" "What's important about this scene?" "Do you have any impulse to turn away from her when she says that?"

Sometimes "I don't know" is the smartest thing a director can say to an actor. Sometimes very smart directors tell an actor "I don't know" even when they do know. John Cassavetes was like that — notorious for refusing to tell actors how to play their roles — but not because he hadn't done his homework and didn't know and understand the characters inside and out himself. Rather because he wanted actors to find the characters themselves, to make them their own. He wanted only fresh, unguarded, and emotionally honest work.

In order to get the use of the full creative potential of your actors you must be prepared for some of the answers to these questions not to be the ones you were expecting. You have to give up your character-in-the-sky and the version of the film you have running on the inside of your forehead. You can learn how to give direction in such a way that the actor ends up feeling that his performance is his own, and yet feels firmly supported by a smart, well-prepared director with an authentic authority, who can offer the crucial "quick fix" because she has done the groundwork.

Moment By Moment

"Of course the film director should know acting, its history and its techniques. The more he knows about acting, the more at ease he will be with actors. At one period of his growth, he should force himself on stage or before the camera so he knows this experientially, too.

"Some directors, and very famous ones, still fear actors instead of embracing them as comrades in a task. The director must know how to stimulate, even inspire the actor. Needless to say he must also know how to make an actor seem not to act, how to put him or her at their ease, bring them to that state of relaxation where their creative faculties are released...

"All in all he must know enough in all these areas so his actors trust him completely." — Elia Kazan

These next chapters will be a journey inside the actor's world, to introduce you to the craft of acting and some ways that actors work. You may feel that I am telling you more than you as a director need to know. Think of it as bounty. I am a great believer in knowing more than you need to know. Creativity is bountiful. If you confine yourself to learning only the things you are sure you will use, you are running amok of the very first principle of creativity, which is bounty.

My approach is intended for directors with a thirst to understand and build a trust with actors. Interwoven with theory, observations, and examples will be specific suggestions of ways directors can connect and collaborate more deeply with actors to make their movies better and their own job more creatively rewarding.

FEAR AND CONTROL

"Almost every actor goes into almost every picture very frightened. He is positive he really can't do it. The bigger the star, the more frightened he is." — **Paul Mazursky**

Actors are in an unrelenting existential spin. A good performance is a thrilling experience — it feels like flying. And it only happens if they let go and float free. Paradoxically the craving to perform well and feel this freeness can trick them into holding on, into reserving a corner of their concentration so they can check on and control their performance, which exactly makes all chances for a vivid, spontaneous performance disappear.

Sometimes asking an actor how she works can be a good way to begin collaborative discussions about the work at hand. But not necessarily. Sometimes actors don't want to discuss their methods, especially with an "outsider," which is how they often regard the director. They may be afraid of sounding foolish. Or they may be superstitious about exposing such subterranean material to the light of day — afraid that once revealed, a technique that has worked a hundred times won't work any more; afraid of becoming self-conscious.

Self-consciousness is a great problem for an actor, because it means that he is uncomfortable about being watched. Self-conscious acting is fussy, strained, thin, actorish; it lacks texture and spontaneity. When an actor is self-conscious, he may start to push or *indicate*. Indicating or telegraphing or *playing a result* occurs when the actor pretends to have feelings, reactions, and attitudes in order to show the audience the feelings, reactions, and attitudes he has decided are right for the character. Indicating shows up as a "false note." It may result from wrong-headed or inadequate preparation, or from fear that his preparation is inadequate, that he will do it wrong, or that the audience "isn't getting it."

The antidote is to put his concentration someplace other than on himself. Without a compelling focus for his attention, the actor's attention turns to his own anxieties. His mantra unwittingly becomes: *"How am I doing? Am I saying this right? Does the audience get it? Does everybody like me?"* Unless the actor finds some other thing to be gripped by, he will be gripped thus by self-consciousness.

It is important for directors to understand how wildly frightening acting can be, how vulnerable you are when you're up there, how painful it is to hear criticism, how easy it is to doubt oneself. The actor's face, body, voice, thoughts, and feelings are exposed. His thirst for a core, existential reassurance and validation is nearly inexhaustible. He looks to the director for this. Honest praise is as necessary to him as water. And so is forthright, accurate, and constructive criticism.

RISK

"I send the actors out to suffer for me every day."
— **Jean Renoir**

When actors can't trust the director for honest and competent feedback, they may become cautious. Cautious acting is not very good acting because in real life people incautiously make a lot of mistakes. In order to bring a character to life, there needs to be risk, mistake, serendipity, idiosyncrasy, surprise, danger. These things give a performance the texture of real life — and "edge." When the acting has risk, it makes drama more moving, comedy more surprising, adventure more thrilling, mystery more suspenseful.

An actor must allow himself to be watched. Great actors love to give, love to perform; like an athlete, they live to compete, they are hungry to perform. A great dramatic actor allows the world to watch his deepest, most private self, transformed by the created reality of the script. Lesser actors hide. They refrain from giving over their whole, flawed, idiosyncratic selves to every role. They rely on formula or cliché in devising their characterizations. They make a safe choice. They don't "put out." Because here's one of life's little unfairnesses: If an actor takes a big risk and it works, it is much better acting than cautious acting. But if an actor takes a big risk and it doesn't work, it looks much worse than cautious acting.

A big risk that doesn't work is called overacting. It is so acutely embarrassing to actors to be caught overacting that many would rather give a flat performance than a risk–taking one. Good actors are not offended when a director catches a false note and informs the actor that he seems to have lost his center of truth or isn't listening and has crossed the line into overacting. They are grateful. They need the director to tell them these things. If the director doesn't tell them, they may feel they must watch the performance themselves, and become cautious.

Success can be an enemy to an actor's creativity. As soon as one has success, one has something to lose and can easily fall into a protective, rather than a risk-taking stance. Actors can be so afraid of looking bad that they make choices they know are wrong for the character. I mentioned in the first chapter the dangers of judging a character, but it is equally dangerous to sentimentalize a character. Fear of hurting his self-image with the audience, or reluctance to find disagreeable behavior truthfully in himself — or plain squeamishness — may cause him to resist the role.

Shelley Winters, in an interview on the Bravo Channel series "Inside the Actors Studio," spoke of the distress she felt on the set of "A Patch of Blue" when she — in her own life a fierce advocate who had participated in civil rights marches — had to play a racist and include a line added to the original script in which she called Sidney Poitier a "nigger."

"It was physically impossible... I just got to that scene and I would vomit. And I would come in every day and I would have some story why this woman got so biased, how she turned out like this, what could have happened..." Apparently the director could see that what the actor thought were attempts to humanize the character were really resistances to the truth of the script and that she was on the road to sentimentalizing the character by injecting an awareness of guilt into the character's behavior. He, together with Poitier, convinced her to take the bigger risk of facing and finding truthfully the behavior of a person without self-awareness, without guilt — with the hollow moral center of a bigot. She won her second Oscar for that role.

A big enemy of risk is the pressure to do it "right." Movies have gotten so expensive, television so driven by ratings, that the fear of making a mistake rules most creative decisions, including those of actors. Actors are expected — and expect themselves — to "nail it" right away. They mistakenly put their concentration on making the producer think they can do it right the first time rather than on a creative choice. Good roles are rare, competition is fierce, and as actors age the parts get smaller. Directors, it seems, are always looking for an instant result, and often are lacking in understanding or patience regarding acting as a process.

Many directors are impressed with an actor's "bag of tricks" — an actor who can cry on cue or go from zero to towering rage in sixty seconds. They may feel their work vis-à-vis acting is done once they have cast someone whose bag of tricks includes an ability to hit a set of predetermined emotional notes on command. But I want to encourage you to look for something deeper, fresher, and more honest.

"Any director's job is to make an actor understand that you're giving everything of yourself to a part... It's kind of a love affair, it really is. You get very close doing movies. It sounds really corny but it's true. There's not a lot that's left unsaid when you go in the trailer with them. They're naked, they're stark fucking naked. We all are. As long as you break down the barriers, and are in it together, then out of that nakedness will come something good." — **Adrian Lyne**

The best work happens when actors are caught in unguarded moments of simplicity and truth, giving a simple, genuine response to a question or remark or event. This is not as easy as it sounds. Whether the script is naturalistic or fantastical, to look like a living person in a situation rather than an actor in a movie an actor has to get below the social mask. Even the most ordinary activities, say, cooking a dinner, when they are scripted in a movie, in order to read and come alive on the screen, especially the big screen, require the actor to perform on himself a stripping of the social veneer. Without this stripping down to essentials, the actor will have no screen presence. Glenn Close calls this stripping down a process of giving herself permission to "disturb the molecules" in the air around her.

Actors often have their own highly private routines to get themselves below the social mask and ready to perform, ready to put out, ready to disturb molecules. Sally Field says that as soon as she knows she is going to be in a movie — no matter whether it is a big emotional role or a lightweight comedy — she begins a process that she calls "rawing myself up." Even if the subject matter of the movie is not painful or difficult, she goes through her emotional and imaginative storage banks to get herself connected to whatever for her is basic about life, to separate herself from mundane concerns, such as fax machines, phone messages, etc. It is a process of disobligating herself to the social realm so she can enter the creative realm. It's a way of turning off the "automatic pilot" that gets one through the routine of daily life, so that she can be "in the moment."

This is the ground on which the director must meet the actor if he wants to have an actor-director relationship based on trust and collaboration. After the best takes, the ones in which the actor is the most unguarded, the actor may feel destabilized and raw. This is a moment of truth for the director, a time when an insensitive response can kill your chances for trust and collaboration — or, on the other hand, when, if you see and acknowledge the actor's psychic nakedness, you can forge an unshakable connection. There is no one thing I can tell you that is the right thing to say at these times. These are the times when the director, too, takes a risk.

HONESTY

"You put your energy, your thought, your imagination, your spirit into something. It's all rooted in who you are. Your skin is what you manipulate to create the illusion of being someone else. And that costs you every time." — Ralph Fiennes

Contrary to popular belief, acting is not pretending or faking. Actors in their work must be more deeply truthful than what passes for honest behavior in the regular world. I want to encourage you as directors to seek out and recognize honesty in a performance.

The great acting teacher Sanford Meisner has an exercise he does with a group of students. He asks them to sit and listen for one minute to the traffic outside the building. At the end of the minute, he asks them, "Were you listening in character, or were you listening as yourself?" If you think about this (you can try it yourself at home), you can see how the idea of listening "in character" adds an element of strain. Listening as yourself, with your own ears — a simple task — is relaxing, centering. It keeps the actor from "acting with a capital A."

The actor must start with himself, he must hear with his own ears, see with his own eyes, touch with his own skin, feel with his own feelings. Then from his study of the script, impulses and understandings start to bubble up from inside him. He makes the character his own. During a superior performance the actor often feels that he inhabits the character's skin, i.e., that he has "become" the character. The audience may feel that too. What this really means is that he is inhabiting his *own* skin, is "in the moment" but has brought choices and understandings to the role that create a sense of belief in the script.

Simple, honest acting is the biggest risk, because being honest means the actor has to use himself, make his work personal. A really good actor understands that when a director asks him for "more" — more anger, more grief, more sex, more humor, whatever — what he really needs to do is get simpler, more elemental, stop "acting with a capital A." In other words, do *less*, make it more honest in order to get out of the way of his deeper resources, which will be the only place he can find the "more" that the director is asking for. If the director understands this too, then she can give her direction in the form of *permission* for the actor to go to the places he needs for the role. Permission is the powerful weapon of the director.

A wonderful side benefit is that when actors are working honestly, they keep coming up with new ideas. Working honestly opens up corners of his brain and psyche so that memories, understandings, and inventions start coming to him that he didn't even know he had. This is called working organically. Some actors do all their script analysis this way — connecting in a relaxed way to whatever they understand about the script and trusting that as they commit honestly to what they understand, their understanding will deepen without effort. Other actors prefer to do their script investigations via their intelligence and then find and fill their organic center. Both Hume Cronyn and Paul Newman have described their own methods as being of the latter type (sometimes called "working from the outside in") and each has expressed admiration for his wife (Jessica Tandy and Joanne Woodward, respectively) for working more organically (also known as "working from the inside out").

Sometimes directors find actors who work organically disturbing. Such actors may look, while they are rehearsing and investigating, as though they don't know what they're doing. Their rhythms and line readings may seem wrong for performance. What they are doing is organically adding layers. Such work pays off in the end.

*   *   *

Some lines are more difficult than others to find honestly. There is a monologue I use in my classes from "The Last Picture Show" in which Lois describes her now-deceased lover, Sam, as the only man who really saw who she was. Then she says, "I've looked, too. You wouldn't believe how I've looked." Students never have any trouble delivering that line believably. It contains a sentiment that most women can find honestly with ease.

On the other hand, actors can easily trip over the line, "I love you." I was once directing a young actor in a play in which he had to say "I love you" to another character. This particular actor always worked with scrupulous honesty (he was incapable of lying in the regular world as well, which caused him to seem somewhat socially inept); he confided to me that he thought I would have to cut the line because he knew it would make him too self-conscious to say it in front of an audience. So I asked him to come early to the next rehearsal. I had him stand on the stage, with me in the audience, and I asked him to tell me how he felt about me. He said, "I respect you. I think you're a good director." Then I said, "Now I want you to say the words of the script, 'I love you,' but let yourself mean what you just said to me. Don't try to make it mean any more than that." When we opened, his performance in that scene was the most beautiful thing in the show. I had given him permission, you see, to feel that whatever he could bring in his own person was adequate to the role, even if he had never said "I love you" in real life (as I suspected was the case). From that point of honest connection, his imagination could be engaged and his performance became a creative thing.

I want to encourage you to prefer from your actors emotional honesty over showy emotional pyrotechnics. One way to talk about this is to ask an actor to keep it simple. "Simple" for actors is a short-hand for emotional simplicity, by which is meant emotional honesty.

MOMENT BY MOMENT

"Just because they say 'Action' doesn't mean you have to do anything." — **Marlon Brando, reported by Al Pacino**

You've probably heard the expression "in the moment" or "moment-by-moment work" applied to actors. You may also know the expression in connection with athletics, or certain spiritual disciplines or the pop psychology of the seventies.

In everyday life not many of us live moment by moment all the time. When we watch ourselves, calculating the effect of our behavior on others; when we censor ourselves and choose our words and actions to meet social rules and expectations; when something painful or upsetting happens and we don't feel sad or angry until later — then we are not in the moment. When we are "in our heads"

57

instead of in our bodies, intellectualizing our feelings and sensations; when, while we are involved in one activity, our concentration is on the anxiety or anticipation we feel toward an activity in the future — then we are not in the moment. Come to think of it, being in the moment in real life is pretty rare.

But it is available on a regular basis if you are an actor. For an artist there are two worlds — the social realm, where we live and work day to day, and the created (creative) realm. They are separate, like nonintersecting sets. The concerns and obligations of the social realm do not apply to the created realm. To enter the created realm one must be — is allowed to be — free of the social realm, uncensored, in the moment, disobligated from concerns with result, following impulses, obeying only the deepest and most private truths.

When an actor is "in the moment," he is relaxed, confident, and alert. He is responsive to the physical world around him, to his own interior world of impulse and feeling and imaginative choices, to the words and subtext of the script, and to the behavior of the other actors. He is available. He speaks with a "real voice," not an "actor voice." He inhabits his own skin. There is "somebody home" when you look in his eyes. "Moment-by-moment" work makes an actor look lifelike and natural even in an extreme plot situation — like Nicholas Cage in "Leaving Las Vegas" or Jessica Lange in "Blue Sky." It makes a performance breathtakingly simple, clean, and unfussy — like Jean-Louis Tritingant in "Red" or John Travolta in "Pulp Fiction" and "Get Shorty." It gives him ease and watchability — like Julia Roberts in "Pretty Woman" or Tom Hanks in almost anything.

Moment-by-moment work is responsible for the tiny flickers of expression that make an actor's face seem alive in between the words. When the actor deliberately tries for such flickers of expression, deliberately tries to hesitate, stutter, wink or grimace, the acting becomes mannered. Mannered acting, by calling attention to the affectations of the actor, takes the audience out of the story. But when such flickers occur "in the moment" they make screen magic, they create a screen *presence*, they confer star quality.

In a 1995 <u>New Yorker</u> interview, John Travolta is quoted: "It doesn't take much for a thought to be seen. I keep having to talk directors out of talking me into overacting. I say, 'You won't see it on the set. You'll see it in the editing room.' I have an ability to be it, and it will read." Shelley Winters quotes director George Stevens as having told her that film acting is "talking soft and thinking loud." It seems to me that "thinking loud" has to mean that the actor trusts whatever he is thinking and feeling to be adequate to the moment. Actors call it "trusting the moment."

Of course there is talent involved here, too. An actor's talent has to do with the expressiveness of his instrument (i.e., his face, body, voice, feelings, impulses) and the truth of his instincts. Travolta's talent is the well he has to draw from — in his case, a deep well indeed. But his *skill* (skill being different from talent, which is given to you; skill being what you do with your talent) in "trusting the moment" while a camera is rolling ensures that his feelings, impulses, and understandings will be believable on the screen.

"In the moment" for actors has to do with freedom. It has to do with fearlessness. It has to do with trust. It has to do with the actor not watching himself. It means that whatever preparation an actor does for a role is done ahead of time. Once the camera starts to roll or the curtain goes up, the actor lets go of his preparation and *allows* it to be there.

Or not! You see, there's a risk that the preparation won't work and the actor will be out there alone, drawing a blank, just saying words, with no inner life, with nothing happening. This is where the fearlessness comes in! Good actors, even after the harrowing experience of a mid-performance loss of concentration, continue to work properly, reworking their preparation and then jumping into the abyss of moment-by-moment work. They continue to trust the process.

When actors lose trust in the process, they begin to push, force, reach for, or indicate what the character is thinking and feeling.

They look like actors, and the audience becomes distanced from them and from the stories they are enacting.

Travolta's quote earlier suggests that a lot of directors are in the dark as to the importance of moment-by-moment work and as to what it even looks like. It would be ludicrous to suggest that this can be taught in a book. But I want to open your minds a little, whet your appetites for further study, and prepare you for the idea that moment-by-moment work is worth making sacrifices for.

Directors can help actors trust their moment-by-moment connections. I have been fascinated by the articles describing the first meeting of Quentin Tarrantino and John Travolta, which led to Travolta's "Pulp Fiction" role and his return to artistic, critical, and box office preeminence. Both men have described it publicly, and I see it as a model for the creative potential of the actor-director relationship. Tarrantino bombarded Travolta with his detailed acquaintance with the minutia of Travolta's career and with his enthusiasm for the actor's talent. "And then," according to Travolta, "Quentin let me have it. He said, 'What did you *do*? Don't you remember what Pauline Kael said about you? What Truffaut said about you? Don't you know what you *mean* to the American cinema? John, what did you *do*?' I was hurt — but moved. He was telling me I'd had a promise like no one else's... I was devastated. But I also thought, Jesus Christ, I must have been a fucking good actor!"

The director here has done three things: 1) he has let the actor know that he *sees* him, the real him, his core being and his shining talent; 2) he has let the actor know he knows the difference between work which connects with that core and work which does not connect with that core; 3) he has let the actor know that his commitment is to that core and to his own core. This type of actor-director communication (as long, of course, as it is heartfelt and *true* and not just Hollywood "love you, sweetie" bullshit) can get an actor "connected up" to his deepest resources and free him to trust the moment and not to "act with a capital A." It gives him a deep confidence.

Jack Lemmon, in an A&E Channel Biography, gives another clue as to how a director can help. He tells a story about working with George Cukor, who kept asking him not to "act." Lemmon tried to comply, but Cukor kept exhorting, pleading with him to do less. "I can't do less," Lemmon snapped back. "If I do any less, I won't be doing anything at all!" Cukor replied, "That's what I want!"

Moment-by-moment work is lost as soon as the actor "puts anything on it" — my teacher Jean Shelton used to call it an "unction." The word "unction" is kin to "unguent" — an oil that lies on top of something and is not incorporated organically. It means playing attitude or faking emotion — laying the attitude or emotion on top of the lines, rather than trusting the preparation and letting the lines bubble up from and come out of whatever impulse and feeling have been stirred up by the preparation.

"The best actors are children and dogs because they're not acting at all." — **Helen Mirren**

The actor who is "in the moment" *is thinking real thoughts and feeling real feelings right in front of us.* This is an extremely radical idea. Because after all, the actor is playing a character, right? So doesn't that mean that she should be thinking the *character's* thoughts and feeling the *character's* feelings?

Not precisely. I invite you to allow characters to have a subconscious — even to have free will (or at least as much free will as any of us have).

It is not possible to decide to play a character whose subconscious mind is doing such-and-such. You can't make conscious choices about what to have going on in your subconscious; it's the very definition of the thing that it is not conscious and not available to conscious control. *So the actor must allow the character to borrow her own subconscious.* Then life between the lines can kick in and the actor can be a bridge between the words which are said and the words which are not said — the subworld.

Think of an iceberg. You know they say that what we see of an iceberg is only ten percent; the other ninety percent is below water. People are like that, too; the words that people say represent about ten percent of what's going on with them, what they're thinking, feeling, and doing. The other ninety percent is the subworld. In order to have full-bodied characters, we need access to that subworld.

In bringing up the subject of free will, I don't mean to raise a philosophical argument. Giving a character free will means that the character makes choices, makes mistakes, takes wins and losses right in the scene as we are watching. The actor, rather than telegraphing to us that the character has made a mistake or choice or win or loss, behaves in the moment right in front of us. This doesn't mean necessarily that the character knows what she is doing; her actions may come out of the subconscious soup rather than the conscious mind. It means that the character says a line or makes a movement because she had an impulse or a need to do so, rather than because the actor learned a line and rehearsed some blocking.

This does not negate the actor's responsibility to the script. But I want to open the possibility of connecting to the script not as an *obligation* but as an *opportunity* to be enriched and enlivened by the facts, images, and events of the script. Then the circumstances and images of the script can interweave with and be informed by the free subconscious inventions of the actor. The specifics of the script are *allowed* rather than *enforced*. This exactly means that actors may be following your direction, and the requirements of the script, and yet their line readings may still be coming out differently from the way you heard them in your head.

To keep from freaking out when this happens, you as the director must feel and believe in the independent life of the characters. When a director does his script analysis homework deeply and properly, he is not threatened when the actors breathe life into the characters. And he has ways to guide the performance in another direction if he wishes.

IDIOSYNCRASY

"The good actors, the professional actors — usually those are synonymous words — are like trained racehorses. They're nervous and skittish. They're high-strung. It's my job to make it as easy as possible for them and to try and get their complete confidence in me." — **Ralph Nelson, director of "Requiem for a Heavyweight," "Lilies of the Field," "Charley."**

I was a young adult in the seventies and I remember well its emphasis on being "grounded," living "in the here and now" — "in the moment." I knew I was one of the many middle-class intellectuals who lived "in my head." I tried to will myself into the "moment," but the effort of will never got me there. When I became an actor, I began to experience being in the moment. It was exhilarating — a high more powerful and more enchanting than any drug. I expect it feels something like what athletes describe as being "in the zone." You are not consciously in control, but you are not out of control. You feel deeply relaxed and confident. You are not thinking about your next line, and yet you know you are going to say it. I was hooked. When the thing was working, when I was "in the moment," it was the nearest thing to a state of grace.

Of course, it wasn't always working. I soon found out that it was hit-or-miss, and the more I *tried* to be in the moment, the less likely it was to happen. How does one stay in the moment? Here are four suggestions:

1) Be strict about following your whims.

It was actually only when I became an acting teacher that I fully understood this. From the very first class that I taught, I always followed the whim of the moment. I always did, precisely and faithfully, exactly what I felt like doing, and said exactly whatever popped into my head — and it always worked out. Being "in the moment" means, for one thing, that you follow your whims without any concern about whether people will approve of you — and *then* they approve of you anyway!

Good actors are disciplined about following their whims. This can make them difficult to be around. People who do not follow their whims sometimes feel threatened by people who do. Technicians on a set can be ruthless in their condemnation of actors who don't meet social norms, who are standoffish or touchy or loud or engage in bizarre rituals to make themselves ready to work. This is terribly unfair.

Now I do not feel that actors or anyone else on a set or in any line of work should be indulged if their behavior is abusive. On a set it is up to the director to set the tone, to draw the line as to what behavior will be permitted for the sake of creative freedom and what will be discouraged or diverted so that everyone can be relaxed and undistracted in the performance of their jobs. In interviews most of the directors that I respect say that it is important to them to maintain a set free of tension.

But maintaining a tension-free set does not mean allowing the atmosphere to be dominated by social concerns. It does not mean allowing the concerns of the shoot to revolve around whether everybody likes each other or is unfailingly "nice." The proper concern of the shoot is always the work. And our work centers not in the social realm but in the creative realm, which permits free and unconventional behavior when it will further the work.

2) Feel your feelings.

To be in the moment, the actor needs to be connected to his own feelings. Sometimes, unfortunately, the only feeling an actor has honestly is anxiety. This can be horrifying for the actor, who may fear that stage fright will make him look unprofessional.

Directors often panic at any sign of insecurity on the part of the actor. In order not to worry the director, an actor can fall into wishing or pretending to feel relaxed and confident when he does not. This is not helpful. It only makes him more tense. Tension causes a constriction of all reflexes and sensation, including our inner vision, or insight. When an actor is tense or in denial of his feelings, he can't possibly go "moment by moment" because his sensory, intuitive, and emotional resources are not available to him. This is what actors are talking about when they say, "I'm just not there."

But feelings are energy. Suppressing or manipulating real feeling does nothing to release the actor's instrument from stasis. Quite the contrary. In order to stay responsive to stimuli that are appropriate to the performance the actor must take the whole kaboodle and stay responsive to stimuli that are not appropriate. Even fear can be used.

Deep-seated, buried pain, anger or fear, which in normal life reveals itself as neurosis, can, with the tools of the actor, be turned into energy and finally artistry. This is the famous joke about actors: "Use it!" In the midst of terrible personal tragedy, the actor brightens up: "I can use this when I play Miss Julie!"

Sometimes, while the camera is running, something unusual happens — a line is dropped, a prop breaks or is missing, a sneeze comes on. Strangely enough, this untoward, unexpected event brings all the actors to life. It is important to make it clear to the actors that no matter what happens, you want them to keep going until you say "Cut," that you make this request because you wish and intend to allow them to be alive and responsive to life in and around them, *and that you are watching their performances so they don't have to.* Not necessarily because you are going to use the take with the sneeze (although who knows?), but because an event/mistake could happen to the actor *interiorly* — a memory, an association, an idea could come to him right in the middle of the performance — and you don't want him to stop when this happens! This is gold.

If an actor comes up to you and says, "I feel terrible. I don't know what I'm doing," the best response is, "I'm glad this happened!" If you can't manage that at first, try "I'm glad you told me." All fears, all resistances, are potential *energy*. Even if an actor is very tired, this can be a good thing. When people are very tired, they often loosen emotional armor and are able to be more relaxed and in the moment.

Sometimes to get the juices going, to break through the armor that is blocking his feelings, the actor does calisthenics or breathing exercises or yelling. Or sometimes he goes off quietly by himself for introspection in order to locate his real feelings — this is what is meant by getting "centered." These approaches may work if the actor gives himself — and is given — freedom; they won't work if their secret purpose is to manipulate or force a particular feeling.

3) Don't move or speak unless you feel like it.

This idea is *not* the same as allowing the actor to wait around or torment himself until he is "in character," that is, until he feels the feeling he has decided is "right" for the character. And I am not suggesting that scripts should be improvised on camera or that blocking and camera moves should not be set and the actors allowed to roam.

This notion of not moving or speaking unless the actor feels like it rather has to do with giving the actor permission to follow an interior sense of timing and impulse. The idea is that the actor speaks because he has something to say, moves because he has somewhere to go, rather than because it is in the script, because the director told him to, or because it is his turn. As a way of encouraging the actor to follow impulses, I find it very helpful to remind students before scenes they present in class: "Don't say the lines unless you feel like it." In fact, I find it helpful to make this reminder every single time. I find that they don't get tired of hearing it. It relaxes them. It gives permission.

4) Forgive yourself for mistakes.

What is risk but freedom to make mistakes? We are mistake-making creatures. A mistake is a moment when we see the abyss open beneath our feet. In beginning acting classes often the best moment of a scene is the moment when a student forgets a line. The look of concentration on his face is real — possibly the only real moment of the scene.

Good actors use these moments, these glimpses of the abyss, to ground themselves in the here and now. And directors can help by giving actors unconditional love and freedom to make mistakes. I often find that when an actor is having a hard time remembering lines that I know he has worked hard on learning, as soon as I tell him, "I don't care if you get the lines right," if he takes my permission to heart, he can remember them easily.

*   *   *

Staying in the moment takes a lot of courage and faith on both the part of the actor and the part of the director. Staying in the moment is not for sissies.

The main reason why I am taking so much time to suggest ways to stay in the moment is that directors should do it too. During one "Acting for Directors" session in Europe, I was suddenly overcome by a spell of homesickness and despair. I allowed myself this thought: "If it is really important to me to do so, I could quit. I could give them back their money, change my plane ticket, and go home tomorrow." As soon as I said that to myself, I relaxed. I didn't quit, of course, but I felt my real feelings. Allowing myself to *feel* as though I could quit was rejuvenating. And it made me know that I was staying out of choice, not obligation.

FREEDOM

"On the set, [Woody Allen] leaves actors alone, he's always about loosening it up, and I tried to do the same. I don't like too much direction myself, it stops me from thinking or feeling... If somebody talks to me too much I clam up." — **Diane Keaton**

In order to work well actors need a tremendous amount of freedom. In order to trust their impulses they need support. They need to be relaxed, free of tension, *free of obligation*.

Obligation is absolutely always the enemy of art — how could it be otherwise? One of my acting teachers years ago, Wendell Phillips, used to say, "Dare to be boring!" We students made fun of him behind his back for such a ridiculous precept, but when I became a teacher myself I saw how profound it was. He was inviting us to release ourselves from the obligation to entertain; only then could we surrender fully, deliciously, to the moment.

It turns out that *obligation*, the need to do things "right," *servicing* the script is so inappropriate to acting that it is better for an actor to place a full, relaxed concentration on the "wrong" thing than a tense, strained concentration on the "right" thing. Let's say an actor playing Hamlet suddenly starts noticing that a wrinkle in his sock is rubbing irritatingly against his foot during shooting. Giving his full inner attention to the discomfort of the wrinkle, in other words letting the words come out through the sensation of the wrinkle, might actually result in a better performance than if he tries to ignore the sensation and struggles to look as if he is thinking about his (Hamlet's) murdered father! I know this sounds like a bizarre lapse in concentration. But the only thing really that makes the sock distracting rather than enriching to the performance is if the actor starts *worrying* that the sock is ruining his performance; in other words, if his attention goes to the audience (do they get it? do they like me? am I doing this right?), and he starts wishing or pretending that the sock problem were not there.

A genuine imaginative or personal connection to the situation of a person whose father has been murdered would of course be beneficial to a performance of Hamlet. It is the *reaching for* or *pretending to* that connection that does the harm. It is the *denial* of present physical reality that takes him out of the moment, not the bad luck of an "inappropriate" reality.

Now of course, actors need to stay within the camera frame and make very exact moves so the camera can follow and photograph them. The freedom I am talking about is an interior freedom, which is all the more important precisely because the actor has such strict logistical parameters to follow. Paradoxically, it requires a strict discipline on the part of actors to maintain their interior freedom.

When I was taking classes from Gerald Hiken, and the work was bad, he would say, "Do it wrong! Whatever you do, for God's sake, stop doing it 'right'! It's better to do it wrong than to do it right!" He would then ask the student, "Okay, what's the right way to play your role?" And she would say (for instance), "Lady Macbeth is very angry and contemptuous of her husband because he's getting cold feet about the murder they've planned." "All right," Gerry would say, "let's run the scene again. This time, do it loving and playful." And damned if it wouldn't come out better! Not just a little bit better, but a thousand percent better. It would have the revelation, the magic, of a moment-by-moment performance *just because* the actor, released from obligation to do it right, had nothing to lose. Disobligation is that powerful; it can make even a sweet Lady Macbeth believable.

Gerry would constantly egg us on, "Go ahead! Think your most private, embarrassing thoughts *right in front of them*!" He meant the audience. There is a kind of arrogance to the uncensored creativity of an artist. For an actor, who must say the lines as written, and move as directed, this arrogance and freedom must apply *interiorly* to his unspoken thoughts and feelings. He must give himself what Stanislavsky called "solitude in public" — an unconcern for what anybody thinks of him. The magnificent paradox is that if an actor is free and uncensored, uninterested in whether or not the audience "gets it," we, the audience, will believe anything he tells us, anything he does! Freedom gives his voice and person *authenticity*.

And it allows humor. A performance without freedom is a humorless one. Anytime in real life that people are loose and free, humor is bound to bubble up. Nothing is less entertaining than an actor who is straining to be funny.

Not only that, but sometimes more freedom is the right *choice* for a character. If it appears that a character is self-centered, instead of trying to play that judgment, the actor asks himself, What is the behavior of a self-centered person? Sometimes, since they are unconcerned with the feelings and needs of others, their inner life is very *free* and uncensored.

I have seen it over and over again as an acting teacher — that the solution to most blockages for actors is *more freedom*. In order to inhabit his own body while making choices, in order to come up with ideas, in order to access his truest truths, deepest feelings, and most inventive imagination, an actor needs freedom.

Paradoxically, actors *protect* their own performance by being completely free and present and unself-conscious. An actor is more believable and more engrossing when he is free and present in the moment, even if his emotion or attitude is "wrong" for the scene, than when he is tight and strained, desperately holding on to the "right" emotion or attitude. A director who understands this can get his actors to do anything because they will know that you are willing to protect their performance by allowing them to be free and real and in the moment no matter what else you ask of them.

CONCENTRATION

"*I only want to skate a clean program, and to have fun.*" — Oksana Bayul, Gold Medal Figureskating Champion

Actors need concentration, but concentration is not an abstract item. When a director hears an actor agonizing, "I can't get my concentration," it might be helpful to ask him, "What are you concentrating on?" Concentration doesn't exist by itself. There is no concentration without something that is being concentrated *on*. The point of concentration may have to do with the actor's choices or it may be something in the here-and-now immediate reality. In other words, if the actor is playing Hamlet, his concentration may be on Hamlet's dead father, or it may be on the wrinkle in his sock. If the

70

work is properly done, the audience won't be able to tell which the actor is concentrating on, only that he is concentrating on something.

When an actor is concentrated on her own private created reality, the audience will want to get in on it. I don't know if you've ever tried to get the attention of a child by coaxing, begging, or demanding that she pay attention to you. It doesn't really work, does it? But if you are deeply involved in some task of your own, say fixing a clock, and if the task fascinates and energizes you, and if you unself-consciously allow the child to watch and partake of your fascination and energy, the child will soon come to your side. This is the function of concentration in an actor's relationship to the audience. This is the actor's *solitude in public.*

Many people have the idea that you can't concentrate unless you are relaxed, but it's really the other way around: having a simple task to concentrate on is relaxing. A good actor thinks of her craft not as something she has to do, but as something she gets to do. Finding a compelling, singular point of concentration or attention unlocks the actor's imagination and opens for her the created reality. It's like stepping through the looking glass. Craft — or technique — is the way the actor marshals her concentration, and finds the thing to concentrate on. Craft, of course, does not replace good instincts. Craft does, however, replace superstition and mysticism.

Good acting doesn't look like acting. When acting is good, no one can see the technique; the portrayal is seamless, magical. So sometimes people get the idea that such performances are created without technique, that on some magical occasions the actor simply "becomes" the character. Sean Penn, whose performance in "Dead Man Walking" unquestionably meets the standards of "seamless acting," said in an interview for National Public Radio after the movie's release that all his work is built on a steady accumulation of detail that he arrives at through his craft. "I could do nothing without my craft," he stated.

When actors do not have a reliable craft they may put their concentration on the wrong thing. They may concentrate on producing a given effect, such as a mood or emotion or judgment. Or they may concentrate on their appearance, their clothes, or the image that they think the audience expects of them. Or their concentration may be on doing it "right" for daddy/mommy director (that's you). If they have done a good audition or good rehearsal or good first take, they might put their concentration on re-performing that earlier work. This will be a disaster.

A "re-performance" *will be bad*. This is an existential truth. Every event, every moment in life, once it passes, is over. We cannot have our lives back after we have lived them. When a director tells an actor, "That was perfect. Do it again just like that," he is asking for something that is just not going to happen. If the actor tries to "re-perform" she will only be straining, controlling — *aiming*. As a young acting student, I once heard a radio baseball announcer observe to his partner, "They're going to have to take that pitcher out. He's starting to aim the ball." The strangeness of this remark caused it to stick in my mind. I didn't know much about baseball, and I kept asking myself, "What's wrong with aiming? How can he throw the ball over the plate if he doesn't aim?" I sensed somehow that the answer was important so I pondered it until I realized that it was like acting — the pitcher works on his mechanics (for the actor, this means script analysis and rehearsal of playable choices) ahead of time and he creates a connection to the strike zone (the actor's "sense of belief in the created reality"). And then he lets go. Trying to do it "right," trying to control the result, to re-perform a good pitch or a good take, automatically makes the performance self-conscious, takes the performer out of the moment, and causes the pitcher or actor to "lose his stuff."

Everybody knows what to do when he or she is in the zone, when inspiration is striking. You don't have to think about what to do; you feel impulses, and you follow them. A wrong place for an actor to put her concentration is on *trying* to be in the zone. When acting is good and the actors are in the moment, enjoying solitude in public, gripped by the created reality, they often don't notice anything outside of that created reality. It's almost a kind of altered state. An airplane overhead, a cough or sneeze of a technician, will go unheard. They may be playing a hot summer scene in the middle of winter and not even feel the cold. Sometimes actors start to think that the goal of their preparation is to get to that altered state. But you can't aim for the zone. Concentration cannot be commanded, only invited.

A good actor follows the rules, concentrating on listening, on playable choices and on physical life; if he hears the airplane or the breathing of the camera operator or the creak of his shoes, he lets the character hear it. He shuts nothing out; he *uses* everything to keep himself in the moment and give his performance the texture of life. If a director observes an actor agonizing because he can't shut out present reality in order to feel the created reality, it might be a good time to take him aside and ask him, "What are you concentrating on?" Perhaps the image, objective, or given circumstance he has chosen is not strong or specific enough, and by asking him questions you can guide him to a juicier choice. Or perhaps the best course will be to assure him that you would rather have him in the here and now than torturing and manipulating himself. The performance may well be fresher and more honest if he lets the distractions in instead of fighting them.

Now what I said here about not aiming for an altered state may seem contradictory to what I said earlier about actors needing to go below the social mask in order to work well. What can I say? Piercing the social mask frees the actor and is a good thing; aiming for an altered state creates strain and is a bad thing. Does it sound like it would be easy to mistake one for the other? Well, it is. This is (one reason) why the really good actors, who know the difference, get paid so much.

The reason I discuss this in a book for directors is not because you are expected to always know exactly what's wrong with a performance and be able to tell the actor how to fix it. But I want to give you some feel for the kinds of things that can go wrong — do go wrong even for the best actors once in a while — so you have an understanding that they are failures of technique and not mystical emanations. Of course, a director who, watching from the other side of the camera, *is* able to troubleshoot these delicate areas is, to an actor, a wonderful creature.

When two actors are in the zone together — when they are "cooking" — they often feel a kind of rhythm to it. In the next rehearsal or performance or take they may try to play that rhythm. But a rhythm is not a playable tool for an actor so the relationship will lose the life it had when they first "discovered" the rhythm. Let me take just one minute to explain why a rhythm is not playable. It's because the actor loses track of what the character is talking about and why — i.e., his subtext and his situation. This is why many people find performances of Shakespeare incomprehensible, because the actors are *playing the poetry* instead of letting the lines mean something and playing the situation. When actors play the poetry or play the rhythm, the audience can't even make sense of the words.

"Learn the lines and don't bump into the furniture."
— **Spencer Tracy**

When a performance needs to be repeated and lines delivered over and over again — in rehearsal or in coverage — each time they must be spoken as if for the first time. Some actors, like Charles Bronson or Frank Sinatra, in order to keep their deliveries fresh, refuse to do more than one take. If the actors started sounding "canned" or "rehearsed," director Frank Capra would simply change the line. Robert Altman, who has an overruling passion for the honest creativity of actors, does not require the actors to say the same lines in every setup of the same scene. Marlon Brando no longer learns lines; he has the lines read to him over an earpiece. He does this, he says, to keep from getting stale.

These tactics are designed to keep the actors from falling into line readings — preconceived ways of delivering the lines. The extreme opposite of working in the moment is to decide ahead of time how the line is going to be spoken, to orchestrate a performance by deciding on and then delivering a set of line readings. This makes a performance stagy, pat. It puts a little frame around each line, sort of like a person who always seems to be speaking in quotation marks. Getting stuck in a preconceived line reading is *the worst thing* that can happen to an actor.

Many actors and directors are opposed to rehearsal for this reason. If actors use rehearsal to set line readings, then rehearsal is a very bad idea indeed. Most modern actors do not deliberately set line readings, but unless they apply craft deliberately *not* to set them, they may fall into them.

All of us have a tendency to fit new things into the familiar. We see the line "You always do that," and we automatically hear an attitude. Without even realizing he is doing this, an actor may learn the line with the cadence "You always *do* that," (or, "You *always* do that") and after a while the cadence becomes the line for him.

Many actors do their work on a role as they are memorizing their lines, finding beats, subtext, intentions, adjustments, images, and associations as they bring them off the page and into their experience. Doing this is not the same as learning them with a particular line reading, which gives a set cadence or intonation to the lines. When the actor repeats a line every time in a set cadence, the line will automatically have less and less life every time it is spoken. It won't have had much life to begin with either because the set cadence prevents him from being affected by his partner or by his impulses of the moment. Sometimes it gets so bad that an actor who habitually locks into line readings will actually lose his place and think the wrong line was spoken, if an actor opposite him changes the way she says a line!

Taking the lines off the page includes taking them off their punctuation. In real life we do not pause necessarily at periods and commas. We pause when we need to take a breath, or to think of what to say next. These things don't necessarily — and in fact don't usually — occur at periods and commas. It is necessary to have punctuation in a script because punctuation makes it easier to *read*. But in order to bring lines *off* the page and into life the actor must wrest from them their punctuation.

If you want an example of how this works, check out Spencer Tracy's opening soliloquy in the original "Father of the Bride." One of the things people often say about Tracy's work in general is that he gave his speeches unexpected readings and rhythms. What this means is that he put the meaning of the character's images and situation ahead of the author's punctuation. If you need further proof that abandoning punctuation sounds more natural, eavesdrop on ordinary people in conversation.

Overacting can easily follow from getting stuck playing set line readings or punctuation. Because once the line reading is set, if the actor attempts to give the line more spark he only succeeds in adding emphasis. Sort of like the stereotypical American who, when attempting to communicate with someone who doesn't understand English, merely repeats himself in a louder voice.

The worst thing about line readings is that they are so often accompanied by a superficial understanding of the line. Unless an actor commits to the *subworld* of the character, he will have nothing he can do with the line except try to convince us that it is true, and so he falls into protesting or urging the line on us. Some lines fall especially easily into this trap. In older movies of the thirties and forties, an example might be, "I believe that truth and justice will prevail." It's easy to see that in a modern movie such a line would sound foolish or phony unless it was spoken with heavy subtext. But current movies have their own clichés; my own least favorite is, "You just don't get it, do you?" And writers seem never to tire of the line, "You'll never get away with this!" Any of these lines delivered in order to make us believe that the information in it is true — in other words, delivered without subtext — will sound forced and untrue.

Sometimes actors get confused and think they are being honest when they are really urging the line on us, trying to convince us that it is true. But in real life, when people are trying to convince you of the truth of their words, we recognize that they are "protesting too much" — and probably lying.

Not all actors who choose or fall into line readings pick the most obvious, pedestrian choice. An actor of greater imagination might make a more off-beat choice, and an actor with a wide range might be able to be convincing no matter what the reading. But an actor who works "moment by moment" won't lock himself into a line reading at all.

So how will he know how to say it?

LISTENING AND TALKING

"Somewhere along the line, someone — I can't remember who it was — told me to stop acting with a capital 'A,' not to perform, not to be big, not to entertain, just to be. And to ... listen to other people when they're talking. That was probably the most important thing I ever learned." — **Dennis Franz, "NYPD Blue"**

Probably the most powerful and also the most readily available tool an actor has for staying in the moment is the other actor in the scene. Listening to the other person(s) in the scene gives an actor a simple task and a focus for his attention. *Listening* is the best technique an actor has for anchoring himself in the moment. It also keeps his choices from becoming mechanical or forced. Listening relaxes actors. It absolutely prevents overacting. It's what makes a performance look "natural." Listening allows the actors to affect each other and thus to create *moments* — tiny electric connections that make the emotional events of a scene.

If you are directing drama, and you want the audience to engage with the characters and their predicaments and adventures, it is essential that the actors listen. Without listening a dramatic scene is just "my turn to talk, your turn to talk"; it becomes a scene about two actors' performances instead of a scene about a relationship and an event in that relationship.

If you have a funny script to direct and you don't want it ruined, it is essential that the actors listen. When the actors listen to each other and play the situations, the audience can hear the lines, identify

with the characters and suspend their disbelief in even the most out-
rageous situations. When actors in a comedy are not listening, when
they start to play the punchlines or the schtick instead of playing the
situations, the comedy becomes forced and a terrible strain to watch.

*   *   *

The words that characters speak to each other are not the scene.
The scene is the underlying event to which the words are clues. We
only have an event — that is, a scene — if something *happens* to the
characters. When the actors are *listening* to each other, something
can *happen* because they can affect each other. Now it stands to
reason that it is the director's job to make sure that there is a scene
and not just words being spoken. Hence a good director will make
sure that the actors are listening to each other.

In the worst cases of non-listening, the actor may do what is
called "anticipating." This means she may actually react (with a pre-
decided reaction) to the other actor's line before that actor even
delivers it. You don't see this much in movies that are actually
released or television programs that get aired. It looks so bad that
even if a director is so tense or unsophisticated that he doesn't notice
it ("anticipating" is one of the acting problems in the movies of
Edward D. Wood, Jr., for example) *someone* on the set — or in the
editing room — will usually spot it.

**"I think that if you have a talent for acting, it is the talent for
listening." — Morgan Freeman**

You might think listening would be automatic. The actors hear
each other's lines — doesn't that mean that they are listening? But
we are not talking about ordinary listening. It is a term of art. It's
not just listening for your cue, for your turn to talk, it is a special
attention paid to the other person.

The actor is required to listen more deeply than we usually do in
real life. In fact Stanislavsky uses the term "communion" to describe
what I am calling "listening." The term "communion" calls attention

to the deepness of the experience as well as to the fact that listening makes the audience feel the actors are communicating with each other rather than delivering lines to each other.

Eye contact is very helpful to listening. In my Acting for Directors class I begin with a listening exercise; first I ask each student to make eye contact with his partner. The eye contact I am asking them to make is different from regular "looking." When we use our eyes in the regular way, we are checking, evaluating, categorizing — this is not a bad thing to do when you are driving a car, for instance. But the eye contact I am asking for is a giving and a receiving; it is using your eyes in the sense that the eyes are windows of the soul.

It is a surrender, a tiny leap of faith. It exactly means that the actor puts more attention on the other actor than on her own performance. And allows her lines to be informed by that attention, dictated by that attention. The lines *come out* of her attention to the other actor, out of her interest in the response of the other actor, rather than out of a decision how to say them. Now this is key. Listening is not simply hearing the words the other actor says and responding to them — it is allowing one's *concentration* to be on the response of the other actor, on him physically — on the expression in his eyes, the little lines around his mouth, on the *sound* of his voice as well as the words he is saying, on his body, even on his smell.

This is a subtle distinction that absolutely differentiates really good actors from mediocre ones. Actors can get stuck selling the surface of the lines if they think listening is merely responding to what they hear the other actor say. Presumably the scene is written so that it sounds like the characters are listening and responding to each other — the lines answer each other. So actors can fool themselves into thinking that they are listening when they are really only playing the surface of the lines. They think that as long as they are not committing the cardinal sin of "anticipating," they are listening.

When an actor is listening, his facial expressions also come out of his interest in the response of the other actor. If the actor becomes concerned with his own response (perhaps in reaction to a result direction, for example, "I think you should get angry when she says X") there is a tiny hardening in his face, an invisible veil in front of his expression.

Of course true listening can happen without eye contact, but it is easier with it. And eye contact is very underrated as an acting tool. According to his book <u>Making Movies</u>, Sidney Lumet noticed, when he was working with William Holden on "Network," that Holden rarely made eye contact with his acting partners. When it came time to film his big emotional scene the only direction Lumet gave Holden was to look in Faye Dunaway's eyes for the whole scene and never to look away. Emotion poured out of Holden.

"All you have to do is look at Anthony Hopkins' eyes and you get so much, your job is cut in half, there's so much in his eyes. He was lovely, generous, moving." — **Joan Allen**

"[Candace Bergen] has the most beautiful eyes. And not being a trained actor, I'll go right into her eyes when I'm lost. I look at them, and I say the words. It's a wonderful thing." — **Garry Marshall**

Listening is sure-fire, it is the best tool an actor has. And it is simple. Whatever her preparation, the actor puts her full attention on the other actor. But sometimes actors don't listen. Sometimes they are fearful of being caught staring at the other actor; they worry that full eye contact would not be natural-looking. Attempting to give their performances variety and colors, they devise elaborate affectations of response that bear no relation to true listening.

Sometimes actors are working so hard on their inner life that they forget about the other actor. Sometimes they don't like what the other actor is doing and think that if they listen to him it will bring their performance down. Some successful, highly regarded actors think they have to screen out the other actor in order to maintain the luster of their individual performance.

True listening can be frightening to actors. Actors themselves call a fellow actor who is a good listener unselfish. A reviewer called Emma Thompson's performance in "Sense and Sensibility" "considerate" — I think he perceived that she always listens. "Ensemble acting" is another name for listening. You may have noticed that the new Screen Actors Guild awards include awards for Ensemble Acting in every category. This is because actors know, as John Travolta said in his Golden Globe acceptance speech for "Get Shorty," that an actor "can only be as great as the actors around him." Spencer Tracy is known as the "actor's actor" because he always listened.

When actors are said to have "chemistry" together, it means that they listen to each other, they engage, they "play off" each other. Romantic leads don't have to sleep together — they don't even have to like each other — as long as they listen. Cary Grant had chemistry with more leading ladies than probably any other actor in the history of movies — because he always listened, always put his full, relaxed concentration *on his partner*.

Ensemble acting puts the story ahead of showy individual performances, and allows the audience to relax and enjoy the movie. There can be a nagging fear for actors that by listening, by submitting themselves to the ensemble, they are giving something up. They could not be more mistaken. They are caught in the misunderstanding I described above: that of thinking that listening is no more than hearing the other actor's lines and inflections. No. It is the attention, the *concentration* on the response of the other actor. For this, each actor bears individual responsibility. Listening does not detract from an actor's performance — it enriches the texture, substance, humor, suspense, etc., etc. My best advice to young actors is always, "When all else fails, make the other guy look good." It's the simplest, surest way for an actor to improve his own performance.

But when the other actors are also listening, are also giving, and are in addition connected up to their simple, honest understanding of the circumstances of the script — then really superior work can take place. And without that, without *all* the actors giving to each other, an actor who listens and who meets the demands of the role may stand out and still look good, but *really* superior work cannot take place.

You as the director are in a position to turn a group of actors into an ensemble. First of all, you must ask for it. And you need to be able to spot resistances to listening because if even one of the actors is not listening you have no scene, only two performances. And the scene itself turns into a scene about two actors instead of a scene about whatever the script is about.

Of course sometimes the reason actors are not listening is because they are trying to follow a result-oriented direction. Result-oriented direction takes the actor's concentration off his partner and puts it squarely on himself. The actor starts worrying: "Am I as angry as the director wants me to be? Did I have the right reaction, the right expression? Did I say the line right? Was I quirky enough?" When his concentration is focused thus on his performance, rather than on a playable choice, which can connect him to the other actor, his performance is ruined.

It can be hard for an inexperienced director to tell if actors are listening. Superior listening skills are invisible to the untrained eye. Actors like James Garner, Peter Falk, Mary Tyler Moore, Spencer Tracy — all actors of superior listening skills — seem simply to be the character, with no visible craft.

When John Travolta says that a director "won't see it on the set. You'll see it in the editing room," it's a bit intimidating, isn't it? Makes you feel left out. Dennis Hopper, while directing Robert Duvall in "Colors," was terrified because it didn't look like Duvall was doing anything! It looked boring! Fortunately he was more terrified of looking foolish by telling a superior actor like Duvall to do "more," so he didn't say anything — because in the rushes, it was all there.

Now that you know about listening, you have the secret! You can see it on the set, if you know what to look for. The main reason why directors don't see "it" on the set is that they don't understand about listening, they don't appreciate the source of the tiny emotional events that read like gangbusters on the big screen.

It is astonishing to me that nowadays so many directors — including directors who should know better — position themselves at the video monitor while a scene is shooting. You're not going to like hearing this, but it's my job to tell you: *You can't tell from the video monitor whether the actors are listening.* You must be next to the camera, watching their naked faces.

In most movies where the acting is bad, the thing that is wrong is the actors were not listening to each other. In student films and first features this is the most glaring defect. Problems of pace and timing, lapses in energy, false notes, lack of "build" to a scene, actors who are flat, stiff, cold, cardboard-y, "walking through it," "phoning it in," actors who seem to be "in different movies" — all these are examples of problems that usually are listening problems. Likewise when actors are overacting. When directors tell actors to "do less" what they probably should be telling them is to listen more.

If the actors are not listening in a two-shot or master, the shot will turn out to be unusable because if there is no listening, there is no relationship. And if there is no relationship, there is nothing to watch in a two-shot. But listening is also crucial to a close-up. People think of the close-up as the chance to see the character's reactions, his inner life, which they figure the actor can create all by himself. But a performance in which the actor is acting "all by himself," while it may be showy and impressive, takes the audience out of the story, to watch the impressive acting. So in close-ups equally as in two-shots and masters the actor must be listening. Listening gives life and colors and expression to the close-ups. Listening creates the tiny expressive movements, the sense that the character is thinking about what to say next, and feels something about what he is saying. Listening makes the audience care about the characters and what happens to them.

Sometimes a shot is so tight or so complicated that there is no room for the other actor to stand in the eyeline of the actor whose close-up is being shot. Sometimes the director of photography will tell you that in order to get the two-shot you want, the actors' eye-lines will need to be elsewhere than looking at each other. I'm not saying that you should block every scene so that the actors are always looking at each other. I'm talking about scenes which are staged so that the characters are meant to be looking at each other but, because of technical demands, the actors playing the charac-ters cannot. Your reasons for deciding to arrange the shot this way may be important enough to you that you decide to forego the freshness that two engaged actors (provided they really are engaged, and are really playing off each other, and not just "acting all by themselves" even though they are standing face-to-face) can give the scene. But you should understand that you are making a choice, a trade-off. If, when you get to the editing room, you don't see "it" — you don't see the relationship or the emotional events of the scene — then what? The one thing I don't want you to do at that point is say, "I had no choice."

Directors often want to know how to work with actors who have been trained in different ways. The answer is simple: get them to talk and listen to each other, get them to put their concentration on each other, keep each one from acting "all by himself" and screening the other one out.

*   *   *

How can directors learn to tell whether actors are listening? No book can give you this skill. You need to be able to see and feel it. And you need to be able to see and feel it not just on a movie screen but while it is happening in front of you. In other words, you need to be in the moment; you need to be able to listen, too. Your eyes must be open, relaxed, and soft, able to receive. This is how you will be able to catch false moments. Sidney Lumet says in his book <u>Making Movies</u> that he can tell if the acting in a take is good enough or not by simply watching in a relaxed way. Then whenever his atten-tion wanders, he knows the actors are not engaged and the take is not good enough.

Here's another way to tell whether the actors are listening: *When actors listen, their performances on each take are going to be slightly different.* This idea is frightening to directors. It takes tremendous courage and skill to trust this process. Each take the actor does of a scene has to be slightly different if the actor is listening. And there's more: If the actors are listening, the readings of the lines are likely to come out differently from the way you heard them in your head. If you want good acting, you must favor listening over preconceived line readings. I tell you this flat out.

"It took me years to understand fully why [my teacher] was right, and...never to plan how I would say a line, only to think of the situation, and listen to the other actors...What is hard, and really has to be worked at, is being able to go with whatever comes up from other actors or the director at each moment of a performance and not to try to force a repetition of something that went well the day before....The real work of acting is letting go." — **Vanessa Redgrave**

Some actors are "naturals," that is, they are good listeners without having to think about it. Most actors are aware of listening as a technique and make a habit of reminding themselves to listen. It can help a lot if the director, before rehearsal and before each shot, mentions it in some nonthreatening way, by saying something like, "No need to push, let's take it easy, just connect with each other."

Then while you are watching the actors work, you need to monitor whether they are listening. When actors are not listening, you as the director need to talk to them about it. You may not want to use the term itself because, as I mentioned above, some actors understand the term "listening" incorrectly. If told that they have not been listening, they might fall into exaggerated or fake listening. There are two kinds of fake listening. One is a studied casual attitude; it's not really listening, it's an attitude of listening. The other is an overwrought pop-eyed intense thing; what's wrong with this is its strain. There is an ease to real listening; the actors who understand its magic are truly liberated by the simple act of putting more concentration on the person they are talking to than on themselves.

Here are some examples of how to ask the actors to listen more: "Give the lines to each other." "Keep it simple." "Stay with each other." "It's okay to relax. Let yourselves connect." "Communicate." "Just talk and listen." "Let yourself hear what she's saying." "I like it when you play off each other." "You can pay attention to each other." "Watch her eyes." "Play off her energy." "It's okay to engage, be affected by her. You can relax. Don't say the lines until you feel like saying them." This is language of *permission* rather than enforcement.

Producer Polly Platt reported to me that director James Brooks says to his actors, "Just remember, everything you are saying is true." Glenn Close, in her interview for the program "Inside the Actors Studio," said that Mike Nichols' words were, "Bring your day in with you." These are ways of saying, "Keep it simple. Be a person, not a character. Don't act with a capital A. It's okay to talk and listen." Sometimes actors have a false sense of responsibility: they feel, even unconsciously, that they're not doing their job unless they hang on to their preparation, that giving themselves over to the other actor is neglecting their responsibilities to their character. It's almost a case of "How can something that feels this good (as listening) be good for you?" You can be the one to give the actors permission to let go, to connect. Woody Allen, in a 1994 <u>New York Magazine</u> article, disclosed that the reason he uses one wide shot for most of his whole scenes is partly because it is quicker and cheaper, but mostly it is for the actors, because it is a way to "let them talk," and to allow overlapping.

If you are more deeply into rehearsal or shooting and the actors are losing their connection, you might try: "I think this is the kind of script that only works if we have ensemble playing." "It's okay to put your concentration on each other." "You two have everything you need. You can give it to each other now." "The listening is really all I care about. I know you can get the rest of it." "Don't worry about what you're feeling; concern yourself with what your partner is feeling." "You don't need to screen her out. You can let what she's doing feed you." "I believe you but you're keeping it all inside, it's very internal. Let it out, give it to the other actor." "I think you're getting worried about your performance. It's all there. You can trust it." "Keep your attention on her, check out her response."

It can be hard for an actor who listens and gives to work opposite an actor who is not listening. It's depressing, because the listening actor knows her chances for a really great performance are going down the drain. Sometimes she tries to "save" her performance by pulling back, thinking that relating to the other actor's wooden performance will bring hers down. A director needs to deal with these situations delicately. Actually she will save her performance by continuing to give and to listen. And of course the scene itself (the director's responsibility) will get even worse if she stops listening too. In a deteriorating situation like this, you might take the more experienced or better actor aside and tell her frankly your concerns, enlist her help so she doesn't feel left out to dry by the other actor's "nobody home"-ness. You need to assure her that if she continues to work full out and to stay engaged that you will make sure that the scene works.

And then you have to do it. You need to do something to change what the other, lesser actor is doing, or the better actor will start to lose faith in you. Usually the problem is that the lesser actor is "acting with a capital A" and you need to get him to be simpler and more present in the moment so he can put attention on his partner. You might do this by changing the interpretation of the character, even if earlier you had agreed on a certain interpretation. Or you might be able to say directly (but privately) to him, "You're doing too much acting. It's not believable."

If you are desperate you might even try an outright trick, such as: "You're doing great, but I'm worried about your partner. I need you to help me here. Try to help her stay loose." Anything to encourage the actor to relax and stop acting up a storm and instead put his concentration on his partner should be done.

It makes me nervous to put such a thing in print, because the last thing I want to do is encourage arrogance in young directors toward actors. When I am directing, the only reason why I would engage in such a tactic is because I love actors and I trust the process. An actor may hear a flat statement that he is not listening as an accusation, even an attack on his personality; this could cause him to shrink. When I give direction, I am always trying to make what I am asking the actor to do sound to him like something he can do rather than like something he can't do, like change his personality. I believe that the condition of relaxed and vibrant listening is a natural condition, and that if I give permission and confidence to the actors they will open toward it as a flower toward the sun. This belief of mine allows me to always see their resistances and acting problems as things that are in the way of their true selves rather than character flaws. And I can always find a way to give direction that doesn't damage their confidence, even though I am like a dog with a bone when it comes to not giving up on something I think is important.

When actors are struggling, I always look for the way to concentrate on what is going right instead of what is going wrong, to see the glass half full instead of half empty, to offer guidance and encouragement instead of criticism and commands. I get laughed at for the circumlocutions of my "relentlessly positive" adjustments, but they work.

*   *   *

Inexperienced directors, and even a lot of experienced ones, do not realize how important listening is. Even as you are reading this, you may be saying to yourself, "Okay, sure. What's the big deal?" It is one of those things that is simple but not easy. It can take discipline on the part of the actors to put concentration on the other actor and not be distracted from listening by concerns for making the "right" effect. It takes great concentration and skill on the part of directors to be able to tell whether true listening is taking place instead of actors just saying lines because it is their turn. And it takes a director secure in his talent and skills to be able to put concerns for listening ahead of concerns for hearing the lines come out the way he expects them to.

Probably the most important difference between a good director and a mediocre director is whether she can tell if the actors are listening. I urge you to investigate this further in your own work and perhaps in a class situation. "Just talk and listen." My own teacher Jean Shelton used to say this to us until we were tired of hearing it. Sidney Lumet uses this expression as well. Talk to a person. Listen to a person. Be a *person*, not a character.

Listening is the most important element of performance. It is the most important thing a director should be looking for. Some of the things I say in this book are controversial, but this is not. Every good director and every good actor agree on this point. Even if they don't always do it, they know they should.

ACTORS' CHOICES

"Most actors' problems, professional or amateur, deal with tension and there are a lot of devices and ways of eliminating it. In a very professional actor the tension is because they haven't made a choice that has taken enough of their mental interest. In other words, they haven't made a vital enough choice; it's not up to a level that will engage their imagination and get them into pretending unself-consciously."
— **Jack Nicholson**

The last two chapters have concentrated on the "right-brain," improvisatory, unpredictable stuff — "in the moment," listening, risk, freedom. I've been harping on giving up preconceived ways of saying a line, but now it's time to talk about structure — choices that fulfill the material. Directors often want to learn "actors' language," but adding a few "terms of art" or jargon to your vocabulary will not make you a good director. What's needed is a new way of looking at behavior.

Constantin Stanislavsky, the actor, director, teacher, artistic director of the Moscow Art Theatre, and author of <u>An Actor Prepares</u>, formulated acting techniques that were objective and quantifiable but could activate the subconscious and mysterious. It became possible to create structure that made a performance repeatable while preserving moment-by-moment reality, emotional truthfulness, and the actor's inner freedom.

91

Before Stanislavsky, acting training consisted of instruction in voice, movement, and selecting a vocal pattern and gesture deemed appropriate to various character types. Certain gestures denoted annoyance or rage; a rising or falling inflection would call attention to the punch line of a joke; a catalog of postures and gaits identified class distinctions and personalities. For example stooping and hand-wringing denoted a pitiful character, nose in the air a haughty character, etc. Stanislavsky charged that this work resulted in posing, stereotype, and cliché that in no way resembled actual human behavior.

Stanislavsky's ideas are still brilliant and radical today — radical both in the sense of going to the root of things and in the sense of their defiance of conventional wisdom. It is still hard for producers, directors, writers and even actors to understand and trust that if an actor commits to a playable choice rather than to a decision about vocal inflection or facial expression, the movie will be better.

*   *   *

Powerful actors must connect with something powerful in the script or else they can't commit their imaginations. A good actor who is uncommitted imaginatively will look like he is "walking through" a role. It may not be possible for an actor to engage and listen with the other actor(s) until he has worked out the choices that illumine the emotional center of the script. For a really professional actor, a poor choice — a choice that does not fully realize the material — reads as a false note. That is, when the material offers an opportunity to make a choice and the actor has missed that opportunity and failed to "fill" the words, there will be a "dead spot." The scene at this moment will seem slow.

The choices an actor makes activate his inner life. The trick of an actor's preparation is to find choices that 1) connect to the deepest and freshest meaning of the script, and 2) turn him on, capture his imagination, so that 3) he can connect to them with emotional honesty and get to the places he needs to go. The actor looks for choices that are objective, playable, and that engage his own subconscious so that he can be in the moment, thinking real thoughts and feeling real feelings.

Imaginative choices are practical and idiosyncratic, not academic. They are secrets, gateways into the imaginative subworld. They are not something the audience is supposed to "get." Although they are inspired by the script and illuminate its deepest reaches, these choices are not in service of the author of the screenplay; they are in service of the actor's concentration. If they work and bring the script alive, they are good ones; if they don't work, they're bad ones.

Choices create behavior. This is where not having gotten stuck in preconceived ways of saying a line pays off, because the *behavior* dictates the way the lines are said. The lines *come out of* the choice. Sanford Meisner puts it this way: "The emotion of the scene is a river and the words are like boats that float on the river."

An actor's work on the script is to find his choice, a "what is to be acted," a "something of his own" from which to listen and play off the other actor. The choice the actor gives himself, the "something of his own" must be so simple, so compelling, so present that he need not step out of the moment to find it. Choices that are arrived at ahead of time are really ideas or probabilities; choices must actually take place in the moment, or they become forced or mechanical. Choices must be specific, private, and eccentric to each actor. When the performances are private, the experience of each audience member watching the film is a private one. Thus the more the actor achieves specificity and simplicity, the more the performance achieves universality.

QUESTIONS

"Finally, you know, I consider that my profession as a director is not exactly like a supervisor. No. We are, simply, midwives. The actor has something inside himself but very often he doesn't realize what he has in mind, in his own heart, and you have to tell him. You have to help him find himself." — **Jean Renoir**

The best route to making choices is asking questions. It may surprise you in discussion with actors to hear them asking questions with answers that seem obvious to you. I have seen directors get panicky and conclude that the actor is at a loss. The opposite is probably the case. As he works, an actor keeps a performance fresh by continuing to ask questions, opening up corners and crannies of the character's world, feeding himself, adding layers. Of course, actors do not always share their questions with their directors. They may do this work privately. If they do ask you, as director, a question, don't answer unless you have an answer you believe in. Not all actors' questions need to be answered anyway. The asking of questions is part of a *process*.

Often the most helpful response you can make to an actor's question is to turn it back, to say, "What do you think?" Often actors know the answer already, but are insecure. Or, sometimes they know the answer but don't know they know it. Let's say the actor asks, "Why doesn't my character tell his wife about the letter?" Perhaps the director says, "What do you think?" and the actor replies, "I don't know, I haven't a clue," or even, "It doesn't make sense to me." The thing to do next is to look at some possible reasons why a person might behave that way. Why would a man not tell his wife about a letter? Maybe he forgot. Maybe the letter contains a guilty secret he doesn't want his wife to know about. Maybe his wife is ill and he doesn't want to burden her. Maybe he had something else on his mind that was so pressing that the letter seemed unimportant by comparison. It's very helpful to look at as many possibilities as your imagination offers up.

Now what if the actor asks you a question about the letter, and you reply, "What do you think?"; then the actor responds, "I think it's a guilty secret" — and you think that answer is wrong! Maybe in doing your script analysis you have considered the possibility of a guilty secret but decided that adding a guilty secret to the subtext would make the movie too melodramatic, and that the lighter choice of "he forgot" will actually add more to the mystery and suspense.

Well, at this point, you the director have some options. Your least attractive course would be to contradict him. Saying things like, "No, I think that's wrong, here is the right answer," or even, "Here is what I want" may work if you have a very close relationship with the actor, but usually they make the actor feel dampened and/or argumentative. It can be more helpful to say, "Yes, that's possible. What else might it be?" Or, "Yes, that's possible. Or maybe he forgot! That happens to me all the time; I forget the real reason why I do things, and get into all sorts of trouble." Depending on your relationship with the actor and your own personal charisma, sometimes just saying, "Well, that's possible" in a thoughtful way might induce the actor to wonder if there isn't a more provocative choice and to keep exploring and rethinking.

Sometimes it is tempting to go to the writer and ask the question, or even demand that the writer put the answer into the script. Try to resist! The fact that actors have questions is not a bad thing — it is a good thing. Questions can be truly magical. Sometimes you need to figure out the answer in order to solve the scene and unlock the choice that releases the actor's attention. But sometimes just asking the question is enough. The character may not know the answer himself! The character may himself be wondering why the hell he didn't tell his wife about the letter. Characters, like people, most of the time probably don't know why they do what they do. The actor can use his own perplexity to engage his sense of belief.

If you think of answering actors' questions as an obligation, your answers will be plodding explanations, probably dead-on the surface meaning of the lines. You will neglect to look for opposites.

OPPOSITES

"I'm interested in the flip side, the B-side of people. As an actor, your challenge is to get your mind around the psychology of another human being — and the bigger the polarity, the more dramatic that is." — **Ralph Fiennes**

Opposites are an actor's best friend. They are a great tool of script analysis — as soon as you come up with one idea, consider also its opposite. Whenever you're not sure what to do with a line, find an opposite. If a scene isn't working, do it wrong! An opposite choice keeps the actor in the moment because it is surprising, even to him. A good actor keeps himself entertained and alive — in the soup — by allowing a conflict between the words and his inner life. And if the actor is alive, the material will make sense even if the inner choice is not logical.

When a character says one thing and means another, that makes him complex. Best of all, the duality makes him more real. People are not especially logical. They often mean quite the opposite of what they say. We see it in real life: a person who says, "I'm very open to your proposal," with arms and legs crossed, looking at you from the side of his eyes. His body language is saying that he is the opposite of open.

An actor who gets stuck in the logical, "on the nose" choice will never look like a real person. The off-kilter, illogical choice is usually the truest one. People don't know who they are or what they want, and they don't do the right thing to get it. One actor who uses opposites constantly and very effectively is Gene Hackman. He often says a line exactly the reverse of the way it might look on the page: for instance, "I'm going to kill you," said with a smile (i.e., with the action verb "to charm").

JUDGMENT

"It's easy to sit back and judge someone, but I am not in a position to judge Nixon. As an actor, I can't judge because moral judgment gets in the way of the characterization. If you start doing that, you end up playing the character like a zombie or a vaudeville villain." — **Anthony Hopkins**

Obvious ways to judge a character are to decide that he is a "perpetual loser," "weak," "vicious," "an anal-retentive type" or "stupid."

But there are tiny judgments that creep into an actor's thinking almost unnoticed: a condescension to the character, an evaluation that the character is just a little less self-aware, or more naive, or more weird than the actor herself. Now these evaluations may even be true, but they are not playable. They cause the actor to stand outside the character and describe and explain her to the audience, to comment on her — to editorialize and to play *at* her — rather than to live her life moment by moment and allow the audience to draw its own conclusions.

Lili Taylor in the movie "Rudy" had the small role of the high school sweetheart who wanted Rudy to settle down instead of following his dream. With the words she was given to say she could easily have fallen into a stereotype of a clingy, manipulative suburban matron-to-be, and become "the person who doesn't want Rudy to follow his dreams" instead of a real person with dreams of her own. Taylor found the character's grit and humor instead of making a judgment and managed to make a not very deeply written character human and watchable.

Really good actors do not ever judge their characters. The imagined world is too fascinating to them, and the opportunity to leap into it too precious. Glenn Close says that she "falls in love" with every character she plays. This doesn't mean that she must condone the character's behavior or abandon her own values or personal ethics. But it does mean she creates the character's behavior using her own impulses.

Sometimes a director in my Acting for Directors class complains to me when I ask him to try a certain adjustment, "But I would never do such-and-such." Okay, I believe you. What I don't believe is that you can never know the impulse to do such-and-such. Every one of us carries somewhere inside us the impulse (perhaps so deeply buried that it will never express itself in behavior) to do anything that any human being has ever done. It is the actor's job to find that impulse and surrender to it honestly in the created reality. You see he finds the *impulse*, not the deed itself. Because it is not real reality, it is created reality, an illusion. We, as filmmakers, are not trying to make the audience believe that the events depicted in a movie are actually happening to the actors on the screen.

Ralph Fiennes has said of his performance in "Schindler's List," "People are always trying to think that in order to play a sadist you have to be one. I was not required to hurt [anyone] when I was playing Amon Goeth. I tried to put myself in a place where I could imagine what it was like to have a form of prejudice that was so extreme that certain groups of people became equivalent to cockroaches or rats." By not judging the character Fiennes gave us the revelation that the face of evil is a human face. This made the Nazi he portrayed far more chilling than the one-dimensional Nazis that are sometimes found in movies.

*   *   *

NEED

Spine / Objective / Intention / Verb

Spine, objective, intention, and verb are all expressions of what a character (person) needs. All creatures — not just human creatures, but all living creatures, all living things — move toward what they need. Plants grow toward the sun. This is the principle behind these actors' tools.

The objective is what the character wants the other character to do, and the action verb is what he is doing to get what he wants. "Intention" is virtually interchangeable with either term, and is sometimes called "the emotional intention."

The character's spine, or super-objective, is what he wants during the whole script; you could call it what he wants out of life. It is the one specific thing that a character needs more than any other, will sacrifice the most to have. Sometimes people call it the character's life-need; you may also hear it called his core, his through line, his want, the red thread, the thing that drives him, what he is fighting for, what is important to him.

Each character has *one* overall spine throughout the whole movie. In each scene, although the action verb may change frequently, each character has one objective. In life our needs don't turn on and off haphazardly. We don't necessarily stop needing something *even when we do get it*. And we certainly don't stop needing something just because we realize we can't have it.

In his "Inside the Actors Studio" interview Paul Newman referred to "active verbs" which are the same as the "action verbs" I talk about. Michael Shurtleff's book <u>Audition</u>, widely read by actors, exhorts them always to connect to "what the character is fighting for" — this is, by another name, the objective. I have heard actors refer to a "driving energy" or finding the character's "agenda" or "motor" — also objectives. You can use any vernacular for it. It isn't necessary to use the terms of art in order to take advantage of these tools.

SPINE

There is often confusion between "spine" and "transformation," also sometimes called "arc." Many directors, when I offer them the liberating and invaluable tool of one spine per character per script, persist in the notion that the character wants one thing until "X" happens, and then he wants something else. This is not a spine; it is an attempt to describe the character's transformation.

You might hear someone describe a character by saying that when his best friend dies, he "learns the value of friendship," that is, he transforms from a person who only cares about himself into a person who is capable of love, or unselfish action, or whatever. It is helpful for an actor to know the character's transformation; it is definitely imperative for the director to know all the characters' transformations. But it is a big mistake for an actor, after figuring out the character's transformation, to set out to play "a person who learns the value of friendship." This leads him to playing the end of the script at the beginning.

Let's take as an example, the character Michael Corleone, played by Al Pacino in "The Godfather." What do you think might be Michael's spine? When I ask students this question, they often suggest that he wants "power" or "control" or "family loyalty" or "to get revenge for the shooting of his father." None of these will work for the whole script. When I say that I think Michael's spine is "to please his father," or perhaps, "to make his father proud of him," students sometimes protest that in the beginning of the movie Michael wants to separate himself from his father and be his own man, and that it is only after Don Vito is shot that Michael wants to make his father proud of him.

But look at the facts. In the beginning of the movie Michael is pleasing his father and making him proud by becoming a lawyer. Don Vito has three sons: the eldest (Sonny/Santino) is to succeed him as godfather, the second (Fredo) is to be active in the business, although his activities must be scaled to his rather severe personal limitations. The youngest (and favorite), Michael, is to become a real "American" (he even has the only "American" name) and make his life and his living outside the family business. Michael's independence *pleases* his father. By the end of the movie Michael is not only in the family business but has taken his father's place as don; this is his transformation. The transforming event, I think, is Sonny's death. After Sonny's death there is no one else (certainly not Fredo) who can succeed Don Vito. So Don Vito makes his peace with the notion of Michael heading the family business, and that becomes the way Michael can please him.

Michael's spine "to please his father" doesn't change even after his father's death. We know from real life that this can happen, that a person might still be driven by a need for a parent's love and respect even after the parent is dead. Perhaps the theme of "Godfather II" is exactly this: that continuing to live driven by the need to make someone happy when that person is no longer alive to respond to one's efforts, robs life of its zest and creates a hollow in Michael's heart.

The spine is *who a person is*. It may even be partly genetic. This is the reason why many actors seem to play every role the same. Being able to believably play a spine different from one's own is quite a feat. Some actors who play the same character in every movie are operating out of a "secret identity" spine, different from their own, but for some reason easily and deeply accessible to their imagination. For example, Charlie Chaplin was in real life quite different from the "little tramp" character he most successfully played, whose spine might perhaps be described as "to stay out of trouble."

There are several ways an actor uses spine as a tool. One is while reading a script and deciding whether to take the role. A good actor when reading a script looks (among other things) for a playable spine — a hanger or hook from which all the character's actions depend. When he finds a believable spine he knows that a real character has been written, not a patched-up plot manipulation.

Once it is found, the actor uses that spine to design the role. This is the way an actor can play a major, complex role when it is shot out of sequence. Every decision, every choice made about the character relates to the spine, including the objectives of each individual scene. But the relationship may be indirect. For instance in "Last Tango in Paris," even though the Brando character in each scene with Maria Schneider has the objective to push her away, or to hurt or humiliate her, it seems to me that his spine (super–objective) is to find love. The pushing away is a series of tests to see if he can trust her. Her scene-by-scene objectives, on the other hand, are nearly all to get affection from him, to get closer. And yet I think her super-objective is not love, but to grow up, to become an adult. She must draw him closer in order to overthrow him, the father figure. The moment when he gives up testing and surrenders to her (at the tango parlor) is the same moment that she gathers strength to reject him (these are their moments of transformation).

Must the actor and director agree on the spine of the character? Yes and no. The choice of a spine must be supported by the script, but it is a secret choice. Sydney Pollack compares the spine of the movie to the armature of a sculpture; it keeps the thing together, but no one sees it. If what an actor is doing works, what does it matter if the spine she has chosen is different from your idea? But if you are not happy with a performance, bringing up the subject (via a question, such as "What are you thinking of as the spine of this character?") can be a useful way to begin a discussion about shaping or changing a performance.

On the other hand, some directors prefer to make all the decisions about spine. Independent British filmmaker Ken Loach, in an L.A. Times interview, said he doesn't give actors a full script ahead of time, and instead feeds them a couple of pages at a time, because he wants them to give a simple, unrehearsed response to each circumstance of the script as it arises. I should think that the success of this approach must depend on the director casting people who have the same life-spine as the characters.

OBJECTIVE

A character's *objective* for a particular scene can be very specific and very simple. For example: I want him to leave the room; I want him to kiss me; I want him to laugh; I want him to cry. The simpler it is the more playable it is. The most playable objectives have both a physical and an emotional component.

The physical component means that, if you achieve your objective, you will know it because of a physical event — the other actor would cry or laugh or kiss you or leave the room, whatever. So you have a point of concentration that is physical and real, a simple imaginative task.

Part of the emotional component means that getting this objective, or not getting it, will constitute an emotional event in the relationship, a win or a loss. To be very simple–minded about it, if my objective is to get someone to leave the room, when he leaves the room, I win; if he doesn't, I lose. In either case our relationship has undergone a small (or a big) change.

The rest of the emotional component is that the objective arises out of the character's needs and feelings. Needs and feelings are subjective. Actors who feel deeply but fail to connect their feelings to intention can become general or self-indulgent. The simple intention — an inclination toward having some effect on the other person — leads to engagement. Although simple listening has already engaged the actors, endowing the characters with a *need* to interact raises the stakes of the relationship. It also makes it possible for the actors to listen and play off each other even if the characters are not listening to each other. Objectives make possible conflict and a sense of *event* in the relationship, because the actors are doing something *to each other* rather than doing something to the lines.

ACTION VERBS

If I want you to leave the room I might *invite* you to leave the room. If that doesn't work, I might *demand* that you leave the room. If that doesn't work I might *beg*. If that doesn't work I might *whine, tease, punish*, etc. The intention, or verb, might change often, even in the middle of the line, or it might be the same for the whole scene. The verb changes because of the exchange between the two characters. Complex characters may change their verb often or make wide swings from, say, soothing to punishing in one speech.

You will notice that the verbs on the Short List of Action Verbs all carry an intent to have an emotional effect on the other person; thus they are sometimes called "emotional intentions." Verbs stimulate emotion. Honestly committing to any one of the verbs on the Short List will put the actor *at risk* (in a theatrical sense).

UNCONSCIOUS OBJECTIVES

A director should be able to determine what intention or objective an actor is playing, even if the actor doesn't know it herself. If an audition, rehearsal, improv, or take has gone exceptionally well, very often the actor doesn't know what she has done, because she was in the moment and not watching her performance. It can be very useful for the director to mirror it back to her. If you want a change in the performance, you might say something like this: "The thing I liked about the last rehearsal was that you seemed to be putting [the other character] at ease. This time it seemed as if you wanted his approval."

Actors can fall into the unconscious objective "to say my lines effectively." Or "to make the director/producer think I'm a good actor," or "to remember my lines." Any of these objectives take the actor's attention off the *work* and hurt the performance. Sometimes an actor intellectualizes his objective and winds up showing us that he has such an objective instead of allowing it organically to impel his words and movements. In other words, he has the unconscious objective "to have an objective."

Finding the character's objective is preparation. The actor analyzes the script, finds something playable, and makes it real for himself. Then he lets go and plays the moment. If the actor falls out of the moment or loses concentration, he has something to fall back on. If his objective is to get her to laugh, he can look at his partner and ask himself, "Is that a little smile around her lips? Am I making any headway in getting her to laugh? What shall I try next?"

What if his objective is "to be forgiven," and the other actor has a line late in the scene, "I forgive you"? If he makes his objective "to make her say she forgives him," he hasn't got enough to do, hasn't got an important enough *task*, because she's going to say the line no matter what he does. This is called a "soft" objective. To keep his objective alive he needs to keep his concentration on something physical, such as her eyes and body language. That's where one really experiences forgiveness — not in mere words.

So once she says the line, does his objective change? No. We look for an objective the actor can hang the whole scene on, that can be true from the beginning of the scene to the end. That is the truth of this tool, and the way to make it useful.

CHOOSING OBJECTIVES

We want to find objectives that are active. Another kind of soft objective is, in a boy-meets-girl scene, deciding that the boy "wants her to talk to him." Unless the actor playing the girl forgets her lines, she's already going to talk to him! An objective that would be more likely to work might be that he "wants her to take her clothes off."

Sometimes students are shocked when I make this suggestion. But I'm not talking about how to stage the scene but rather an interior adjustment for the actor. It doesn't mean that he has any notion that he's going to achieve that objective; it doesn't mean that he is doing anything overt to achieve it. It's his *inner life*, it gives him an inner point of concentration. This particular idea may give the scene a subtle undercurrent of sexual sizzle. It depends on the actor, however; for another actor that interior adjustment might make the character look depressed and anxious.

The objective is not the result. It is not a blueprint for the scene. Perhaps you were surprised earlier when I suggested that the spine for Chaplin's little tramp might be "to stay out of trouble," since the little tramp was always *in* trouble. The lines or plot contain clues to the objective, but the objective relates to what is not being said, the subworld. In the case of the little tramp, humor results from the incongruity of intention and result.

The interesting thing is that if the character was a real person and you asked him what he wanted from the young woman, he might truthfully answer "to talk to her." His need to be alone and unclothed with her might be deeper than his conscious intent. Which intent or need should the actor use in the scene? Whichever one works. In rehearsal, he can try them both.

"Get him to acknowledge you" is a soft objective. Try instead, "get him to look you in the eye." Instead of "get her sympathy," consider, "get her to put her arms around you." It's more physical and specific, and closer to the way these situations really feel when they are happening.

Directors (actors too), when asked what a character's objective might be, often come up with all kinds of things the character *doesn't* want (e.g., "He doesn't want to hurt her"). This is usually a weaker use of the imagination than phrasing the objective as a positive ("He wants her to smile").

"She wants this but she also wants that." Human beings can't do more than one thing at one time. If an actor tries to want two things at once, the two will cancel each other out and make the performance flat. There is always something that a person wants the most, will sacrifice the most for. It is the skill of the actor or director to unlock this mystery and find the singular playable key. "He wants X but he knows he can't get it." A cop-out. Knowing we can't get something doesn't stop us from wanting it. People want what they want, however irrational. Don't forget that very often they do the wrong thing to get it. Sometimes, for instance, a person wants respect but constantly seems to be apologizing for his actions. Avoid the construction, "He is trying to get her to..." Instead say, "He wants her to." The word "try" may add a strain.

The most important thing to understand about choosing an objective is not to get stuck making us believe the truth of the words spoken. If I say, "I really want you to understand this," my intention is probably not to have you *believe* that I want you to understand, but to actually have you understand. "I need you to love me" comes out very differently if my intention is to make you believe that I love you, rather than if my intention or need is to be loved.

In the film "Last of the Mohicans," Daniel Day-Lewis has a line where he tells Madeleine Stowe that he will find her. This moment was used in all the trailers, but so out of context that it sounded like a declaration of his intent, as if he were playing the intention "to get her to believe that he would find her." It seemed to me like a cliché.

106

Later, when I saw the movie and the line was said in context I could see that Day-Lewis, an excellent actor, had not made Hawkeye's intent "to get her to believe that he would find her," which would have been the hackneyed "movie" choice, stuck on the surface of the words. Although I have no inside information as to how Day-Lewis works, it looked to me as though his choice was something more visceral, perhaps "to calm" or "to soothe" or "give her courage" for the ordeal ahead.

Sometimes it is helpful for the actor to concentrate on what he is doing — the action verb — the simple task. Often it is more helpful for the actor to create for himself a strong sense of need or objective and then not think about when to change action verbs, but rather let the changes come out of his interaction with the other actor. Some actors prefer not to think about objective or intention at all, on the grounds that the character probably doesn't know what he's doing or why he's doing it.

But whether or not the actor uses this tool, the performance, in order to be believable, must have a through-line and a sense of intention. The actor doesn't necessarily have to be aware of it or be able to label it (he may be working some other way), but it must be there. When the director monitors actors' performances, this is one of the things he should be monitoring. If you can discern whether an actor operates out of a need, can play the verb rather than playing *at* it, you will have an invaluable tool for casting. If you become adept at discerning actors' unconscious objectives, you may become known as an "actor's director." The caveat, as usual, is that reading about objectives, intentions, and spines is only a start. In order to understand and effectively use them, you need to practice and see them in action.

IMAGES

There are images in the text and images behind the text. By images in the text I mean every person, place, or thing that the characters mention in their dialogue. By images behind the text I mean the things the characters don't talk about — the people, places, and things that inhabit their subworld. This includes not only visual images but impressions of all the senses — what we see, hear, smell, taste, and touch.

An actor when studying a script examines all the images in the text and makes sure he understands them. He puts them in the context of the facts of the script, of course, but he also makes them real to himself; that is, he relates them to his personal experience and observation and allows his imagination to weave through them and be captured by them. He does this in order to be sure he is talking *about* something, not just talking about words. This is an important cornerstone of a believable performance.

The content of what someone is saying is not the *words* themselves but the image those words evoke. Let's say the character has a line, "There was rain today." To give life to the image "rain," the actor invests or *endows* it with sensory associations. Of course everybody knows what rain is, but an actor who works deeply with images would adopt a "beginner's mind" and not take anything for granted. She would make a full sensory exploration of all the images of rain that she could conjure and connect with. This would involve memories of rain, all different kinds of rain: hard, needle-like rain; soft, sweet, warm rain; cold rain; rain squishing in your shoes; being indoors in a rainstorm; the sound patterns as the wind brings the rain in gusts; the sight of rain streaming down the window; the condensation on the inside of the pane; mud; the sound of splashing; the taste of rain; the smell of rain; rain on wool; rain running down one's collar. Besides memory, the actor might add imagined associations of rain. Even if a person has never been inside a tiny mountain cabin during rain, she can imagine it; if she has never stood naked in the rain, she can imagine it.

As soon as I let myself take some time to think about rain, I remember my New England childhood, where summer rain was usually accompanied by thunder and lightning. A warm summer shower without lightning was a special event, since it meant no danger of electrocution! My mother would let my brother and me put on our swimsuits and play outside in the rain. It takes time, but I can recreate many sensory details of that experience, and what I don't remember, my imagination easily fills in. And what feelings it brings back!

This is all preparation. When it comes time for the actor to deliver the line "There was rain today" in front of the camera, the word "rain" has some emotional weight; there is an image behind it. The actor is not working to have the image while the camera rolls, he is not stopping the scene to remember his image; he has already done the work and the image will be there. Or maybe it won't. If the image is not there when the actor gets to the line, that means it wasn't strong enough, wasn't meaningful enough, wasn't present, private and compelling enough. Or perhaps that it wasn't sensory enough. If the actor has mistakenly intellectualized the idea of rain rather than connected to the sensory experience of it, then the image won't come unbidden when the actor arrives at the word. In that case he goes off by himself before the next take and reinvestigates it.

Dealing with images is a way to give a word emphasis and color. Michael Richards, Kramer on TV's "Seinfeld," will give an ordinary word some strange twist in the way he says it, and suddenly it's a funny word. I don't know what he does to achieve his amazing effects, but I can't help wondering — is it possible that he prepares by riffing and free–associating in a similar way to the "rain" associations above? Could he have created some idiosyncratic imaginative stand-in for, for instance, "beta-carotene"? What I mean is that I picture him, when he says the words "beta-carotene," imagining something other than a vitamin — maybe a person whose name is Beta Carotene, a woman, perhaps petite, with red hair, a great figure, and very firm opinions!

Images can be imaginative or they can arise from the personal experience of the actor. That is, the actor can make a *substitution*. In a scene in which the character is talking about her ex-husband, who is not present, whenever she has a line mentioning him, she would substitute in her own mind the image of her own ex-husband. Of course she may not have an ex-husband. She may never have been married, but she can still play the role. She can substitute for the ex-husband someone from her own life.

Substitutions do not need to be exact, but they need to be specific and strong. They need to capture the actor's imagination, so they can be surprising, even opposite. Usually I would say that the actor in the above example, when substituting for an ex-husband, should pick somebody important in her own life, an ex-lover or ex-friend. But if the character's ex-husband was selfish, the actor might substitute a selfish person who is not a man or an ex-lover at all; for example, she could substitute her mother if her mother was a selfish person. Or she might substitute her own ex-husband even if he wasn't selfish. It doesn't really matter what the substitution is, as long as it captures her and as long as she is talking about a *person*.

She could even substitute for the ex-husband a person she met in a store yesterday; that would give the relationship less emotional investment, and thus a different attitude. This would create an adjustment that she's gotten over the relationship, or that it was never very substantial to begin with, or that she is in denial about her true feelings. The substitution is an emotional parallel to the character's relationship. The parallel need not be exact if it is done honestly and simply and with full commitment. The audience will believe the relationship because they will believe that there is *some* relationship, and they will suspend disbelief and fill in the blanks.

The purpose of substitution is honesty in a performance. If at all times the actor is talking about something real, then the audience can hear that in the words. They don't know what the substitution is; that is, they don't know *what* truth is being spoken, but they hear truth being spoken. Lines spoken as lines in a script, without images connected to the words, have little effect on an audience. So, paradoxically, when the actor is substituting — that is, in his mind he is speaking about something *other* than the words of the script — the audience can hear and believe the words better.

A few years ago I performed a demanding lead role in a stage production in which my character had long monologues on the subject of ironing her husband's shirts. (She was not ironing on stage; she was actually in a police station, but she was talking about ironing.) Although my mother ironed my father's shirts and taught me how, I had never, as an adult, ironed men's shirts. In early rehearsals I tried my best to focus on images of ironing shirts during those long monologues, but they did not carry the emotional weight for me personally that the writing clearly meant them to carry. I was dry. So I made a wholesale substitution and as I spoke the images of the monologue, which had to do with the steaming ironing board, the texture and colors of the cotton shirts, I focused instead on a sensory experience of wrapping a present for someone I loved. (It was my choice about the character that to her the ironing was an act of love.) I made my images very specific: a specific gift, a certain person the gift was for, the wrapping paper, the tape, etc. I quit worrying about getting the right image, and instead gave myself completely to the substitution I had found. And eventually, the ironing image did kick in! The steam from the iron and the crispness of the cotton began to take hold of my imagination. During many performances, I could feel the steam on my face and in my nostrils. I did not try to make the audience believe that I felt the steam, it was just there. The substitution gives the actor a springboard into the imaginative realm — the "magic as if."

The actor also makes sure that there is an image in place for the *facts* or *events* he is speaking about. In the 1995 version of "Cry, the Beloved Country," one of the characters has a line "I am a cynical and selfish man. But God put his hand on me." In order to make this strange and powerful line his own, the actor must be sure that he is not speaking in generalities, but is speaking specifically of something in the character's past that might cause him to say such a thing. The work of the actor is not to decide whether to say this line piously or defiantly or sarcastically, but rather to determine what specific events of this character's life make him call himself cynical and selfish. Perhaps it is something he did that he knew was wrong but escaped punishment for. What is it?

There are no further clues in the script as to what this event might be, so the actor goes to his own imagination, and also to his own life and the lives of people he has known. I happen to know someone who went to jail for manslaughter. Meeting this person made a tremendous impression on me. Perhaps I would borrow his experience and substitute it as my own when it came time for me to say this line. I would not need to do that of course. I could recall the time when I was nineteen and lied to my parents that I couldn't meet them for dinner because I was sick. In fact I wanted to see my boyfriend, of whom they disapproved. That evening we were in a serious motorcycle accident. In the Bellevue emergency room there was a kind nurse. Recalling her face and eyes might well start me on the road to creating a reality behind that line.

Besides substituting the things he is talking *about* the actor can make a substitution of the person he is talking *to*. If the character is talking to a person who has betrayed him, instead of working himself up into a phony, actorish rage against the other actor in the scene, the actor can substitute for his scene partner a person from his own life who has betrayed him. The substitution gives him a truthful need to speak, and the results may be surprising. The words may not come out with rage at all; they may come out with sadness, or even perhaps with very little emotion.

When a character has a telephone conversation, the actor needs to create the image (a sound image as well as visual image) of a voice on the other end that he is responding to. When the actor has a close-up or eye-line that prevents him from eye contact with the actor he is playing the scene with, even though they are supposedly face-to-face, the actor creates an image of the face he is in dialogue with. These images can come from his imagination or from his own life. In either case, the more specific and sensory (the wrinkles around her eyes, texture of her skin, her fragrance, etc.), the better.

Even if there's only one character in the scene, the actor is always talking to someone. Under what circumstances do people talk when nobody else is around? Take the "Twilight Zone" episode in which Burgess Meredith, wearing thick glasses and the only survivor of nuclear war, finds himself in the ruins of the public library. The whole script has only one character, and this character speaks out loud during the whole episode. Why does he talk? He must be talking to someone. He could be talking to himself, in which case he imagines himself as a separate person to talk to. He could be talking to objects (the books). He could be talking to an imaginary person, someone he wishes were there to see him now. This is necessary also for voice-over narration. Narrators of documentary (or fiction) films need to give themselves one particular person to whom they are telling their story.

An image can impel an intention. Perhaps Daniel Day-Lewis, playing Hawkeye, rather than articulating an intention for himself, as I suggested earlier, instead endowed his line "I will find you" with an image of Madeleine Stowe's future rescue and safety — the strength and warmth of his arms around her, for instance — and put his concentration on transmitting that image to her, making her see and feel and share it, to give her courage and hope. This image could be connected to the imaginative circumstances of the frontier setting of the story. Or it could be personal to the actor — a picture, the sound of a voice, a fragrance, that conjures up for him safety and love. If the image is strong, the actor doesn't have to think about his intention, or even to make a decision as to what it is; he uses the image instead of an intention.

That's an example of an image behind the words. Other images outside the writing may be the images of the character's world that characterize the period and culture he lives in, his social class, and occupation. If an actor is playing a knight in medieval times, he will of course be given the appropriate costume, props, and set decoration for the period. But a thorough actor will also create for himself images of objects and experiences that relate to his period and occupation, things which he may have no lines to talk about, but which nevertheless inform his life.

Many actors get emotional colors through images. Images have a big effect on all of us. If you start thinking about the backyard of your childhood home, creating a detailed image of the swings, the hiding places, the tear in the screen door, it's going to have an effect on you. Even if actors have not been specifically trained to work with images, it's just true. That's why they are such a useful directing tool. Franco Zeffirelli gave Glenn Close this image for her portrayal of Gertrude in "Hamlet": "The walls of the castle are filled with her perfume."

Images are the poetry, the resonating sensory subworld of the text. A dedicated actor or director will always connect images with associations that are rich both in personal meaning and in imaginative breadth. She will read extensively, especially biography and fiction, go to museums, concerts, to meadows, mountains and deserts; she will ask acquaintances for the stories of their lives, talk to strangers, eavesdrop, spend time with children, in order to constantly replenish her repertoire of images and associations.

I find that many novice film directors have filled their imaginations exclusively with images from movies and television. This is a mistake. It's true that there is fun to be had in movies that reference other movies, if it is done in an original way, but to build a real career, and to grow as an artist, one must have access to images from other sources.

Who knows where Vanessa Redgrave got the images for the shimmering scene in which she describes her memories of Howard's End to Emma Thompson? Wherever the image comes from, she lets the words come out of her commitment to that image, without deciding how she will say them. The more private, specific, and real her image is to her, the more we (the audience) are able to journey in our own imaginations to our own Howard's End.

OBSTACLE

An important reason for using a personal substitution is that it gives the actor an obstacle. An actor might win the role of a person who after many years of hiding her feelings finally confronts her father about the distance in their relationship. Actors are usually thrilled to be approaching such a meaty role. They jump in feet first, confronting away, acting up a storm. In real life, of course, confronting one's father about the deficiencies in the relationship is likely to be a painful experience, one that, indeed, most of us would put a lot of energy into avoiding. Substituting her own father in the imagined circumstances of a confrontation that she perhaps has never experienced will give her the obstacle that can bring emotional truth to the scene.

Sometimes the productive way to talk about a character's need is to talk about the character's "problem." The concept of "problem" incorporates the sense of need with a sense of obstacle. Concentration on a problem creates a sense of *task*, and keeps the actor's attention forward, not focused on whether he is doing the role "right."

Again, as with determining the objective, it is a good idea not to come too dead-on to the lines of the script. Let's take as an example the opening scene of "Driving Miss Daisy." You might say that Dan Ackroyd's problem is to get his mother to agree to hiring a chauffeur. This might work (I'm not claiming any clairvoyance into Dan Ackroyd's mental or creative processes) if he has a good enough substitution, but usually the actor will ask himself some questions to lead himself to a problem more under the surface. For example, have they had this discussion before? What were those other conversations like?

Perhaps her dismissals of his well-meant suggestion make him feel that she doesn't respect his opinion, that she still treats him like a child, not a man. This could give him a problem — a grown man, a successful businessman, who is treated like a child by his mother. A completely different tack might be to give him the problem that he has received complaints (which he knows would upset his mother if she found out about them) from the neighbors that his mother has been driving over their lawns.

These two different imaginings of the character's problem would be two different character choices. The first one might create a deeper undercurrent to the relationship. The second one might make the character of the son more superficial. (Or it might not. You could add another obstacle that no matter what, he will not expose her to humiliation by letting her know about the neighbors' complaints. This could add a tenderness to his concern for her.) But at this point I don't want to discuss the merits of these choices. I think a director could have reasons for preferring either one.

First of all, I want you to note that they are *choices*. There is nothing in the script to prove or disprove either one. Second, I want you to notice that exploring these choices is different from asking the actor for these results. If you, as director, ask for the result — for example, to bring a deeper undercurrent to the relationship, or to make his character more superficial — you are hoping that he searches his imagination and experience for ways (such as, though not limited to, the ones suggested above) to create a believable sense of problem around your request. But if you are interested, you could engage in discussion and experimentation with the various ways of looking at the character's problem.

You should understand that if you engage in the problem with the actor, the performance might or might not end up with the result you have in your mind. To work successfully this way, you will have to be process-oriented rather than result-oriented.

Sometimes actors forget that an obstacle is a good thing, not a bad thing. Of course an actor needs to be confident about his choices. But sometimes actors cross the line into wanting to stay in their comfort zone. Sometimes they make a choice that enables them not to engage, not to be affected by the other actor. This doesn't work for a scene. Both characters have to be affected by each other, even if they struggle against it, even if they struggle to preserve their composure and keep the other guy from knowing that they are affected. There has to be something at stake.

Sometimes actors make bargains with each other ("If you are really mean to me in that scene, then I will be able to cry"). Such bargaining drains the scene of life, because the actors are servicing each other. The concept of "servicing" or "cooperating" is slippery. I have been carrying on about the importance of listening, of generous acting, and now I am saying that cooperating is bad.

Cooperating, or bargaining or servicing each other, means the actors collude on the emotional subtext of the scene. The actors may have agreed on what lines will be spoken and what blocking, even the *emotional structure* of the scene — i.e., the through-line and the beats. But each actor's *emotional subtext* must be sovereign, unpredictable, in the moment; otherwise the scene loses a sense of obstacle, and the emotional life becomes a connect-the-dots drawing instead of an event. It is a very good idea to ask the actors not to discuss the work with each other. When actors discuss their characters together, it is like gossip — fun, perhaps, but nothing creative can come of it.

Sometimes actors bargain with the director, requesting that another actor stand closer, or a prop be changed so it is easier to handle. If you are working with stars, such situations can easily become political, and sometimes political considerations will force you to respond to such requests with political solutions. In the best of all possible worlds, however, you would respond to all such requests in terms of the work, and physical obstacles can be the best thing that can happen to the work. If the character wants someone to kiss him, and she is standing way across the room, it could add to the dramatic tension — or to the comedy — of the situation.

Or actors may bargain with the writing ("That line is too hard to say," or "My character wouldn't say that"). This calls for a decision on the part of the director. Sometimes the writing should be changed. Sometimes the writing will have a "false note" — something the writer has put in for reasons other than the inevitabilities of story and character. A superior actor, one who is intelligent and is working honestly and organically, will stumble on such lines and be able to call them to the attention of the director. This can be very valuable input.

On the other hand, sometimes the writing is solid, and the actor has not made the connection necessary to see the life in the line. If you have the time and the skill (the more skill you have, the less time it takes), you can give his performance a huge boost by insisting that he find a way to meet the line, enter its subworld, and find a way to *justify* it. And if you are really skilled, you will be able to give suggestions on how to do that.

Budd Schulberg, in a 1994 <u>GQ</u> article about the shooting of "On the Waterfront," reveals that Marlon Brando was unhappy with the taxicab scene and pestered Elia Kazan for a rewrite. The rumor reached Schulberg, who insisted he saw no way to change a word. Kazan called them together for a reading of the scene. Brando's problem was the point at which Charlie, played by Rod Steiger, pulls out the gun. Brando said, "I've got all that stuff where I say 'I coulda been a contender' and that my brother and Johnny sold me out, all those dreams of what I could've been — how can I say all that with a gun pointing at me?" Schulberg says that Kazan responded, "What if you just reach out quietly and push the barrel down a little so it's not pointing at you?"

This is an important story. Anyone who has seen the movie will, I think, agree that it would have been a mistake to change any lines. And yet, Brando's point was a valid one. It seems to me that Brando was objecting to the pitch of melodrama that he felt would result from the situation of a man pouring out his heart with the obstacle of a gun pointed at him.

What is the scene about? It's about two brothers. Kazan's direction goes to the heart of the scene, because when Terry gently pushes the gun away, we see the inarticulate depth and strange tenderness of the relationship; we see that whatever failures Charlie has made as a brother, Terry knows Charlie will not use a gun on him. Pushing away the gun becomes the transforming event of the scene. After it, Terry opens his heart to his brother, and Charlie is moved to love and shame — indeed, he then sacrifices his own life. This was a major directorial insight, but it was also a correct way of working with a good actor who is having a problem with a well-written script. (Interestingly, Brando, in his autobiography, claims to have improvised that whole scene! But to me the two versions of the story are not really in conflict. The question raised by Brando was central to solving that scene, and certainly it is fair to say that the actor created, i.e., improvised, the scene's emotional life.)

118

I think you can see, from the "Waterfront" example, what a mistake it would have been for the actor and writer to meet without the director. It is the director's job to mediate any concerns the actor has about the writing, or the writer has about the acting. I feel strongly that actor and writer should never meet without the director present — even when the writer and director are the same person! If you are both the writer and the director, when you need to talk to an actor about script changes, you should do so with your director's hat on, not your writer's hat.

Sometimes an actor objects to a line because he is resisting some facet of the character. This used to happen to me. In every role I undertook, there would be a line, sometimes a whole scene, which I didn't get, or didn't like. Since I was trained to theater discipline, I never tried to get the line changed, but often I was secretly sure that no matter how brilliantly I performed, it would not work, since it was really the line that was wrong, and not me. But every time, sometime in rehearsal or performance, I would finally understand, "solve" the line or moment, and that solution would give me the whole character. What I had been resisting was *a part of myself* that was central to the character. Such resistances carry a lot of energy. When the resistance is pierced, tremendous emotional and psychic energy is released, and insight and connection result.

Now if you have a rehearsal period, the director can allow the actors time to work out such resistances at their own pace. Organically working out the resistances of the actors is one of the purposes of rehearsal. Without rehearsal, actors may need help from the director or else sooner or later the line they are resisting will probably have to be cut or changed, perhaps to something inferior. Such resistances are not bad, but they are obstacles. When they are solved they release energy.

FACTS

A character's through-line can come from the facts of the scene. In that case the actor doesn't have to know the objective. The facts themselves can create a powerful enough sense of need so that it is not necessary to put the objective into words.

I'll give you an example from an improvisation I use in my advanced acting classes. I call it "Danielle and the Doctor." "Danielle" is a female and "the Doctor" is male. (I also have a variation in which the male and female roles are switched, and one in which the actors are two women.) First I ask the female actor to go out of the room, and I speak to the male actor. I tell him that six months ago he graduated from medical school on a scholarship, and has chosen to take his internship in the public assistance hospital of a large city far from his home. Interns work extraordinarily long shifts, at low pay, with little time off. He has made no friends in this new city. He takes extra shifts for other interns when they want time off. Two weeks ago, a young woman was brought into the hospital in a coma, with no identification, a "Jane Doe." The staff of the hospital took to calling her "Danielle." During those two weeks he found himself visiting her room whenever he had time off. He would talk to her. Two days ago she woke from her coma, but she still doesn't speak. The tests have shown that she can hear and that there is no medical reason why she can't speak. It is now late at night, his shift is over, and he has come up to her room.

Then I speak to the female actor alone. I tell her that she woke up in a hospital two days ago and the people there have been telling her she was in a coma for two weeks. I tell her she may or may not remember what caused her coma, that's for her to choose. I tell her that she can speak, but that for the past two days she has not spoken. I ask her to find that place within herself from which she might have no desire or need to communicate. I tell her that many of the hospital staff come into her room, but there is one intern who comes more often and who calls her "Danielle."

"Danielle" prepares and settles herself and the improv begins. The intern comes in. Sometimes these improvs are quite beautiful, but every time, guess what objective the actor playing the intern has? To get her to speak. I haven't told him what his objective is; I haven't told him what should happen in the scene; I haven't told him what he feels. I have given him only facts. And, through my instructions to "Danielle," I have given him an obstacle. The facts by themselves are powerful enough to activate his sense of belief.

SENSE OF BELIEF

"[Acting] is basically a simple exercise of living life truthfully under imaginary circumstances." — **Bryan Singer, director of "The Usual Suspects"**

If an actor has a line to the effect that "this is the first letter I've ever received," as does the title character in "Il Postino," the actor, who has undoubtedly received letters in his own life, must create the given circumstance that justifies the facts behind that line; i.e., create a sense of belief in the situation. What would it be like to be a person who has never received a letter? How would I feel, who would I be, if *I* lived in a tiny village all my life, had no education, and had never received a letter? These are questions an actor might ask himself in order to create a sense of belief in the given circumstances of the character. "Given circumstances" is another way of saying the character's situation, or his predicament. Writers and producers tend to call it backstory. I like to call it the *facts*.

Some actors are in touch with their imaginations enough to surrender themselves to an unself-conscious sense of belief in the situation no matter how improbable. The wonderful film actors of the thirties and forties, who were working before the teachings of Constantin Stanislavsky took hold among cinema actors, would commit themselves to the circumstances of the story, no matter how silly or far-fetched, and were able to infect the audience with their sense of belief. Since the fifties, when the early work of Marlon Brando, Montgomery Clift, James Dean, Geraldine Page, and Kim Stanley seemed to tear open the envelope of the emotional depth an actor could give the audience, we now demand of our dramatic film actors an inner life and moment-by-moment authenticity of feeling that the film stars of the thirties and forties did not always have. But they had a great sense of belief, a great will to believe in their characters, and a will to make us believe with them.

All actors, no matter what techniques of script analysis and preparation they favor, to one extent or another, exercise belief in an imagined reality. All other techniques, such as objectives and substitutions, are really means to an end, which is to kick in the sense of belief. If he does not allow himself to believe in the scene on some simple level, he is likely to fall into the trap of trying to prove to the audience that he does.

A wonderful example of a pure sense of belief at work, it seems to me, is the performances of Tom Hanks and Tim Allen in "Toy Story." Now I don't know how they worked; maybe they mapped out through-lines and beats and adjustments and subtext, but somehow I doubt it. They seemed to make a wholesale imaginative leap into their created personas. That the characters are not even people, but toys, seems only to have made the imaginative leap all the more graceful. I can picture these two talented men allowing themselves an effortless imaginative journey back to childhood, when acting out the inner lives of their toys was daily bread.

ADJUSTMENTS

Some people use the term "adjustment" to refer to any choice or shading of a performance. For instance, a director may say, "Let's try a different adjustment. Let's say that you want to pick a fight with him." That's really an objective, right? But sometimes people call it an adjustment. There's nothing wrong with that. When I gave the "Driving Miss Daisy" example of adding an obstacle for the son, that could be called adding an adjustment.

An adjustment arises as a way of interpreting *facts*. In Tennessee Williams' "Orpheus Descending" (the movie "The Fugitive Kind"), there is a scene in which Lady and Val first become acquainted. Val had arrived in town that afternoon, stopping briefly in Lady's mercantile store, leaving his guitar there. It is now the middle of the night. He has returned to the store and he is standing in shadow as Lady, who that afternoon brought her invalid husband home from the hospital, descends the stairs to place an emergency call to the druggist. She hasn't slept in days and has lost her sleeping pills. They surprise each other in the dark store and their acquaintance begins.

There is a fact central to this scene: Val was in the store earlier in the day when Lady arrived with her husband from the hospital. The only words the husband spoke were words of criticism toward Lady. One way to approach playing the character of Val would be to look at that fact; he first saw her while she was involved in the task of getting her sick, demanding husband upstairs to bed and keeping her business running.

How does he perceive her, based on the events of that afternoon? There are several possible choices, based on the facts:

1)   He perceives her as a woman in trouble who needs help;
2)   He perceives her as a woman with power who owns a store, commands respect and could help him (he has no job);
3)   He perceives her as crazy, a difficult, dangerous woman;
4)   He finds her attractive;
5)   She is the same age as his mother.

Making a choice about his first impression of her that afternoon (if you go back and reread that scene, there are no clues about this and that means the actor can make a choice) will give the actor an adjustment to the other actor that creates a relationship between the two.

Adjustments can be a way of adding imaginative backstory to the facts of the script — a "what if?" Using the "Driving Miss Daisy" example, the idea that the neighbors might have complained about tire tracks on their lawns is an imaginative backstory idea. It's not in the script. It's a "what if?" as in "What if one of his business associates lives next door to his mother and made a nasty joke during a meeting about Miss Daisy's driving habits?"

Adjustments are ways of talking about the character's behavior without using adjectives. Instead of saying that character A is "respectful" toward character B, you might say his adjustment is that "B is an important man," or, if you want to raise the stakes, the adjustment could be that B carries a weapon, and has been known to shoot people he feels are disrespectful to him. This is an imaginative adjustment; it is used for a script in which B does not in fact carry a gun or have anything to do with guns. The imagined gun is a secret the actor playing A gives himself in order to justify the relationship and the need to speak. It can also be phrased as an "as if" — "as if B is carrying a gun and will use it if he perceives any sign of disrespect from me." You see how this could create the same effect as deciding to be very, very respectful (or deciding that the character is irrationally paranoid), but it puts the actor's attention on the other actor, not on himself.

If you feel the need to discuss the character's emotion with an actor, you make the direction less result-oriented if you connect it to a metaphor-type adjustment. So you might say, "It's not like the rage you would feel if a drunk driver killed your child. It's more like when the phone company won't come out to fix your service until next Thursday and insists that you be there all day."

The actor can make an off-the-wall imaginative adjustment to *justify* a difficult line. The actor in "Il Postino," in order to say believably the line about receiving the first letter in his life, might make the adjustment that what he is really saying is, "This is the first letter I've ever received from the President of the United States." You could also call this an imaginative subtext.

SUBTEXT

Subtext is the thing that is not being said. If the line is, "Please shut the door," there can be several different subtexts to it: "Please shut the door (you stupid ass)." "Please shut the door (so we can begin our business meeting)." "Please shut the door (so we can finally be alone together, darling)." "Please shut the door (and keep that maniac out)." The line itself would be the same each time, but it would come out in different ways depending on the subtext. In a sense the different subtexts give it different line readings.

Subtext is what the person is really saying, what she means. It happens in regular life all the time. "You got your hair cut (finally — it was looking like hell)" vs. "You got your hair cut (I wish you hadn't, it looked better before)." It can be the reverse of the meaning of the lines. I'm sure we have all occasionally heard an "I'm sorry" whose subtext was "I still think it was really your fault."

Subtext is useful as another way to create a sense of intention or need. On the Short List of Action Verbs I have put what I call anchoring subtexts next to each verb. If you want the actor to play the verb to belittle, for instance, you might say, "The subtext is, 'You're worthless.'"

Sometimes I tell actors to play a whole scene as if everything they are talking about is really about sex. I tell them to be specific and graphic, but not to say it out loud, to let it be the subtext. This works especially well if the scene has nothing whatever to do with sex. My intention is not to actually make the scene be about sex, but to keep the actors interested in the scene and alive to each other.

There are scenes with interaction between characters but no dialogue; for example, the scene with Cary Grant and Deborah Kerr at the ship railing in "Affair to Remember." They have no words, and yet their facial expressions make it clear that they are communicating. They are communicating with subtext. If you want the actor to give a "look" to another actor, say a skeptical look, and if you want to avoid the adjective, you could use subtext — "Are you serious?" You need to watch out for subtext communications that cross the line and become mugging; that is, the actor performs the subtext communication for the benefit of the audience rather than for the benefit of the actor he is communicating with.

PHYSICAL LIFE

The objects of a person's life are very defining of who she is. An actor creates a sense of belief in her character's life by creating a relationship to the objects of that life. Giving life to the objects and activities of the character's world is as important as finding her inner needs and impulses. Objects have tremendous power to create energy. When directors define the physical staging of scenes, they become significantly involved in the actors' physical life. It is very helpful to involve the actors organically in the creating of blocking and stage business.

It is important for actors to think of props not as obligations but as opportunities to add to the richness of their portrayals. If a character is playing cards, the actor must really deal with the cards, look at them and make decisions about whether to draw or hold — not turn them over because the stage directions tell him to.

When an actor is presented with the prop handcuffs he is to wear in a scene, he needs to make a connection to that object, and give it life. If he gives the object life, it gives life back to him, almost like another actor in the scene. To a prisoner who in real life is hand-cuffed the handcuffs would feel completely different from the way they would to an actor, who can take them off when the scene is over. The actor has to make an adjustment to the cuffs in order to believably play the prisoner. To a prisoner who is handcuffed for the first time the handcuffs would feel different from the way they would to a prisoner who has worn them many times before. Rather than deciding the result — that the character is submissive or defiant — the actor makes a physical adjustment, perhaps that the coldness of the steel deadens all feeling in his hands, or that it cuts him like a knife, or reminds him of a frightening childhood experience. Or perhaps the familiarity of the cuffs is almost a comfort.

It is via objects and activities that a sense of period or class distinctions is grounded. People's needs and feelings are no different throughout history and throughout social classes. It is the activities and objects of their lives that change. An object can also be a kind of emotional lightning rod, to keep a relationship from coming across too dead-on. Once in a class two students were enacting the confrontation scene from "I Never Sang for My Father." The student playing the father was acting up a storm, confronting the son in a way that was very dramatic and probably satisfying but not believable. I gave him a newspaper and told him I wanted him to read the paper during the scene, and not merely use it as a prop. I instructed him to be able to tell me after the scene was over what the article was about. The scene then played beautifully. Objects are wonderful as a way to bring actors into the moment, out of their heads. If they concentrate on the task of, say, making a sandwich, that concentration can impart to the emotional life a sense of task as well. This allows the emotional event to take place without actorish posturing.

Physical life grounds a performance. An objective can be played through an object, and become a physicalization of the character's inner life. Brando, in "A Streetcar Named Desire," created a physical relationship to every object — the radio, the dishes, Blanche's luggage — in that little apartment. This gave a physicalization to Stanley's spine, which was to keep possession of all his property. In "On the Waterfront" he added to the first scene with Edie the business of picking up her glove and putting it on his own hand. The glove business physicalizes their relationship: it is boy-like; it gives him his intention (to tease her); it reveals the differences in their education and manners; it is a sexual metaphor. And it gives Eva Marie Saint a playable objective for the rest of the scene — she wants her glove back!

Most actors love costumes and makeup. There is more than a grain of truth in the "Wings of Desire" scene in which Peter Falk, playing an actor on his way to a location shoot, is brooding because he has no ideas for the character he is about to play, but consoles himself with the possibility that they might have a good costume for him. "That's half the battle," he says.

There is a difference between connecting to the physical life of the character via costume (which is good), and "playing the

127

wardrobe" (which is bad). For instance, if the production designer decides to put all the female characters in white (as in "Crimes of the Heart"), then each actor needs to make a choice for each costume change as to how she happened to choose that outfit that morning. This physically roots her in the character's reality; then whatever thematic significance the production design is meant to have can be experienced by the audience as integrated to the story and theme, rather than presented to them as an intellectual idea.

Morgan Freeman's character in "The Shawshank Redemption," released from prison and wearing a suit for the first time in forty years, looks odd, uncomfortable. In the following few scenes we see him gradually wear civilian clothes more naturally. Instead of demonstrating to us that the character feels awkward, Freeman makes his attention to the suit physical. Morgan Freeman the actor is familiar with the sensation of wearing a suit jacket, but the character isn't. If the actor puts his attention on the sensation of shoulder padding, this creates for the viewer the illusion that the shoulder pads are unfamiliar to him. Or perhaps he puts his attention on the arm-holes, tighter than those of prison blues. Or perhaps on the hat, understanding that the character would lack a sense of where a hat would sit well on his head; wherever it sat would feel unfamiliar.

An important part of creating a character is finding activities and behavior for her. Does she knit? Chew gum? What objects are her allies? Her enemies? Watch out for clichés.

Actors sometimes do interior physical work. They create characters of varying degrees of sensuality through physical awareness of the intimate parts of their bodies. In order to play a graceful person, they may create an inner life of physical pain. They may work on physical centers: an intellectual person has his center of energy in his head, for example. A belief in the character's physical life can give you the whole character. Actors sometimes have "magic keys" that open up the character for them. Often these "keys" are physical choices. This is called "character work." Dustin Hoffman has said that he found his magic key to playing the elderly Jack Crabbe in

"Little Big Man" when he realized that the guy "probably hasn't had a decent bowel movement in twenty years."

In a <u>Los Angeles Times</u> interview, Martin Landau described the physicality of his characterization of Bela Lugosi for the movie "Ed Wood": "My face is very alive, and he had a certain limitation to his face. I had to learn his face. When I put the makeup on, I would learn to subordinate certain muscles in my face. I open my eyes wide. He rarely does. You see a lot of teeth when I smile; you see no teeth when he does. He held his head at certain angles, he had a certain walk which is different from the way I walk." Do you see the subtle difference it makes that Landau does not say about Lugosi, "he squints"? Instead he says, "I open my eyes wide. He rarely does." His concentration is physical, specific, and sensory — not judgmental!

All character work, whether accompanied or unaccompanied by makeup, should be sensorial. Sometimes complex and difficult character work is done in meticulous detail, like Daniel Day-Lewis in "My Left Foot," or Tracey Ullman in her myriad personas. Sometimes, like Jeff Bridges in "Starman," the actor makes only a very small physical adjustment that suggests his otherness more symbolically than naturalistically. But when, as Bridges did, he commits fully and simply to it, the audience gladly goes along for the ride.

Sometimes character work is a function of the style of the movie. The movies of the Coen brothers demand stylized acting. Stylized acting can be wonderful as long as the style is internally consistent; and as long as all the actors are listening, and are connected to their need; and as long as all physical adjustments are created organically in their bodies, not as an intellectualized *idea* of the character, which becomes a judgment.

Actors can sometimes fall in love with their "business" and start to play it for its own sake. It becomes shtick. Or they may start playing their character choices for their own sake — "playing character" or mugging. The director needs to monitor these things and ask the actor to give up business or character choices if they get in the way of telling the story.

WHAT DO YOU MEAN "SPECIFIC"?

All good actors work to some degree instinctively. There may be some very good actors who don't consciously use any technique, who instinctively listen, instinctively play intentions, and instinctively create a sense of belief in the facts, images, and physical life of their characters. But, to be blunt, there are some actors who claim to work "instinctively," and pride themselves on never having had an acting lesson, who are capable of better — that is, more specific — work. The purpose of technique is not to smother or hobble the actor's instincts, but to find ways to make character choices more and more specific.

"Specific" is a concept that a lot of people have trouble with. I know I did when I was first studying acting. The reason it is hard to grasp is that there is no one definition for it. The way to make acting "specific" is specific to every situation!

If an actor A is directed to make her performance more "stern" in a scene opposite actor B, actor A could make an imaginative *adjustment* that earlier in the day she heard actor B telling an offensive joke. Already this is a more specific choice than trying to "be stern." She would continue making this adjustment specific by imagining the details of the experience, or by recalling the details of a parallel experience of her own. She would recall or create the hallway or room where it happened, the sound of his voice, the heat in her face, etc. This adjustment would only work if actor A is actually bothered by such jokes. If that is not the case, then she must make some other choice. She is looking for a choice that impels simple, truthful behavior in the moment, so she doesn't have to demonstrate a clichéd, general attitude of "sternness."

Finding more specific choices is called "filling" a performance. It's also known as finding "colors," "levels," or "layers." Paul Newman, on "Inside the Actors Studio," spoke about what to do when a director tells actors to pick up the pace. He said the actor should go off by himself and work more on the part, "fill" it better, ask himself questions, find beats, add adjustments, opposites, change the rhythms, add more specific detail. After the next take, when the director says, "Great, just what I wanted," Paul says to check with the script supervisor on how long the two takes were. "A hundred times out of a hundred," he claims, she will reply that the second take was longer than the first one — the one the director said was too long!

This means that in the initial take the actor was "rushing," not connecting to the subworld of the lines, possibly because he has not investigated that subworld adequately. "Rushing" paradoxically can make a scene feel slow, because if the subworld of the scene is not coming alive, the scene becomes boring and generic and the person watching can't help but wish it finished and done with as soon as possible. In fact it needs to be slowed down in order to find the details of inner life that will make it worth watching.

In Paul Newman's example, in which the actor is actually rushing, the direction "Pick up the pace" was a result direction, that is, a direction that if followed blindly, would make the scene worse instead of better. But sometimes the direction "Pick up the pace" is a playable, on-target direction. Sometimes when a scene seems slow it really is slow.

In rehearsal the actor needs to go slow to figure out the transitions. After some rehearsal, however, the transitions, if they are working, should start to go more swiftly, the way they do in real life; but the actor may still be stuck in the exploratory rehearsal rhythm. In that case picking up the pace will simply feel more natural than staying with the rehearsal rhythm. Picking up the pace will also bring the scene alive if the actor is laboring the transitions or listening to himself act. In that case he needs to stop thinking, let go, and spit it out. If the actor goes off to think up more transitions, this will be a disaster. Sorry about that, but I warned you there was no cookbook!

What are the responsibilities of a director in these cases? Is he supposed to know and fix every problem of every actor? No. It is the actor's job to make all direction her own, and fill it with her personal and imaginative associations. So why should directors bother to learn how to give playable (choice-oriented) direction? Because it puts things on the right track. It engages actor and director in a process; it keeps their attention forward. Even good actors who routinely translate or fill all result direction, when subjected to a constant barrage of it, can get worn down and confused, while inexperienced actors can easily lose their bearings. So it helps when the director can come on the journey with them and give direction in terms that suggest playable choices.

My first professional job was for director John Korty. We were shooting a made–for–television movie starring Stephanie Zimbalist. I was playing the sister of Stephanie's new boyfriend. In the first scene we shot, I was to bring cups of coffee out to the porch and sit down on the step next to her. While we were rehearsing he said to me, "You can sit closer to her, because you want to welcome her into the family."

Later as I learned more about moviemaking I realized that he probably wanted to be able to put a tighter frame on our two-shot, but instead of asking me for that result, chose to give his direction in terms that related to the characters' relationship. Or maybe his mind connected instinctively to the created reality of the characters' interests and needs. I was on the set for four days, and interestingly, I never saw anyone on his set put down a piece of tape for the actors' marks. He set all the positioning by giving direction that related to the characters' situations and relationships. And his technicians never grumbled. Everybody loved him.

When directors can use imaginative adjustments well, actors adore them and will do anything to work with them. But an inexperienced director forcing his ideas — however properly phrased in the language of imaginative choices — on actors may be seen as a foolish busybody. That's why it's a good idea to try these things out in a class situation or with actors with whom you are friendly. The goal is not to replace one catch-all phrase ("edge," or "take is down") with others, but to allow yourself to think and feel more deeply, more specifically.

STRUCTURE:
TRANSITIONS, EVENTS, AND
THROUGH-LINES

Actors get into a lot of trouble with transitions, the emotional changes and events of a role. Transitions are the places where actors feel the most self-conscious, worry the most about whether they are going to be able to "hit it." Directors often exacerbate the anxiety by using the result direction of asking actors to hit a certain emotional "note." It is in the transitions that bad acting is most likely to show up.

Transitions, or shifts in thought or feeling, in real life are utterly unconscious, one of the most spontaneous, organic things we do. We do not plan to change our minds, have a new feeling, undergo a change of heart, react, realize, or go off on another train of thought. We may ignore, repress, or refrain from acting upon such tiny inner events, but we can't prevent them from happening or summon them to our will. They are set in motion by what is going on in our subconscious.

Actors' transitions are another matter. They must be prepared. But how? First, here are some things that can go wrong:

1) The transition is not there, because the actor hasn't found it in the script, hasn't understood, or doesn't believe that there is a transition or event at that moment.

2) It is indicated or fake. The actor decides on a transition and demonstrates it to us rather than creating it honestly and organically, or *allowing* it.

3) It is forced. The actor intends to make the transition organically but does not get there and, at the last moment,

133

out of a feeling of obligation, pushes it rather than not make it at all.

4) It is flat, because the actor is worried about forcing or pushing, and is afraid to overdo or overact, so at the last moment she drops out.

5) It is overprocessed, labored, telegraphed. This is a variation on playing the end of the scene at the beginning. We see the actor "winding up," anticipating the next emotional event, letting us know that even though right now she is in a rage, she is getting ready any moment now to break down in tears. In real life there is no process or motivation involved in the experience of transitions at all. They are unexpected, lightning quick, and like lightning they seem to come "out of the blue."

6) It is too logical, too dead-on. In other words, however well executed, it still looks planned, because it lacks the idiosyncrasy of a real-life transition. The actor has made a choice that is pedestrian or obvious.

A transition is an emotional event. Sometimes it is called a "moment" or a "beat change." Now a discussion of moments or "beats" is always complicated by the fact that so many screenwriters use these terms as stage directions, in lieu of the word "pause." When you see a parenthetical "beat" or "moment" in a screenplay, that means the screenwriter has in mind a very brief pause at that moment. It has nothing to do with the beats and events I am discussing here.

A moment means the actors stop each other, and affect each other. Sometimes a genuine moment catches the actor so off-guard that she momentarily forgets her lines. An actor should never stop the scene when that happens. Such inner accidents create a lot of energy. She should allow this inner accident to be an emotional event, and she should continue the scene and do something with the energy that has been released. The forgotten line is likely to come back within a few seconds. The director, of course, must be open to this idea, must be able to tell the difference between a "dead spot" and an energy-releasing inner accident and must allow a climate in which creative accidents are welcomed. Sometimes actors forget that a moment is an event, not a feeling; it is not an end point. When a moment occurs, the actor must then *do* something.

Emotional events for characters can be wins or losses, discoveries, choices or mistakes — not realizations or reactions, which are not playable. By the way, when I say that a character's emotional event might be a "choice" made by the character, this is a different use of the word from when we talk about actors' choices. "Actors' choices" are also called "character choices," i.e., choices that create the inner life of a character. A choice made by the character is something different, however; it's an emotional event in the scene.

Transitions need to happen in the moment. The character's wins, losses, discoveries, choices, and mistakes need to be made in the moment. We want them to emerge spontaneously from the subconscious, the way they do in life. They need to *count* — or *read* — on the screen, because the emotional events tell the story, but we don't want them telegraphed or emphatic. We want them to be spontaneous, vivid, and subtle all at once.

What is needed from actors is connection, engagement, a willingness and ability to affect each other and to be affected, to deal with each other and with the environment. This is achieved by having a *through-line*. The through-line is what makes a performance simple and unfussy. Meeting the transitions in the moment is what makes the performance nuanced.

What is needed from the director is that he or she *structure* the scene (and the full script). The tools for understanding (via script analysis) and then creating (in rehearsal) scenic structure are what the scene is about, or its central event; its beats; the sub-events leading up to and resulting from the central event, that is, the events of each beat; and the characters' through-lines. These tools will be examined in detail in the Script Analysis chapter. For now, what I mean by an event, from the director's point of view, is *what happens*. This is not exactly the same as a plot event — it is an emotional event, for example, an apology or a seduction. An emotional event in a relationship might be "No matter what she does, she can't cheer him up." When the audience feels this event, is taken up by it, connects

135

to it (whether or not they would describe it that way), they wonder, "Will this couple stay together?" In other words, "What happens next?" The director is responsible for putting the events of the scenes together to make a satisfying story, that is, keeping the audience interested in what happens next.

The events, however well understood intellectually by actors and director, only really work if they happen in the moment. When a scene is structured properly, actors can commit to choices, then abandon themselves to the moment. The scene will then naturally and inevitably "build," achieving its proper pace and flow. The "how" of an actor's choices — for example, how he gets the other actor to leave the room, or give him comfort — comes from the moment-by-moment interaction between the actors.

This is the ideal: solving the scene by finding one simple choice (through-line) for each character that all his behavior can be hung on, like a hook, and then allowing the actors to play off each other. But often, once that central problem of the scene has been solved, there are still transitions here and there that are not working, that need to be sharpened, deepened, or cleaned up. This is the most dangerous place for a director to use result direction. When a director wants to ask an actor for a transition but doesn't want to use result direction, he can use his "Quick Fix" tools, thus:

Images

The best way I can think to describe how images and associations work in creating transitions is to relay Stanislavsky's anecdote, from An Actor Prepares, about a woman who has just been told her husband was killed in an accident at the factory. She stands in place for minutes, not moving. The question going through her mind while she's being told this is, *What will I do with the dinner I've prepared if he will not be there to eat it?* The mind works in such incredible ways, especially when information is coming in that one can't deal with or accept. The image "husband" connected with the image "dinner" and her mind would go no further. The most useful images in this regard are off-kilter, out of context, even bizarre, because that's the way people's minds work.

Verbs

An excellent way to make transitions is to make a simple full change of action verb, without thinking about the why of it. If an actor changes suddenly and completely from begging to accusing, we (the audience) will know that a transition has taken place. And it will be more believable than if it is made by dragging us through an actorish "process."

When the director is describing such a transition to an actor, he should leave out connective phrases. So instead of saying, "Here she is pleading with him, and then *something makes her* start punishing," say, "She pleads with him all the way to here; then she punishes."

Physical activity

If an actor is not getting the emotional event or transition interiorly, the director can suggest it with exterior means. Standing up from a chair, putting down a newspaper, even turning her head away can, if the writing is strong enough, suggest the moment quite adequately and avoid the pitfalls of an overwrought transition.

In any case, one of the worst kinds of result direction is to tell an actor what he realizes at a certain point or *what* reaction he is supposed to have. If you can't come up with some specific playable direction, such as a through-line, playable event, image, verb or physical activity, then the best thing to say is something like "I think there's a change here," or "I think there's a transition we may need to make here," and let the actor figure out how to get there himself.

*   *   *

Through-lines give the actors a sense of history, risk, or need among the characters. A through-line can be an objective (spine/need), a verb, an adjustment, a problem, a given circumstance (fact), a subtext, an image. Another way of thinking about the through-line is as a *primary engagement* or *focus*. So it could be an object, as in a scene, for instance, in which a character returns a stolen ring to a friend. The ring itself, first burning in her pocket and finally shining on her friend's hand, could be the primary focus, or through-line. The primary engagement of a character could be with a memory or image. It could be with drugs or booze.

Or it could be with a third character. Most two-person scenes have an absent third character, someone who is crucial to the relationship of the characters who are present. In "Days of Wine and Roses," most of the scenes are between Kirsten and Joe; in some scenes, the absent third character is Kirsten's father who has loaned them money; in some, it is their young daughter, asleep in the next room.

Concentration on the through-line keeps the actor connected to the other actor, but *with something of his own*. Having something of his own, a strong choice, makes him able to listen and play off the other actor *without picking up the other actor's tone*. Unless you are directing soap opera, you don't want the actors to pick up each other's tone, since it becomes melodramatic. In real life we often pick up each other's tone. We unconsciously adopt our antagonist's reality and start defending ourselves or explaining ourselves in relation to his agenda. This is a place where we want movies to be more surprising, emotionally cleaner, and more revelatory than real life. It's what people mean when they talk about an "edgy" quality or the "heightened" reality required of acting. "Edgy" or "heightened" are, of course, very vague and general and would not be helpful directions to give an actor.

A movie can have a non-naturalistic, heightened *style* without being fake and caricatured as long as the verbs, facts, images, events, and physical lives of the actors are all alive and centered in a reality. *Heightened* is achieved by making the choices and transitions crisp, specific, and committed, not wishy-washy. And also engaged. While the actors are committing to something of their own they need to be sure that they take energy from each other, that they don't screen each other out, that no matter what the other actor does they make an adjustment that allows them to keep playing their own intention; they use what the other actor is giving them as a playable obstacle. This is how scenes of confrontation — so common in movies and so rare in real life — can be alive and believable. This is how comedic or fantastical situations can carry us with them.

"Heightened" also has to do with making choices that are not obvious and pedestrian. This means finding a truth deeper than everyday actuality, seeking insight. I think when many people talk about heightened reality they mistake it for putting a frame around the performance — this causes a performance to look pushed or faked or overdone. Heightened means *more* honest than we are in real life.

When actors find the deeper truths of a script, it is always best for them to maintain a privacy. When the actor confers with his director about such ideas, the transaction needs to be delicate. And actors should not talk about these ideas with the other actors. It becomes casual, a kind of gossip; it dissipates the energy of the idea and damages the actor's concentration. Meryl Streep disclosed in an interview with Gene Siskel that for every role she gives herself a *secret*, something which her character would not want others to know, and which she herself conceals from her co-stars; in "Kramer vs. Kramer" her secret was that she never had loved her husband.

When actors keep secrets from each other, when their transitions are crisp and clean, their images private and idiosyncratic, their intentions (verbs) opposite to the obvious surface meaning of a line — a performance may have "edge." And the actors' performances can contribute to the style of a film.

ACTORS' RESOURCES AND TRAINING

"I...build on my own experience, on that of others — on everything I have heard and seen...The day Ingmar gives me the manuscript he also gives me the right to feel that henceforward I understand the part best. She becomes my reality as much as she is Ingmar's." — Liv Ullmann

The really great actors love their craft. They experience acting as a kind of laboratory of the soul, a means to exploration and growth, a path. Acting can be a great act of love, a sharing of the most important things one knows and feels about life.

There are excellent actors who have never taken acting lessons and instead have developed a private technique of their own. There are other actors who think of their teacher almost as a priest or guru. I think that the best actors recognize and seek out true teachers, and steal and learn from everyone and everything they encounter.

This chapter addresses ways an actor brings moment by moment reality to his choices. For this task, the actor has four resources:

1) memory, or past experience;
2) observation;
3) imagination;
4) immediate experience, or the "here and now."

MEMORY (PERSONAL EXPERIENCE)

By *memory* I mean the actor's personal memories and experiences — things that have happened to him while living his own life. The reason an actor uses his own life and experience is not that his particular life and hard times are any more significant or worthy of note than anyone else's. The goal of using personal experience as an acting resource is not self-indulgence but honesty.

No one can experience another person's life. Each individual is essentially unknown to all others. Hence, when an actor properly uses his own experience he can do work that is *original, specific and emotionally truthful.*

Memory is the resource actors are using when they make personal substitutions or when they work with the technique of affective memory. *Affective memory* (also called emotional memory) is based on the technique of *sense memory.*

Sense memory is the creation of imaginary objects via the memory of your five senses — what you see, hear, smell, taste and touch. In a sense memory exercise the actor recalls physical sensation. She allows the memory to occur physically (in her body) rather than intellectually (in her mind). In a beginning sense memory exercise a student holds in her hands an object, say a cup of hot coffee, and puts her attention on the sensory impressions it makes on her: the weight of the cup, its temperature, its contours; the sensation of steam against her face; the smell of the coffee, etc. The attention needs to be sensory, not intellectual — that is, what she is registering is not an intellectual evaluation of the temperature ("it is pretty warm," or "very hot") but rather the pure sensation against her fingers and palms, her cheek and nostrils. She tries to be as specific as possible about the individual sensations of different areas of her skin. Once she has given thorough attention to the sensory impressions of the object, the object is taken away and she works with an imaginary cup of coffee, that is, a sense memory of the real object. She imagines the weight, temperature, texture, aroma, etc., with as much detail as she can summon, but — this is important — *without strain.* The goal of the exercise is not to demonstrate the object to anyone watching, but to train one's sensory concentration.

When I lead sense memory exercises in my classes I usually ask the students to close their eyes, because in regular life we overuse our eyes as sensory portals and it's hard to abandon ourselves to our sensations of touch and hearing and smell when sight is available. Also, in regular life our eyes are used primarily for evaluation and categorizing, whereas this use of the senses is a surrender.

For an *affective memory* exercise, the student selects an emotionally charged event from her own life. She recalls not the emotion itself or even the event itself, but her sense memories of the physical life surrounding that event, i.e., the color of the walls, the smells of the kitchen, the feeling of the upholstery under her legs, the condensation on the glass she was holding. Affective memory (or "emotional memory") was developed in this country as a technique for actors by Lee Strasberg, founder of the Group Theatre, and the leading light of the Actors Studio. The idea was that by selecting an event with a significant emotional charge, and by practicing to revisit the sensory life surrounding that event, an actor could bring herself back, at will, to the emotional life of the event.

Substitution is a kind of brief affective memory. The "magic as if" is another approach to a personal substitution: "As if my own job is in jeopardy." "As if my own sister has just shot her husband." It's a way to talk about raising the stakes of the relationship. It's also a way to keep the work simple and real. Sometimes a director can say to an actor who is overdoing, "Forget about the character. Play the scene as if it were you." An actor needn't use the technique of affective memory or substitution or the "magic as if" *per se* in order to bring his own memories and experience to bear on a characterization. Actors have many private ways to inform their work with their own understandings of life.

OBSERVATION

In addition to his own experiences, an actor understands what makes a character tick from *observing* others. An actor may use observation of the behavior and physical characteristics of people he has

143

come in contact with to play characters that are different from himself. Using observation as an actor's resource is sometimes called working "from the outside in." An actor may be playing someone of a certain social class or occupation; he needs to find the physicality of, for instance, a person who has lived all his life as a farmer — gestures and behaviors that differ from a person who, say, has always worked behind a desk. Playing a character who ages in the film, like Cecily Tyson in "The Autobiography of Miss Jane Pitman," or Dustin Hoffman in "Little Big Man," an actor uses his observations of elderly people to create that physicality: there is often a stiffness in the joints, a tendency to walk and stand with the feet farther apart. An actor keeps an inventory of the different kinds of drunkenness he has seen — quiet drunks, sloppy drunks, happy drunks, angry drunks — and can create a particular physicalization for the kind of drunk he feels a particular character is.

Working from the outside in is more associated with British acting and university drama departments and movie actors of the 1930s and 1940s. An actor might plan gesture, facial expression, and line readings, even practicing them in front of a mirror. When I was studying acting in the early seventies, American actors had a tendency to label this kind of acting "technical acting"; the slightly pejorative ring to that term was intentional.

There have been mighty controversies about whether actors should work "from the inside out" or "from the outside in." The danger of working from the outside in is that the work, relying on external skill rather than engagement and surrender, may become superficial and stagy. Working from the inside out is associated with Stanislavsky, and with most acting technique taught today in the United States. What about the term "The Method"? Stanislavsky himself called his work a new "System." In New York and Los Angeles when people refer to The Method they mean the work of Lee Strasberg and specifically they mean the technique of affective memory. In other parts of the country — in San Francisco, where I first started acting, and in Chicago and other major cities — when people say Method they mean any kind of acting training that follows or purports to follow the teachings of Constantin Stanislavsky; in other words, any kind of acting training that favors working from the inside out.

The funny thing is that Stanislavsky himself would probably be appalled to find that his teaching was thought to be restricted to working from the inside out. Although the first book in his trilogy of textbooks, An Actor Prepares, concentrated on ways to reliably and truthfully activate an actor's inner life, the second, Building a Character, concerned itself entirely with creating characterization by physical means — makeup, costume, vocal patterns, gesture, gait. The confusion is I think made complete when we notice that the introduction to An Actor Prepares, supposedly the bible of the "inside out" crowd, was written by John Gielgud, a classically trained British actor and an "outside-inner" if there ever was one!

Surely the best actors do both, work from the inside out and also from the outside in. Marlon Brando is known as an actor who works from the inside out, but who actually also works from the outside in; it was he who insisted on stuffing his cheeks to play the Godfather. Anthony Hopkins, although he is associated with British acting and thus working from the outside in, acknowledges in his interviews working from the inside out as well; Shelley Winters claims to have spotted him sitting quietly in the back of Actors Studio classrooms during the seventies.

A character may remind an actor of someone she knows. She can then adopt physical and emotional behaviors of that person. Shelley Winters, for her role in Stanley Kubrick's "Lolita," had to play a woman she considered different from herself. Kubrick suggested that she find someone she had known that she could identify the character with. She picked a "pseudo-intellectual lady" she remembered from her childhood in Queens and adopted what she remembered of that woman's physical behaviors — the way she moved her hands, her feet, the way she wore clothes. Actually, Shelley calls this process "substituting," a different use of that term from the process I described in the "Images" section of the chapter on Actors' Choices. It's an empathy, really. An actor can sometimes adopt whole cloth the persona of someone she has known. I had a television role once which I decided to play as my mother. It has to be someone the actor is very involved with, either personally or imaginatively. It's a kind of emotional transference, but based in physical observation.

In order to become imaginatively involved with a character, an actor often does research. To find the physical details he brought so vividly to life, Martin Landau watched thirty Bela Lugosi movies and numerous filmed interviews with the deceased star he played in "Ed Wood"; he also researched and studied a Hungarian accent. Actors who have been cast as policemen often spend time riding in patrol cars with real officers in order to understand how a police officer relates to the physical paraphernalia (uniform, holster, etc.) of the job.

IMAGINATION

Many actors are drawn to the profession because of an overdeveloped access to the *imagination*. For many of us (I must say "us," of course, since I am one), imagined reality (i.e., the lives of characters in books and plays and movies) is as real as life itself, and more compelling. A sense of belief in an imagined reality gives the actor solitude in public, allows him to be absorbed in the created realm and reprieved from the duties of the social realm.

All of us, actors and nonactors alike, are sitting on a vast iceberg of submerged resources — memories, observations, feelings, impulses, images, associations, meanderings — that are not useful to our daily lives and have been filed away, to all practical intents and purposes no longer available to us. These are the resources of our story imaginations. Stella Adler included among the riches of the subconscious the resources of the "collective unconscious."

When I use improvisation as a teaching technique, I see released the depth and range of my students' unconscious resources — much vaster than what is available to our conscious minds. I've seen students instantly go believably to the controls of a spaceship or to the jungles of Vietnam, in an improv, when only moments earlier they had been miserably struggling to place themselves in a family kitchen, and believably say the lines of a character who is actually very much like them. I am a great believer in improv for engaging an actor's imagination and sense of belief.

Also daydreaming. Sanford Meisner in his book On Acting advocates daydreaming as an actor's resource. What does this mean? Sometimes nonactors tell me they are analytical and don't have good imaginations and don't understand what I mean by daydreaming the life of a character. It's something most actors do automatically: the mere mention of an idea sends them off and running, building images and associations and backstory (both imaginative and personal) around it. They start having ideas for the character's spine ("I think he's in love with death!"). Or for ways to physicalize: "I'll grow a mustache for this role!" "Can I knock over the chair on this line?"

Imagination is precious. It's a bubble of belief. The bubble of belief is punctured by result direction. Actors are suggestible and kid-like. Directors are the parental figure. When the actor is told, for instance, that "at this point in the arc of the script, we need an ominous note," it's like being reminded of the adult world. It's the director's job to pay attention to what is needed "at this point in the arc of the script." It's the actor's job to play.

IMMEDIATE EXPERIENCE

An actor uses the resource of *immediate experience* by being alert and awake to what's happening in the here and now, to the stimuli he's getting from the other actors and from the environment. This is "moment-by-moment" work. Some people call this an attention to "outer reality," to distinguish it from "inner reality," the imaginative subworld of image, need, and adjustment.

Sanford Meisner invented the "repetition exercise," a teaching technique that promotes moment by moment aliveness and engagement with a scene partner. It is described in his book, Sanford Meisner On Acting. Two actors sit across from each other, giving each other relaxed attention. When one of them has an impulse, he may say something — either an observation of the other actor or a statement of his own feelings — such as "Your eyes are brown," or "My stomach is tense." The other actor repeats exactly what the first actor has said, and the two of them keep repeating the same phrase until one of them has an impulse to say something else, which then gets repeated in the same way.

The exercise must be carefully supervised, to make sure the participants are speaking out of true impulse, not because they think it is time for them to come up with something, or because they feel a need to entertain those who are watching the exercise. But the beauty of it is exactly that: you can participate in the exercise even if you have no impulse or idea for something to say, because you can repeat what is already being said. The exercise, when properly supervised, gets the actors out of their heads and away from watching themselves, and into the moment.

The repetition makes the "lines" of the exercise a kind of nonsense, so there can be no pressure to say them "right." The exercise allows the actors to be engaged without any responsibility to a text or even a situation. Typically in a Meisner oriented class, the students are only allowed to improvise situations after several months of repetition exercises.

In my own classes I use a variation on the classic Meisner technique which I learned from David Proval. The two participants sit across from each other, looking at each other, relaxed. After a while one of them is asked to say something about the other person, but specifically using the form, "You have..." and refraining from any descriptive adjectives. For example, if the participant has the urge to say, "You have beautiful eyes," he instead must say, "You have eyes." The other participant then repeats back, but changing the pronoun to "I." After a while the participants are invited to say how they feel, only using the form, "You make me feel..." which is repeated, "I make you feel...," etc. The important rule is that the "you make me feel..." is a *form*. The participants are to say how they actually feel, regardless of where the feelings come from. In fact, no analysis will be made of where the feelings come from.

It's quite a remarkable exercise. Without manipulation or bullying, students "go places" emotionally, with full, instantaneous transitions and a simple, deep "solitude in public." The purpose is to build their confidence so that even when they have memorized lines to say, they will be able to give the lines the moment-by-moment life of an improvised emotional subtext. They will generate energy from their honest, real feelings and a concentration on their scene partner. Their transitions will be full and unforced.

When actors have confidence that they can trust their feelings and the other actor, they receive all stimuli as energy. If the actor is irritated with the direction or doesn't like the other actor or is shooting on a hot sound stage a scene set in the Antarctic, the actor can still be alive to the "here and now," using everything as energy, instead of shutting it off, screening it out, pretending it's not there. If the actor has a headache, he lets the character have a headache. If the actor is nervous, he imagines what the character might conceivably be nervous about.

Some actors use direct experience as preparation; that is, rather than imagining the experiences of the character, or finding parallels from their own experience, they put themselves through some part of the character's experience themselves. Eric Stoltz spent two months in a wheelchair to prepare for his role in "Waterdance." Oliver Stone led the actors through a kind of boot camp to prepare for "Platoon." Holly Hunter has described her preparation for a scene in "Copycat" in which she was supposed to enter a room distraught; she asked a group of extras on the set to do an improv with her, in which they pushed her around physically, just before the scene was shot. Dustin Hoffman is known for insisting on experiencing the reality of the character. On the set of "Marathon Man," the story goes, he arrived one morning to play a scene in which his character had been up all night. "I stayed up all night to prepare for this scene," he declared to his costar, who happened to be Laurence Olivier. Olivier's legendary reply: "But my dear boy, why don't you just act it?"

*   *   *

SENSORY LIFE

Adding sensory detail deepens and keeps fresh any actor's choice. The brilliance of affective memory as a technique is the understanding that it is the sensory life (e.g., the pattern of the wallpaper, the sound of the voices in the next room) that recalls the emotional event far more vividly than pondering the emotion ("I felt frightened," etc.) or even the event ("My mother was screaming," or whatever).

If the actor is using a substitution, he starts from a relaxed condition and explores his memory for true sensory detail about the person or event he is substituting. He uses all his senses: sight, hearing, smell, taste, touch. If he is substituting, say, the kitchen table of his own childhood for the kitchen table the set decorator has brought in, he recalls its color, its scratches, the chewing gum his sister left under it, etc.

Objectives and intentions stay fresh and vivid via the here-and-now physical reality of the other actor's *physical* face and body: for example, "Do I see forgiveness in her eyes, hear it in her voice (not just in her words)?"

Sensory life is necessary to bring to life the resources of imagination and observation too. Let's say the movie is set in medieval times. The actor does reading and research to get ideas for his physical life, which will be entirely based on imagination. But the imaginative work should still be sensory. When he imagines himself sitting in the wooden chairs of the period, he lets himself feel the rough wood against the backs of his legs. When he imagines wearing armor, he doesn't just *think* about armor, he lets himself feel its weight on his

150

body. If actors do not root their imaginative preparation thus, in sensory life, their work may become intellectualized and stagy.

Character work based on observation must also be sensorially rooted. If an actor plays a character with a limp, there may be a temptation to make a mere imitation or demonstration of the outward appearance of an uneven gait. Making it sensory has to do with making it specific — not a generic limp, but a specific limp, which originates in a specific stiffness or soreness in the hip or knee joint. The actor puts his concentration on a sensation of stiffness or soreness, but not with any sense of strain or obligation to *feel* it. Concentration is the operative word. If the concentration is five or ten percent successful that is plenty; imagination supplies the rest.

Sense memory exercises can be very freeing. I find in my own classes that sense memory exercises, as long as there is no strain or fear of failure attached to them, offer students a kind of reprieve from the stresses of daily life which distract us from our creative resources. They return us to a child's sense of concentration on very simple things, such as the color of the inside of a seashell or the texture of a rose petal or the temperature of a cup of tea as it cools in our hands.

Sense memory has very practical uses for actors. When a character in a scene burns himself on a hot stove, the actor playing the role does not touch a stove that is hot; he touches a cold stove *as if* it were hot. Sophisticated special effects require actors to perform in front of the blue screen *as if* they were on a precipice or airplane wing. And since Shakespeare's time, the actor playing Macbeth has had to be able to see a dagger where there was none.

An actor working from the outside in might scan his storage banks of observation for the physical movement of someone touching a stove that's hot, and borrow or imitate that movement. Working from the inside out, however, the actor creates the sense memory of the sensation of burning, and then lets his hand follow its own impulse and move whichever way it wants to, in response to this created, imagined stimuli. I think you can see that for film, especially the big screen, a sense memory is going to be more believable.

151

Does this mean the actor actually feels the pain of a burn? Not at all. That's the wonder of all this acting stuff; the *concentration* creates an imagined reality; the audience is invited to fill in the blanks with their own experience or imagination.

FEELINGS

"I think that to sing the blues you have to feel it." — Billie Holiday

Is an actor supposed to "feel it"? If so, does he feel it as *himself* or as *the character*? If the character is scared, should the actor really *be* scared or should he merely *look* scared?

A dozen actors will answer these questions a dozen different ways. My own answer is, yes and no. I think that when Billie Holiday said (in a radio interview) that to sing the blues you have to feel it, she was talking about authenticity. Authenticity — not feeling, exactly — is the goal, but authenticity is unlikely without feeling. Whatever truth the artist gives us must be true on a feeling level, not just on an intellectual level. An actor needs to surrender to the emotional honesty that is required for a role rather than crank up its emotional intensity. I urge all directors to take an acting class yourself so that you can understand some of these issues at gut level.

Feelings don't hurt people. Sometimes directors are afraid of deep feelings and this holds them back in their communication with actors. For actors, expressing deep feelings can be cathartic; they may have chosen the profession for the very reason that it offers the opportunity to go to dark and difficult places. Does the director have to go with the actor to these dark places? Yes and no. You can let yourself deeply imagine the characters' inner lives, and respect the courage of an honest actor while also respecting his privacy.

Emotions are energy. There is no need to manipulate, bully, shame, or abuse an actor into going to the places you feel are required for the role (even though some of them won't mind it if you do). You can invite them to invest more in the images of the scene, in other words, to make the work more personal. Or you can offer them freedom, give them permission to "let go even more." You need in the next breath to promise that you'll be watching to make sure the performance is not overacted.

Emotion must never be indulged, or even attempted, for its own sake. When actors enjoy their tears and hold on to emotion for the sake of its effect, showing us how much emotion they have, the acting becomes bad. Whenever an actor feels something, he must harness that energy to a sense of *task* or predicament. In real life, as I mentioned in the first chapter, people don't try to have feelings, and frequently they try *not* to have them. Performances are usually much more successful when actors play *against* whatever feeling they have. It can be funnier when an actor tries *not* to laugh at a funeral (like Mary Tyler Moore in the famous "Chuckles the Clown" episode of her long-running TV show); more poignant when an actor holds back his tears; more frightening when his rage is contained.

TEACHERS AND GURUS

It was via the Group Theatre of the 1930s that Stanislavsky's teachings became disseminated in the United States. The history of the Group Theatre is described in Harold Clurman's The Fervent Years and the documentary film, "Broadway's Dreamers: The Legacy of the Group Theatre," made by Joanne Woodward, as well as (more briefly) in A Dream of Passion by Lee Strasberg and A Life by Elia Kazan. It had a far-reaching effect on American acting. Four Group Theatre members, Strasberg and Meisner (whom I mentioned earlier), Bobby Lewis and Stella Adler, became teachers who taught or influenced, directly or indirectly, almost every American actor and the current generation of acting teachers.

As it happens the resources I described earlier correspond in a very rough way to the approaches developed by the great Group Theatre teachers. *Memory* is emphasized by the Strasberg Method, *observation* by British technique, *imagination* by Stella Adler; and Meisner's Repetition Exercise emphasizes the value of *immediate experience*.

Affective memory has for some people a kind of "black magic" status, and they sometimes have violent objections to it. The good things about affective memory are that it makes memory (a resource all actors use, one way or another) sensory rather than intellectual, it makes substitution specific, and it helps actors get below the social mask.

The potential problems of affective memory, voiced most vehemently by Stella Adler, are these:

1) It can be dangerous. It can turn into a kind of therapy without a license. Often the events used for the affective memory exercise are traumatic events from deep childhood. Students may be pushed into emotional areas they are not equipped to handle.

2) It causes the actor to bring the role down to himself instead of bring himself up to the role. In other words, the actor makes every role be about his own miserable childhood instead of about the circumstances of the script.

3) In Strasberg classes students practice an affective memory that brings them to tears, anger, or fear a certain number of times. The theory is that it then belongs to the actor and will always work, but it may not. We are a little different each day from the day before. Using affective memory is itself a kind of discharge of emotion, and thus changes the emotion attached to the event being remembered.

4) You can't be in two places at once. It can take the actor out of the moment to concentrate on his substitution rather than his scene partner.

5) The actor may fall into playing "general emotion."

Method actors can hang onto feelings, and the work may become subjective, too inward, not expressed in intention or physicalized in activity — or at worst, self-indulgent. In my classes I always ask students to tie an affective memory exercise to a need or objective or relationship, rather than an emotion. The actor must play the situation (the predicament, the problem, the task), not the emotion. The words, the situation, the physical life, the needs of the character — plus what he is getting from the other actor — bring him to a feeling or they don't.

This makes me more influenced by Stella Adler than by Lee Strasberg, although I find affective memory and sense memory invaluable teaching tools. I am equally devoted to the Repetition Exercise, and to finding any way possible to get my students to awaken and engage their imaginations. The line between memory and imagination is in fact very thin. In practice, most actors use both personal experience and imagination. And observation. And direct experience too. (An actor could do an elaborate sense memory or imaginative work in order to carry an empty suitcase if it were full, but why not instead put something in it?) At some point in his work on a role, the actor needs to explore personal experience and associations. Working honestly this way unlocks the imagination. Sense memory itself is an imaginative exercise. All acting technique is in service of creating a spark.

Let's look at Anthony Hopkins, a wonderful actor who, I believe, uses all his resources. For the movie "Nixon," Hopkins did not try to imitate Richard Nixon physically, but he chose to focus on a few specific physical behaviors of the man — shoulders, chin, hands, some vocal work. He also made observations (which he has discussed in the press) of Nixon's emotional life on which he based the character's inner life, in particular the insight (shared by director Oliver Stone) that Nixon was an "outsider." Hopkins has said that Stone cast him because the director sensed "my isolation as a person and thought I could relate to Nixon... I was surprised when he said that, but I guess I've been a lone wolf my whole life. It started when I was still a child in school." It seems to me that this thinking may have led him, consciously or unconsciously, to use, in creating his characterization of Nixon, the spine "to build a wall against the pain of being on the outside."

In any case, to create his Nixon he used a combination of *observation* and *personal experience*. His creation of Hannibal Lecter, on the other hand, is surely the work of a vivid, sharp, playful *imagination*. He always uses *direct experience* — always gives and takes with the other actors. The "book" scene with Emma Thompson in "Remains of the Day," for example, contains remarkable moments of pure chemistry and real psychological event; this is because they both *give* the scene to each other.

Any acting technique can be used improperly. I have heard of repetition exercises, if supervised imperfectly, becoming indulgent, even out of control. Actors who rely on observation and imagination to the exclusion of memory can turn in work that is shtick-y or merely slick. At any rate, different techniques work for different people.

In England, live theatrical performance, including Shakespeare, is incorporated more naturally into children's education. The Shakespeare plays themselves, when met fully (not recited stagily) by an actor, are lessons in emotional openness, imaginative invention, risk-taking, and clean, specific emotional transitions. Vanessa Redgrave has pointed out that she feels her classical British training in fencing had to do with actors learning to give and take; in other words, to listen.

There are excellent American acting teachers who are not as well known as the Group Theatre titans. Peggy Feury and Roy London never became household names but were beloved teachers who taught many excellent actors. Some acting teachers are dogmatic about their teaching methods. Some are tyrants and bullies. Getting below the social mask can be difficult; most of us have characterological and social armoring that prevents us from deep feeling. Acting teachers sometimes take it on themselves to attempt to pierce this armor by bullying and manipulating students. Actors unfortunately are often wounded souls who expect and respond to such bullying. I have found as a teacher that the opposite tack — more freedom and permission to fail — works better.

Acting class should be, among other things, a place where the imagination is stimulated and creative freedom is encouraged and where it is very safe to be open and honest and to reveal feelings. It is appropriate for an acting class to be therapeutic but it should not be therapy.

STRETCHING

"By taking on roles of characters that were unlike me, I began to discover those characters in me." — **Al Pacino**

What if an adjustment doesn't work? What if an actor tries a given circumstance, then an imaginative adjustment, then an objective, a substitution, and nothing seems to get him to the place needed for the script? Take the example of the actor asked to make her performance more "stern." What if she makes the imaginative adjustment that she heard the actor B (opposite her) make a racist remark, and that adjustment doesn't make her behave sternly toward him; instead it makes her feel upset and anxious? Well, she might then try adding a substitution of the actor opposite being someone she is less fond of (or less threatened by), and that might give her the stern response. Or she might look for another adjustment, say, that actor B has made a mistake that is going to make the production go into overtime and she will miss a social event she's been long looking forward to. But what if that doesn't work either?

What if "sternness" is foreign to her nature and emotional vocabulary? What if she never behaves sternly in her own life? By now she should have translated the result direction "sternness" into a verb: possibly to teach, to preach, to disapprove, or to punish. Then she should take another look, and make another emotional inventory. Has she really never had the impulse to disapprove or to punish? We have all had the impulse, even if we never act on it. The actor gets to find it and then act on it in the created world — to behave in ways she would never behave in real life — and get away with it!

The actor must make his choices his own, must connect with the choice in such a way that allows his own subconscious to kick in. The actor can play characters that are different from himself by making character choices that are different from his in real life, e.g., choose to beg in a situation where he himself would not beg. It's a playable choice. He needs to "beg" honestly, of course, the way he himself begs when he does beg. This can allow the pure, delicious freedom of getting to do something one doesn't get to do in real life, that is, to achieve the actor's liberty to kick in, as it seems to for Ingrid Bergman in her robust portrayal of the belittling mother (opposite Liv Ullman as the daughter) in Ingmar Bergman's "Autumn Sonata." Allowing herself to complain, demand, and exert her will as no one ever gets to do in real life gives the performance great zest.

One doesn't need to sleep with one's leading man or lady. One can play a murderer without having murdered someone. Lynn Redgrave has said that her best work is in roles that are not at all like her. Glenn Close has said the same. Under what circumstances would I be capable of murder? Everybody draws his own line. An actor catches hold of a corner of a scene's reality, unlocks some tiny part of it, and imagination captures the rest. Holly Hunter calls it "living on a terrain that I know something of, but is not where I live."

A good director can be the key — can provide the invitation to stretch, the deep permission to "take a chance," to play — that unlocks the doors to an actor's resources.

STAGE ACTING VS. FILM AND TELEVISION ACTING

Glenn Close has called the performer's condition a condition in which one allows oneself to disturb the molecules in the surrounding space. On stage the actor "disturbs the molecules" up to the last row of the balcony. For film, the actor must disturb the molecules of the camera lens. These are very different experiences for the actor, and require adjustments to his energy and concentration. There are stage actors who don't connect to the camera, who are, in a way, afraid of the camera, and there are film actors whose work doesn't read at all on stage. But the ways that stage and film actors prepare are similar. The goal of an actor's preparation is always the emotional truth of the role. Acting that is too fake and stagy for film is, to me at least, too fake and stagy for stage. (Four-camera television comedy — rehearsed for five days and then filmed or taped in front of a live audience — is both a stage performance *and* a film experience for an actor.)

Stage actors (and four-camera comedy actors) must put together in rehearsal a fully structured characterization, complete with spine, transformation, through-lines, and beats. Since film acting is done in bits and pieces, a whole performance can be patched together with tricks and quick fixes. Some directors prefer to work this way, rather than by allowing the actors to create a full characterization, on the theory that the demands of a full characterization will conflict with moment-by-moment freshness. Sydney Pollack, although he comes from a stage background and used to schedule lengthy rehearsals, has said that in recent years he prefers to work without rehearsal, confident that he can get the moments he needs with a word or two just before the camera rolls. Certain directors, such as Ken Loach and sometimes (reportedly) Woody Allen, don't give actors a whole script.

On the other hand, since film acting is done in bits and pieces, an actor who knows how to craft a full characterization (Meryl Streep, for one) can be an exciting collaborator with a confident director. Directors as diverse in their rehearsal and shooting methods as Martin Scorsese, Sidney Lumet, Robert Altman, Jane Campion, and Quentin Tarrantino all rely heavily on the actors' contributions.

PROFESSIONALISM

"Skillful actors acquire great expertise, and the greater the expertise, the more difficult it becomes to [surrender]."
— **Vanessa Redgrave**

Besides learning the craft of acting, film and television actors also learn camera technique. This includes hitting marks, finding their light, and not blinking. Over time, their familiarity with these technical tricks can make their acting slick and less exciting to watch.

Actors can also burn out, get sloppy, or general. They may even take roles they are not particularly interested in just for something to do.

Actors often develop a bag of tricks, a set of effects they know they can reliably produce. My teacher Jean Shelton used to call this "tap dancing." She meant a reliance on showy emotional or comedic shtick *for its own sake*, at the expense of listening. It is also called mugging. For example, romantic comedy heroines Carole Lombard, Irene Dunn, and Claudette Colbert invented and brought to its peak the screwball, "quirky" comic heroine. They were great ensemble players, great listeners. They always played off their partners; they never demonstrated "quirkiness" for its own sake. But it's a great temptation for an actress who wants to entertain the public to establish for herself a set of glances, shrugs, and inflections that become a formula to produce an effect of quirkiness, and to put her concentration on producing these effects rather than on the response of her partner. This is called playing her bag of tricks.

It is also called buying a moment "cheap," or trying to "slip a moment through the back door," as Tom Hanks, in an interview with Roger Ebert, described his trick, in some early movies, of punctuating a dramatic moment with a "half-look-away, half-eyes-to-the-sky" number. He then expressed his gratitude to the directors who knew enough to call him on such gimmicks. You should understand that actors with a well-developed bag of tricks are usually highly talented people, and that honesty and listening will not cost them their inventive facility, but will enhance it. Secretly they know this. These actors are capable of wonderful, honest work. Sometimes they just need a director with guts enough to ask for the good stuff and they'll put it out.

In addition, from being on many sets with lots of time on their hands, experienced actors may learn the following: how to watch themselves in dailies; how to judge material; how to design lighting and camera angles, especially those that will present them and their work most effectively; how to get respect. You may notice that some of these things, like lighting, camera placement, and watching dailies, are usually considered director's jobs.

160

It's hard to direct people who can fire you. I think a young director has to cope with the situation head-on, meet with the star, and have a frank discussion. You've got to let actors know that you love and respect them and you want to make the best use of their talent — that's why you're there. If you've gone ahead on a project with an actor that's been foisted on you and that you don't even like, I don't have any advice. But if you've gone with somebody that you know might be difficult but that you think will bring excitement to the project — dive in! Go after it. Go after the relationship. Good actors know that if they do their job and if you do your job they'll look better. Sometimes you have to prove to them that you know how to do your job.

Actors at a high level of expertise are very canny about scripts, know a lot about directing, and usually show up for work completely prepared and professional. You should not let yourself feel frightened about working with such actors. Don't let yourself resent their power. Find ways to communicate with them and tap into their resources and learn from them, but don't abdicate your responsibilities. The actor is not served by a director who lets him take over directing decisions.

Directors in episodic television have special problems. Unlike Jim Burrows, who directed nearly all of the "Taxi" episodes and who now directs only pilots, most episodic directors are "hired guns" who come into an established show and are expected basically to direct traffic. In this situation the actors can legitimately claim to know much more about their characters than you do, so why should they take any substantive direction from you?

Professionalism requires actors in television series to maintain their characterizations even though there may be different directors every week. That means that their *spines* are set. It would be a mistake for a director to come in and try to change basic characterizations; this would be a disservice both to the actors and to the viewing public.

What do you do when the actors have more professional experience than you do? First, make a script analysis.

SCRIPT ANALYSIS

"...Then there are other directors I watch and wonder why they get out of bed in the morning, because of the stunning lack of homework they do." — **Anthony Hopkins**

It is natural, when you read (or write) a script, to hear the lines and see the characters in your mind's eye, but if you are the director of the movie, this is only a place to start! This is not a completed script analysis. It's all still in your head. You need ways to bring your vision out of your head and into life.

Many directors are primarily visual in their orientation, and their story imaginations are less well developed than their visual imaginations. But even directors who are also writers often have trouble bringing their story imaginations off the page.

The words on the page, the dialogue, and (to some extent) the stage directions are clues to a vast subworld of behavior and feeling which it is the duty and privilege of the director and actors to supply. This is the ninety percent of the iceberg that is below water. In order to understand the script you need to be able to operate in the subworld of these characters, to believe in it, create in it, and trust it.

The tendency people have, once they have heard the line, to adhere rigidly to that line reading or interpretation, is very detrimental. Instead directors need to know the characters and the script structure inside out. The purpose of script analysis is to find out who these people (characters) are and what happens to them, to become the teller of their story. Then you won't have to remind yourself to phrase your direction in the correct vocabulary or jargon; you will have insight and understanding that you can *communicate* to the actors.

You will be able to think of characters in your movie scripts not as conventions, stereotypes, pawns, movie elements, or theatrical devices to be manipulated — but as people. You may notice that I use the terms "character" and "person" interchangeably. I think of characters as people. I allow the characters I meet the same independence and privacy that I allow the people I meet in real life. As a result, characters step off the page and take on independent life in my imagination. This makes directing actors actually fun.

I have a set of tools which will help you go deeper into the lives of the character. They work for every genre, and are helpful both for good scripts and mediocre scripts. Good scripts are complex with a rich subworld hinted at and not overexplained; you need a script analysis in depth so you can dig out every delicious tidbit, but you must do the same work with a bad script. Bad scripts are often over-explained and obvious, so you need to create something behind the words, to flesh them out and give them a texture of life. Although no actor can really be better than her material (and you must be careful not to burden the script with profundity it cannot carry or it could become pretentious), borderline or mediocre material can be made more lively and entertaining by using the same script analysis tools you use to dig out the riches and layers of a good script. (Helen Hunt seems to have done this in "Twister.") One of the most important adjustments I want you to make is, once you have decided to direct a script, to treat it as if it is a good script. You must stop judging and begin to engage.

This kind of script analysis is *not* a competing approach to any of the various ways that screenwriting teachers talk about script structure. Writers may find it useful to understand the tools directors and actors use, and they may find some of my exercises helpful for getting their creative juices going, but my script analysis discussions are not meant as a way to design a script you are writing. They are meant as tools for your design of the *adaptation* of that script for the screen.

That these two processes are very different is exactly my point. This means for one thing that if your thinking about script structure includes ideas such as which character is "hero," "mentor," "enemy," etc., for the purposes of this script analysis I need to ask you to let go of such categories and think of each character as a human being in a situation.

I'm going to refer to a set of charts that I use to teach my script analysis methods. There are four charts, each with columns; they are a teaching tool. For some people the charts might also work as framework for your notes, although I don't use them that way myself. I like to make my director's notes on a lined pad, a paper napkin, or the back of a telephone bill. Script analysis is not really as linear as it looks on the charts. But I believe that all the good directors go through something like these thought processes and do work of this kind.

There is no conflict between preparation and spontaneity. The purpose of preparing is to be ready to meet and trust the moment, and to go through your mediocre ideas, so you will be ready, once you get to rehearsal and the set, for your great ideas.

PREPARING FOR THE FIRST READ

The Skim is what I call the first time you read a script. I call it a "Skim" because I don't believe that the very first time you pass your eyes over the words of a script can be a meaningful reading. Even if you read slowly, you do not, on the first Skim, take in much of the script's possibilities. You may see *that it has* possibilities, but that is not the same as *seeing* the possibilities, because you are sifting what you read through the filter of what you expect to read.

The Skim will leave you with impressions and feelings, of course, and these can be very valuable. Because these first impressions are bound to have more to do with what you already know and feel than with what the script has to offer, they tell you something about the personal investment you may be able to make in the movie, why it might be important to you to do it, what personal and original slant you may give the material — *what*, for you, *the movie is about*. So it's a good idea to make notes of your first impressions. Column 1 of Chart 1 (page 184) is a place for such notations. Don't worry, at this point, whether you have phrased your ideas as a result. Once you have jotted them down, I suggest that you let go of them for the time being, refrain from allowing them to ossify into prejudgments, and prepare yourself to meet the material itself during your First Read.

THE WRITER-DIRECTOR

If you have written the script yourself you may not need the Skim; you may already know what you think the script is about. But I invite you to approach the First Read the same way as a director who hasn't written the script — that is, with an open, fresh beginner's mind.

Directing is an adaptation of a script. You must do this work of adaptation even if you wrote the script yourself. You need to take off your writing hat, put on your directing hat, and treat the script as if it was written by someone else. This may seem almost impossible to do at first, but I can tell you that I have worked with directors who were able to do this, who believed in their characters so deeply that they could allow them to have independent life. They were not threatened by the actors' contributions and they could collaborate with the actors to bring the characters out of their own head, off the page, and into life.

So when I talk about figuring out what the words mean I don't say, "Find out what the author meant." I mean no disrespect to the author when I say that the director must find the meaning of the *script*, not the meaning the author "intended." My intention is not to "deconstruct" the author's intention. Good writing often takes place at the most creative, i.e., subconscious level. In working with writers, I have seen over and over that the author is not always a reliable interpreter of what he has written. His unconscious impulses are often richer than his conscious intention. Adapting the clues of the script into cinematic life is a different process and requires a different talent from the talent of writing. Sometimes a person has both talents, but they are two different talents.

EDITING STAGE DIRECTIONS

Before you actually start reading you should edit the stage directions — and cross out most of them. At the very least, all stage directions should be *adapted* rather than swallowed whole as emotional marks that the actors are supposed to hit. Movie people don't have any trouble understanding that the production designer must adapt rather than execute rigidly the screenwriter's description of sets and locations. It's the same for actors.

There are different kinds of stage directions, some more needful of editing than others:

1) Directions that describe the character's inner life.

"Longingly," "kindly," "livid with rage," "a withering look," etc. These should all be crossed out, for the same reasons that you stay away from result direction. It is especially important to cross out (or at least approach with serious skepticism) the parentheticals: "pause," "beat," and "she takes a moment."

All these kinds of stage directions are adjectives, adverbs, indications of transitions or psychological explanations, or emotional maps ("He cannot look away"; "She makes a decision"). They are not playable. What the writer has done by putting in these abbreviated emotional guideposts is to take a stab at providing the characters' subtext. This is useful to the producers, executives, distributors, and agents who read a lot of screenplays — dozens per week — and need such time-saving devices.

It is exactly the job of the director and actors to create the subworld. Heeding such shortcuts to the characters' emotional life will make the director's and actors' job more, not less, difficult. You might want to keep an uncrossed-out version of the script hidden away to look at at some point during rehearsal, to make sure that the choices you and the actors are coming up with are at least as good as the author's suggestions. But crossing them out first is an important invitation to your story imagination.

The wrist-cutting scene in "Fatal Attraction" contained the stage direction "laughing." Actor Glenn Close tried but could not make it work honestly. Given permission by director Adrian Lyne to do whatever she needed to do, she ended up crying in the scene.

2) *Directions that depict blocking or business with no plot consequences.*

"She struggles with her coat"; "He looks at his watch." These should be crossed out too. Such a stage direction as "She struggles with her coat" is still a shorthand suggestion of the inner life of the character, another version of the first category above. It's better writing than describing the character as "frustrated," but it's really the same thing.

In addition to finding the subtext, finding the movement and activities that physicalize the emotional events of the script is exactly your job, a big part of the creative challenge of acting and directing. In "The Bridges of Madison County" Meryl Streep created a bit of business around fixing the photographer's collar that was the sexiest thing in the whole movie.

If there is a bit of business or blocking in the stage directions that looks interesting to you, that brings to life an emotional event or justifies a character's line, you might highlight it with a question mark, to try in rehearsal. But if, in rehearsal, the actors' connection to the emotional event leads them to some other physicalization (activity), you can consider that as well, and make a choice.

3) *Directions that give us characters' personal objects.*

In the examples above, perhaps we would want to make note of the one character's coat or the other character's watch, as potential personal objects. Objects are very important elements in a person's (character's) life. When we find clues as to the objects in the characters' lives, whether they are in the stage directions or dialogue, we need to circle them, then list them in Column 8 ("Physical Life") of Chart 3.

"On his desk there is a picture in a silver frame of a woman and two little girls." This should be circled as one of the character's personal objects. Any adjectives or adverbs that suggest inner life should be crossed out. (E.g., "A picture of his wife and two daughters has been lovingly placed on the desk." You should cross out "lovingly.") Even if you end up without the picture frame in any shot of the movie, it is helpful and necessary for script analysis. It leads to questions: "What is the history of this framed photo? Who bought and placed it on the desk? Is its presence a gesture that fulfills obligation and proper form, or deeply felt? Are they still married? Is the divorce too painfully recent for him to have put away the photo?"

4) Directions that give us backstory facts.

"The last time a crime occurred in this town was twenty-five years ago"; "He graduated first in his class at Harvard." Backstory facts in stage directions fall into two subcategories: a) facts that are referred to in the script, that is, a line somewhere in the script refers to the fact that the character graduated first in his class from Harvard; and b) facts that are not referred to in the script, that is, there is no line describing his education one way or the other.

In the case of (a), since they are already in the dialogue, you don't need them in the stage directions and you can cross them out. I find it much more exciting and creative to do the detective work of deducing the backstory facts than being fed them.

In the case of (b), since they are not in the dialogue, they may contain useful or even necessary clues. In that case you might enter them on a list of "facts" (see Column 1 of Chart 2 on page 192). On the other hand such statements by the author may be *imaginative choices* which you can use, if you find them helpful, and if not, you can reject and invent your own. In that case they belong in Column 1 of Chart 3 (page 207). For now I suggest that you circle them with a question mark.

5) *Directions that give us an image.*

For example, the feather which escapes Forrest's fingers and floats up into the air during the opening credits of "Forrest Gump." This image was described in the original script, and even if it had never ended up in the completed movie, it would have been circled as an image of the script, and a potential clue to the themes of the movie. It should also be listed in Column 6 of Chart 2.

6) *Directions that describe an emotional event.*

That is, an event with plot consequences (e.g., "He searches through the pile of clothes until he finds a gun"; "They kiss.") These need to be left in, after you cross out any descriptive words (e.g., "He searches *desperately* through the pile..."). You should translate any psychologizing explanations ("He cannot look away") into emotional events ("He does not look away"). Once you have edited and translated the description into an *event*, highlight it. Make sure you are not confusing essential information about the emotional events of the script with optional stage business; optional stage business may be highlighted but should have a question mark next to it. An important reason for crossing out superfluous stage directions and questioning optional ones is so that you can locate and highlight the necessary ones — the ones that tell you an emotional event which is not revealed by any dialogue.

After you do this, you'll be left with very sparse, circled or highlighted stage directions, and some question marks. The circled images, facts, and objects will have been entered on the proper charts. Highlighted material will contain clues to the physical and emotional life of the characters.

Below is the opening scene from the play "When You Comin' Back, Red Ryder?" by Mark Medoff. Before you read on, you might want to look at the scene and do your own circling and crossing out.

ANGEL
Good mornin', Stephen.
(Stephen does not look at her, but glances at the clock and makes a strained sucking sound through his teeth — a habit he has throughout — and flips the newspaper back up to his face. Unperturbed, Angel proceeds behind the counter.)
I'm sorry I'm late. My mom and me, our
daily fight was a little off schedule today.
(Stephen loudly shuffles the paper, sucks his teeth.)
I said I'm sorry, Stephen. God. I'm only
six minutes late.

STEPHEN
Only six minutes, huh? I got six minutes
to just hang around this joint when my
shift's up, right? This is really the kinda
dump I'm gonna hang around in my spare
time, ain't it?

ANGEL
Stephen, that's a paper cup you got
your coffee in.
(Stephen is entrenched behind his newspaper.)

STEPHEN
Clark can afford it, believe me.

ANGEL
That's not the point, Stephen.

STEPHEN
Oh no? You're gonna tell me the point
though, right? Hold it, lemme get a pencil.

171

ANGEL

The point is that if you're drinkin' your
coffee here, you're supposed to use a glass
cup, and if it's to go, you're supposed to get
charged fifteen instead of ten and ya get
one of those five cent paper cups to take it
with you. That's the point, Stephen.

STEPHEN

Yeah, well I'm takin' it with me, so where's
the problem?
(Stephen has taken the last cigarette from a pack, slipped
the coupon into his shirt pocket and crumpled the pack.
He basketball shoots it across the service area.)

ANGEL

Stephen.
(She retrieves the pack and begins her morning routine:
filling salt and pepper shakers, the sugar dispensers, setting out place mats, and cleaning up the mess Stephen
evidently leaves for her each morning. Stephen reaches
over and underneath the counter and pulls up a half
empty carton of Raleighs and slides out a fresh pack. He
returns the carton and slaps the new pack down on the
counter.)
What're ya gonna get with your cigarette
coupons, Stephen?
(Stephen reads his paper, smokes, sips his coffee.)
Stephen?
(Stephen lowers the newspaper.)

STEPHEN

How many times I gotta tell ya to don't call
me Stephen.

ANGEL

I don't like callin' ya Red. It's stupid —
callin somebody with brown hair Red.

172

STEPHEN
It's my name, ain't it? I don't like
Stephen. I like Red. When I was a kid I
had red hair.

ANGEL
But ya don't now. Now ya got brown hair.

STEPHEN
(exasperated)
But then I did, and then's when counts.

ANGEL
Who says then's when counts?

STEPHEN
The person that's doin' the countin'!
Namely yours truly! I don't call you
Caroline or Madge, do I?

ANGEL
Because those aren't my name. My name's
Angel, so —

STEPHEN
Yeah, well ya don't look like no angel to
me.

ANGEL
I can't help that, Stephen. At least I was
named my name at birth. Nobody asked
me if I minded bein' named Angel, but at
least —

STEPHEN
You could change it, couldn't ya?

ANGEL
What for? To what?

STEPHEN
(Thinking a moment,
setting her up)
To Mabel.

ANGEL
How come Mabel?

STEPHEN
Yeah...Mabel.

ANGEL
How come? You like Mabel?

STEPHEN
I hate Mabel.
(Stephen stares at her, sucks his teeth.)

ANGEL
Look, Stephen, if you're in such a big
hurry to get outta here, how come you're
just sittin' around cleaning your teeth?

STEPHEN
Hey, look, I'll be gone in a minute. I mean
if it's too much to ask if I have a cigarette
and a cup a coffee in peace, for chrissake,
just say so. A person's supposed to unwind
for two minutes a day, in case you ain't
read the latest medical report. If it's too
much to ask to just lemme sit here in
peace for two minutes, then say so. I
wouldn't wanna take up a stool somebody
was waitin' for or anything.
(looking around him.)

Christ, will ya look at the waitin' line to
get on this stool.

                    ANGEL
              (pause)
Did you notice what's playin' at the films?

                   STEPHEN
Buncha crap, whudduya think?

                    ANGEL
              (pause)
I saw ya circle somethin' in the gift book
the other mornin'.

                   STEPHEN

What gift book?

                    ANGEL
The Raleigh coupon gift book.

                   STEPHEN
Hey — com'ere.
(Angel advances close to him. He snatches the pencil from
behind her ear and draws a circle on the newspaper.)
There. Now I just drew a circle on the
newspaper. That mean I'm gonna get me
that car?

                    ANGEL
Come on, Stephen, tell me. What're ya
gonna get?

                   STEPHEN
Christ, whudduyou care what I'm gonna get?

ANGEL

God, Stephen, I'm not the FBI or somebody.
What are you so upset about? Just tell me
what you're gonna get.

STEPHEN
(mumbling irascibly.)
Back pack.

ANGEL

What?

STEPHEN

Whuddya, got home fries in your ears?

ANGEL

Just that I didn't hear what you said is all.

STEPHEN

Back. Pack.

ANGEL

Who's gettin' a back pack?

STEPHEN

The guy down the enda the counter.
Chingado the Chicano. He's hitchin' to
Guatamala.

ANGEL

You're gettin' a back pack? How come?

STEPHEN

Whuddo people usually get a back pack
for?

ANGEL

Ya gonna go campin'.

STEPHEN

No I ain't gonna go campin'. I'm gonna go
gettin' the hell outta this lousy little town
is where I'm gonna go campin'.

ANGEL

When? I mean...when?

STEPHEN

When? Just as soon as I get somethin'
taken care of.

ANGEL

When will that be?

STEPHEN

When will that be? When I get it taken
care of — when d'ya think? Lemme have
a donut.

ANGEL
(getting him a donut)
Where ya gonna go?

STEPHEN

Where am I gonna go? I'm gonna go
hitchin' that way (pointing left) or I'm
gonna go hitchin' that way (pointing right)
and when I get to some place that don't
still smella Turdville here I'm gonna get
me a decent job and I'm gonna make me
some bread.
(He picks up the donut
and bites into it.)

177

ANGEL
Rye or whole wheat, Stephen?

STEPHEN
This is some donut. I think they glued the
crumbs together with Elmer's.

ANGEL
Rye or whole wheat, Stephen?

STEPHEN
(with his mouth full)
Believe me, that ain't funny.

ANGEL
Don't talk with your mouth full.

STEPHEN
Christ, my coffee's cold. How d'ya like
that?
(He looks at her. She pours him a fresh cup of coffee in
a mug. She sets it down by him. He looks at it a minute,
then pours the coffee from the mug into his paper cup.)
I told ya, I'm leavin' in less'n two minutes.

ANGEL
That's right, I forgot.

STEPHEN
Yeah, yeah.

ANGEL
You better let your hair grow and get some
different clothes if you're gonna hitch
somewhere, Stephen. You're outta style.

Nobody's gonna pick up a boy dressed like
you with his hair like yours. And with a
tattoo on his arm that says "Born Dead."
People wear tattoos now that say "Love"
and "Peace," Stephen, not "Born Dead."

STEPHEN

Love and peace my Aunt Fanny's butt!
And who says I want them to pick me, for
chrissake? You think I'm dyin' for a case
a the clap, or what? I got a coupla hundred truck drivers come through here in
the middle of the night that said they'd all
gimme a ride anytime anywhere they was
goin'. You think I'm gonna lower myself to
ride with those other morons — you're
outta your mind.

ANGEL

Two hundred truck drivers? Uh-uh, I'm
sorry, I have to call you on that one,
Stephen. If it wasn't for Lyle's station and
his motel, Lyle'd be our only customer.

STEPHEN

You know, right? Cause you're here all
night while I'm home sacked out on my
rear, so you know how many truck drivers
still stop in here, now ain't that right?

ANGEL

In the three weeks since the bypass
opened, Stephen, you know exactly how
many customers you had in the nights?
You wanna know exactly how many,
Stephen?

                    STEPHEN
No Christ, I don't wanna know how many.
I wanna have two minutes of peace to read
my damn newspaper — if that's not askin'
too much! Is that askin' too much? If it
is, just say the word and I'll get the hell
outta here and go to the goddamn cemetery
or somewhere.

Now here is what I would do:

On the first two pages I would circle "newspaper," "cigarette" and "coupon" as personal objects of Stephen's. Since they are also mentioned in the dialogue they are mandatory personal objects for him. In fact they could be circled in the dialogue rather than the stage directions. You may notice that the author didn't write a stage direction "He is drinking coffee out of a paper cup." There is no need for it, because the information is in the dialogue. In order to create a script that was easy and pleasurable to *read*, the author made decisions to leave out a stage direction about the coffee cup and put in the stage directions regarding the newspaper and cigarettes. In order to *adapt* the script to the stage or screen, we need to cannibalize the stage directions for clues, not read them for instructions. So I am crossing out the rest of the stage directions referring to Angel's entrance and Stephen's reaction to it.

Soon the writer mentions some objects (salt and pepper shakers, sugar dispensers, place mats, cleaning supplies) which are potential personal objects for Angel. We might have inferred them anyway, since they are not unusual to a diner. They are not referred to in the dialogue, so they are not mandatory. I'm crossing them out but highlighting, with a question mark, some stage business involving Angel's work-related activities and Stephen discarding his empty cigarette pack for a fresh one. I am tempted to cross these instructions out, because I like to find my own blocking and business in rehearsal, but, to be conservative, I'll highlight this idea with a question mark, to try in rehearsal. On the other hand, the directions "Stephen reads his paper, smokes, sips his coffee" and "Stephen lowers the newspaper" I'm going to cross out. They seem to indicate inner life.

Right after the "I hate Mabel" line, I'll highlight "sucks his teeth" with a question mark, since it provokes Angel's next line, "...how come you're just sittin' around here cleaning your teeth?" Although he doesn't really have to be sucking his teeth; if he were using a toothpick that would also justify the line. I would want to make sure in rehearsal that the actor playing Stephen can suck his teeth credibly before committing to the teeth-sucking business. (If a star is playing the role, there probably won't have been an audition in which to find this out.) At this point, I'll go back to the beginning and highlight "sucks his teeth" there too.

About halfway through, "He snatches the pencil from behind her ear." I would probably highlight that with a question mark. This bit of stage business may have been written by the author but is just as likely to have been taken from the first production of the play. Whether it was thought up by the author or the first director of the piece, you are free to steal it, but you are also free to come up with a different bit of business of your own. As the director, I'm not sure I'd use it, but I might want to at least try it (among other ideas) in rehearsal. All other neighboring stage directions ("exasperated," "mumbling irascibly," etc.) are results, so I cross them out.

When we get to the donut business, I'm going to highlight the word "donut," but I'm definitely going to cross out "getting him a donut," "He picks up the donut and bites into it," and "with his mouth full." Why? They are redundant; the clues to these activities are already in the dialogue. They are therefore mandatory. But I want to take them *off the page*, so I allow a donut to enter the scene almost like another character. In rehearsal we will work out the ways that this new character changes the relationship of the characters already there.

I'm going to highlight the business of her pouring the coffee into a mug, and him pouring it back into his paper cup. Some activity is needed to justify his line, "I told ya, I'm leavin' in less'n two minutes." Also I like it. I definitely want to try this idea in rehearsal. *But I am not married to it.* If it should happen not to work, I'll find something else.

Now the only stage directions left should be either circled or highlighted; the circled ones have also been entered on one of the charts. Even though I have crossed out everything I haven't circled or highlighted, this does not mean that the writer should not have put it in. There are writers whose stage directions are insightful and useful, and the ones in this scene are not bad. But there are also terrific writers who write with minimal stage directions: Chekhov, Pinter, Horton Foote. Shakespearean texts have zero directions, except for the odd "Exeunt"; in Shakespeare's plays all physical movement and business must be inferred and deduced from the dialogue. At the other end of the spectrum there are great writers who lay on the unplayable stage directions with a trowel — Eugene O'Neill, for one.

It's okay for writers to put such directions in for the convenience of the producers. In fact, producers usually judge the writing by the stage directions as much as by the dialogue. So remember that the best-written, most evocative stage directions use verbs, facts, images, events, and physical tasks instead of adjectives and explanations whenever possible (for example, "She takes off her glasses and rubs her eyes," instead of "tiredly"). But once a script has a green light and has been turned over to the director and designers and actors, the writer must send his characters out into the world the way a parent sends out the children when they turn eighteen. You must trust that they have learned good values; you have to believe that you have done all you can.

The important thing for directors is to recognize the necessary stage directions (emotional events, personal objects and thematic images) and either cross out or question everything else. Even the directions I am suggesting that you as directors leave in are not necessarily useful to actors. Many, many actors routinely cross out *all* stage directions, to give themselves freedom to create their characters' emotional lives from scratch.

During a Skim I may glance at the stage directions. But once I have edited them, I forget about them for a while and turn my attention to the dialogue.

FIRST IMPRESSIONS — CHART I

Reading out loud is a good way to access first impressions. You make friends with the words. You may or may not wish to be alone when you read out loud. Read slowly in full voice. Don't whisper or mumble. Don't rush. Don't try to "be" the characters but don't censor yourself. Don't listen to yourself. Enjoy the words. Feel them in your mouth. Don't read the stage directions (even the ones that you have circled or highlighted).

If you are relaxed and open, there are two benefits you may get from reading out loud. You may get new ideas — or questions. Questions are better yet. In any case, you might want to jot them down briefly, because if you are doing this properly — that is, if you are in the moment — you might not remember them later.

FIRST IMPRESSIONS — CHART I

1 IDEAS/FIRST IMPRESSIONS	2 EVIDENCE FOR YOUR IDEAS	3 PARAPHRASE	4 MYSTERIOUS LINES OR EVENTS	5 THREE POSSIBLE MEANINGS	6 THE FACT OR REALITY BEHIND THE LINE

"OWNING" THE CHARACTERS

The second benefit of reading aloud is that this can begin the process of owning the characters. Just as each actor must "own" his own character, the director must own each of the characters, separately. At this point you have not yet begun figuring out what the words mean. You are allowing them to find breath and voice in your own body. You are beginning to take them off the page.

PARAPHRASING

Then you can start putting their lines into your own words. Does this sound a bit radical? I don't know. This idea is based on a very effective exercise I use in my classes. I ask the student to say the lines of a monologue she has learned. Then I ask her to tell me what is going on in the speech, what she understands about the character from it, starting with the words "This is a character who..." I tell her that her paraphrase can be any length: it can be much longer than the speech or much shorter; it can go far afield; in effect, she can say anything that pops into her head. After this I tell her to do the same thing again — again putting the speech in her own words, allowing her impulses to take her wherever they go — only changing the pronoun from "she" to "I" when she speaks of the character.

The purpose here is *not* rewriting the script, but "owning" the characters and accessing your intuition about them. Ideas often surface that you didn't even know you had.

Let's take one of Stephen's speeches on page 4:

> "Hey, look, I'll be gone in a minute. I mean
> if it's too much to ask if I have a cigarette
> and a cup a coffee in peace, for chrissake,
> just say so. A person's supposed to
> unwind for two minutes a day, in case you
> ain't read the latest medical report. If it's
> too much to ask to just lemme sit here in
> peace for two minutes, then say so. I

> wouldn't wanna take up a stool somebody
> was waitin' for or anything. Christ, will ya
> look at the waitin' line to get on this stool."

I have heard students paraphrase it thus: "This is a guy who over-reacts to everything. He's a control freak. No matter what Angel says he has to beat her down and get the last word."

I'm sure you have recognized this as an unplayable judgment on the character; Stephen probably doesn't think of himself as a control freak. When the student takes the next step and changes the pronoun to "I," he experiences a little bit of revelation because he has to say, "I am a control freak. I can't stand it when anyone gets one up on me." Putting it in the first person makes him feel something. Maybe discomfort. Maybe a pang of recognition.

In fact, when he puts it that way, he may realize that there is a little bit of control freak in all of us. Judgments may be accurate, but they are not playable. As long as you own them, as long as you admit that these feelings are ones that we've all had or are capable of, then you're not judging but empathizing. Empathy is the difference between saying "This guy is a control freak — just as I am sometimes (although I may not like it)," rather than "This guy is a control freak — just like all the people I can't stand and who make my life miserable and who are nothing like me."

Another paraphrase of the same speech might be: "I'm tired. I don't want to be here, but I don't want to go home either. My life is not very exciting or very much fun; in fact, smoking cigarettes is one of my only pleasures. And now my mother has got it into her head to nag me about my smoking and she won't let me smoke in the house." This is an example. There could be dozens of other ways to paraphrase the speech. Such a paraphrase gives us a possible subtext of the speech. Or maybe an idea for a backstory choice (the idea of the mother forbidding smoking in the house is not anywhere in the script — I made it up). And it lets us inside the character's experience and feelings.

I think directors during their First Read should do some of this paraphrasing; not every line of the script necessarily, but as much as you have time for. Let it be fun — something you *get* to do rather than something you *have* to do. You can take notes: there is a column (Column 3) on Chart 1 for this. You needn't feel that you have to take notes, however; you can let the exercise be an experience, rather than information. If it starts to feel boring that means you're doing it mechanically, so take a break and go on to another script analysis tool. But paraphrasing does get easier and more fun the more you do it.

The purpose of the paraphrasing exercise is to get you out of your head and able to access your intuition. When they do this exercise people often find themselves saying things about the character that they didn't know they thought. The resources of their subconscious minds are being enlisted in the task of script analysis.

The paraphrasing exercise can be used to gently confront an actor with his own prejudgments (resistances) to a character, or to unlock a static interpretation. If you sense a resistance on the part of the actor, you can ask him, "What do you think of this guy? Do you like him?" If he answers with a string of negatives, you can quietly say, "Say the same thing again, only using the pronoun 'I.'"

"IT'S JUST..." AND "I ASSUME"

I make a big fuss with my students about the words "It's just..." I call them the two greatest enemies of an artist. Instead of "It's just a love scene," say "It's a love scene." Instead of "He's just apologizing to his mother," say "He's apologizing to his mother." Do you see what a big difference that is? A good director inspires the actors. "She's just waiting for the doctor's report." "It's just a confrontation between two friends." "He's just being sarcastic to the judge." You can't expect to inspire anyone when you minimize such important events. Our artistic goal is to illuminate human events, not minimize them.

"Obviously" is another red flag for me. "Stephen is obviously not attracted to Angel." Maybe I'm perverse, but as soon as I hear someone say that something in a script is "obvious" I want to consider its opposite. Nothing in a good script is obvious. Like people, characters are subtle, arbitrary, full of contradictions, and lacking in self-knowledge. Other uninspiring qualifiers are "basically," "potentially," "sort of," etc. Think of yourself as a person who can commit, rather than qualify and hedge all your ideas, and then, when a new idea or information comes in, change your mind.

There are two other words that directors all too frequently use as the sum total of their script analysis: "I assume." "I assume that Angel lives with her mother." Don't assume anything. Investigate. Imagine. Choose.

THE TECHNIQUE OF THREE POSSIBLE

One of the best things that can happen on a First Read is that there will be lines that you don't understand, and that don't fit. An unfortunate tendency in Hollywood today is to rewrite such lines, to make everything fit, without an attempt to find out what they might mean.

Logic can be a serious roadblock to the imagination. In a well-written script (and remember, for the purposes of script analysis, we are considering any script you have decided to direct is a well-written script), such non sequiturs and contradictions — even lines that at first you don't like — can be gold. They can hold the key to some insight you have been resisting; that the key was elusive and the insight hard-won will make its truth all the more powerful.

Anytime you find a line that you don't like or doesn't make sense, I suggest that you make a quick list of three things it might possibly mean. Don't try to find the right answer but, rather, without evaluating your ideas, scribble them down.

Let's take Angel's line, "Who's gettin' a back pack?" Why does she say this (other than to set up the joke of Stephen's next line)? She just asked him what he was getting from the coupon book. Why doesn't she seem to understand that "back pack" is the answer to her question?

Okay, three possible answers. 1) Maybe she has some association with back packs that is so different from her associations with

Stephen that for a moment she can't connect the two. For instance, maybe she has a sister who is a Girl Scout leader and was talking about back packs for her troup yesterday; hearing the term jolts her mind back to that conversation and it takes a moment to allow "back pack" to be part of this conversation. 2) Maybe as soon as she hears the words "back pack" she associates it with Stephen's departure, which perhaps he has spoken of on other occasions. Maybe the image of him leaving is too painful to process quickly. 3) Maybe she engaged in some physical — or mental — activity that requires a lot of concentration. Maybe she is scrubbing the coffee machine. Or perhaps she is totaling the receipts from yesterday or making up the orders for the vendors who will make deliveries today.

Now, I didn't particularly concern myself with making sense but rather with trying to find three ideas that were different from each other. I'm looking for something — anything — to get myself started, so I can feel that I am coming up with ideas — any ideas — rather than listlessly staring at the paper. If I write them down without evaluating them, I may access my deeper resources. What I'm trying to do is not find the right answer, but turn myself on.

I find the "Technique of Three Possible" most useful when I come across hackneyed "movie-sounding" phrases, like "You just don't get it, do you?" or "You're sorry? All you can say is you're sorry?" These are words that people almost never really say in real life but which show up in movies a lot. Such lines require special attention to finding some truth, some subtext, to keep them from sounding clichéd and actorish.

If you open yourself to the idea that any line might have more than one meaning, you won't lose your equilibrium when an actor doesn't relate to something in the script that you have found compelling or beautiful or funny, and you won't panic when the actor interprets it differently. Then, too, you can use the "Technique of Three Possible" with actors who are resisting a line, to get them turned on. When they say, "This doesn't make sense to me," you can ask, "Well, what could it possibly mean?"

THE REALITY (FACT) BEHIND THE WORDS

Another way to understand mysterious lines is to look for the fact or event that they refer to. This goes for lines that you like as well as for lines that bother you. Lines that you like can be especially dangerous; you might fall in love with their wit or poetry and forget to look for the reality behind them. (This is one of the pitfalls of performing Shakespeare.) You have to approach such lines not by looking for the most effective way to say them and thus display their beauty, but by looking for the reality behind them.

For the "Forrest Gump" scene in which Forrest calls the front desk to complain about the noisy Watergate burglars, the director in script analysis (and the actor in performance) must put their concentration not on how funny the scene is going to be but on some reality behind it — for instance, that Forrest is a light sleeper.

MORE READING IDEAS

At some point you might try reading aloud the lines of one character at a time. For this technique, you don't even read silently the words of the other characters or any stage directions, and you don't try to make sense of the scenes. You read all his or her lines one after the other, slowly, in full voice. Something may come to you. Perhaps you may want to read the script with another person. Don't try to act the roles or the scenes. Instead, look at each other as much as possible, switching around roles from scene to scene. Or (this is my favorite) read the whole script aloud to another person. Don't read the character names or any stage directions, even circled or highlighted ones.

Finally, I want to strongly encourage you to reread the script (silently or aloud) as often as you can throughout script analysis, pre-production and rehearsal. Each time pretend it is the first time. Free your mind of the ideas you are coming up with (you have notes so you don't have to remember them), so you can return to the beginner's mind that characterizes the First Read. You may be surprised at the ideas and questions that will come to you.

THE IMMUTABLES: FACTS AND IMAGES: CHART 2

I call the facts and images of the script immutable because they are not subject to interpretation; they are in the script. They are a wonderful place to start for these reasons:

1) You don't have to be creative to come up with them. It's something you can do when you're not "in the mood" and find yourself staring at the page and don't know where to start.

2) They are the skeleton of the script, its infrastructure. You need to know them in order to feel confident that you know and understand the script.

3) They are magic keys into the subworld. Whenever you get stuck creatively you can return to them, ask a few questions, and your creative juices can be renewed.

4) Both are great ways to give direction. The facts of a script are its situation, its imaginative given circumstances — a good jumping-off place for actors. The images are an excellent tool for shaping and deepening performances.

5) They can help you avoid arguments with actors. If an actor brings in an interpretation of the script that does not encompass the facts and images, you can point them out, and they are there in black and white; this is especially useful to keep actors from judging or sentimentalizing characters. You can say, "Yes, but what about the fact that...?" This approach can help keep your egos out of the discussion.

Sometimes an actor brings in an interpretation that is supported by the facts and images, but is different from yours. When this happens you should listen with an open mind to the actor's ideas; they may turn out to be as valid as yours, or they may even be better. If you can tell the difference between this situation and the situation (above) in which the actor's ideas are not supported by the script, you will be much better prepared for discussion and rehearsal.

THE IMMUTABLES: FACTS AND IMAGES: CHART 2

1 FACTS	2 EVIDENCE	3 QUESTIONS	4 DISPUTES CONTRADICTIONS ISSUES	5 RESEARCH A. REREAD SCRIPT B. EXTERNAL C. INTERNAL	6 IMAGES	7 ASSOCIATIONS A FROM STORY B. EXTERNAL C. PERSONAL/ INTERNAL

FACTS AND EVIDENCE

Facts are very powerful for actors — the magic "as if." The actor creates a set of simple circumstances, allows himself to believe them, and then functions as if he were in those circumstances. For the purposes of this exercise we will treat the scene from "When You Comin' Back, Red Ryder?" as if it were a complete script. If we were making this movie, planning a rehearsal of this scene, we would of course examine the full script for facts. Working on one scene as if it is a full script is an exercise to teach you script analysis techniques which in the real world would be applied to a whole script.

Some facts will be clear; others we will deduce. We're not going to insist that the writer spell everything out; instead we'll look for evidence and follow clues. But we're not going to pretend to have any facts that we don't actually have. We're not going to make assumptions, judgments, or jump to conclusions; we're going to stick to facts. This is detective work. In a way we'll use some of the rules of court. For instance, hearsay is not admissible; just because a character says something is true, we won't automatically call it a fact. We will look for circumstantial evidence to back it up.

"Facts" are events that have happened or circumstances that are true before the scene starts — the character's situation. "Events" are things that happen in the scene, but once they have happened they become facts. For instance, Stephen eats a donut; that's an event in this scene. For the scene following this one, "Stephen has had breakfast" would be a fact.

Sometimes students suggest as a fact for this scene, "Angel likes Stephen." That's not a fact. I'm not saying that the role couldn't be played with that *choice*, but anything that has to do with a character's state of mind is not a fact. It is a choice or interpretation.

Often, the first thing students say when I ask them for the facts of this scene is, "Stephen wants to leave." This is not a fact either. Besides describing a state of mind, this statement is contradicted by the fact that he keeps sitting there. So it belongs under Column 4, "Disputes, Contradictions, Issues."

Don't forget — characters, like people, don't always tell the truth. They don't always know the truth. They remember things incompletely or inaccurately. They may not admit the truth to themselves, and, of course, sometimes they lie.

A good place to start in establishing some facts in the "Red Ryder" scene is the characters' relationship. I'll propose this statement for our list of facts: *Stephen and Angel work at the same diner.* Sometimes students call me on this one. They say that if they cross out all the stage directions it's not certain that they both work there; it could be that Stephen works there; Angel could be a friend, girlfriend, or even sister picking Stephen up after his shift. Okay, let's back up a step and look at the evidence.

There is early evidence (Column 2) that Stephen works there (his line, "I got six minutes to just hang around this joint when my shift's up, right?"). There also is evidence that she works there too: She knows about the rules of the place (how much to get charged if you drink from a paper cup); she brings him donut and coffee; her line "If it wasn't for Lyle's station and his motel, Lyle'd be our only customer" includes the proprietary "our." On the other hand, if it is a small diner in a small town and she is known as his steady girlfriend, she might be familiar enough with the place to know the rules and to pour a cup of coffee if the waitress was not there, or even to call the place "our" place. The line in which she asks him what is playing at the films could be seen as evidence that they are friends or boyfriend/girlfriend.

The stronger evidence that she does work there is her final line, "In the three weeks since the by-pass opened, Stephen, you know exactly how many customers you had in the nights? You wanna know exactly how many, Stephen?" The way I understand this line is by looking for the event behind it. First of all I recall what I know about small diners (I used to work in one). At the end of each shift, the order tickets were collected and put in numerical order and stacked neatly so that the next morning the manager could go through them and compare them to the cash register totals. Angel's shift (if we end up proving that Angel does work there) follows Stephen's. So if she does work there, she is in a position, each morning, to count Stephen's tickets; maybe it's even her job to do so. Unpacking the fact behind this line (also called "justifying" the line), and finding that it jells with earlier evidence pointing to the likelihood that she does work there, confirms that deduction.

Proposed fact: Angel is late for her shift.

Perhaps we can accept this hearsay of Angel's because Stephen doesn't contradict it. I think we can be sure that she is no more than six minutes late; if it was more than six minutes, it seems likely that Stephen would comment (Whadya mean, six? It's eight minutes!). Some questions (Column 3) arise in my mind: Has she ever been late before? Is it habitual? Is this the first time?

Maybe she's not actually late. When I was waitressing, the other waitresses used to habitually arrive a half hour early for their shift; if they arrived exactly on time, they considered themselves late, as did the waitresses they were relieving! If I were directing this scene I might want to suggest this little adjustment to the actress, to give her another layer. (See Column 6 of Chart 3, "Imaginative Choices," page 207.)

My idea for this adjustment arose from information I happen to have because of my experience waitressing in a diner. If you are unfamiliar with the customs and traditions of diner employees, you might need to do some Research (Column 5b).

Proposed fact: Angel has a daily relationship with her mother.

The line "My mom and me, our daily fight was a little off schedule today" is strong evidence, although not actual proof, that they live together (they could live separately but speak on the phone every morning). Her calling it a "daily fight" does not actually mean they fight every day, but it might *feel* like it's every day. Her mother, if asked, might claim that she and her daughter never fight!

Is this a fact? *"Stephen doesn't want Angel to call him Stephen."* No. All we can say as a fact is that there has been at least one conversation between the two of them on the subject of his name. Even though he says, "How many times I gotta tell ya...," it still may have been only once; for some people, twice is too many times to discuss certain subjects.

We can't even include as a fact that Stephen was called "Red" as a kid. Even if he claimed it was true, we wouldn't be able to accept it as fact. Interestingly, when we reread the scene carefully (script research, Column 5a), we find he doesn't actually say that. What he says is that when he was a kid he had red hair. Of course we can't be sure that this is true either. There is no evidence for it since now his hair is brown, as even he admits. All we can say as a fact is that he *says* that he had red hair as a kid, and that on at least one occasion previous to this scene he has made a request that Angel call him "Red."

Another way of putting this would be to list it as an "issue" under Column 4. His name is an issue between them. Other issues might be her lateness, if we make the choice that it is habitual; or the rules of the diner, e.g., the paper cup rule.

Actually, as soon as I wrote that, I considered its opposite: maybe the paper cup is not a standing issue between them. Maybe it's the first time this particular issue has come up. Maybe he always uses the prohibited paper cup, but usually she indulges his lapses; today she doesn't. Or maybe he usually uses the ceramic cup and this morning has decided to make this little rebellion. I'm not trying to talk you into any of these ideas. The point is that they are *ideas — choices —* not facts. (At first glance they seem like weaker choices, but you never know. Sometimes an apparently less plausible choice can give a performance a mystery, an edge. It might be something you could whisper to the actor in between takes to freshen things up.)

QUESTIONS

Questions are perhaps the most important product of script analysis, even though you are not going to rewrite the script so all questions are answered. Make a big list of them. If a character says, "Why are you shouting?" instead of assuming that the second character is shouting, ask questions: Is the other guy shouting? Or does the first guy have a low threshold? Could it be that what actually bothers him is the content of what the second guy said?

To me an important question of the scene is raised by Stephen's line "...as soon as I get something taken care of." Characters can lie, so he might be bullshitting — there might be nothing he has to take care of. He might have no reason except his own immobility for staying in this town instead of leaving. But I don't want to stop my script analysis here, because this thinking is likely to lead me into generalities and judgment about Stephen.

What is the thing he has to take care of? It may be that as soon as the thing he is referring to gets "taken care of" there will be another thing to take care of, but even so, it is something specific. With whom does he live? Does he live with his parents? Could there be abuse or alcoholism in the family? Is it possible that he has to fix his mother's life before he can leave?

If you find yourself jumping to a conclusion, I want you to put it in the form of a question. If, for instance, you find yourself saying, "Obviously this has happened many times before," turn it right around and ask, "Has this happened before?" That's always a good question in any case. One question you should always ask is, "What in this scene *is* happening for the first time?"

Anytime there is more than one possible explanation for something, it is not a fact. It may seem bewildering at first to open up so many possibilities. You may feel, "I thought I knew what I was doing and now I have nothing to hang onto." There are two purposes to this seemingly chaotic approach. One is to bring our story imaginations to life. Allowing ourselves to "daydream" around the facts of the script gives us the opportunity to let the material tell us what it is about. The other purpose is to prepare ourselves to make choices. In order to make choices, you need a field from which to choose; otherwise, it's not a choice, it's an assumption. As you get used to this

technique you will find it cleaner, and more liberating than psychologizing, explaining, or gossiping about the characters.

I often hear directors describe characters in terms of what they
are not. "Stephen is not a good employee." "Angel probably
doesn't have boyfriends." As soon as I hear statements like that, I
turn them into questions: Is Stephen good at his job? Does Angel
have boyfriends? If Stephen is not good at his job, what is he good
at? If he is not interested in his work, what is he interested in?
What sexual experience has Angel had? (A good question to ask
about any character.)

Sometimes I hear people say about characters, "She doesn't have
much of a sense of humor," or "He isn't very smart." A character who
is what society calls "slow" is not trying to be slow, so an actor who
tries to show us intellectual slowness is condescending to the character and playing a result (society's judgment of him). What such a
person (character) is usually doing (his objective) is *to struggle to keep
up*. An actor should never *show* us that a character is "slow," but
always involve himself with how the character copes with the cards
fate has dealt him.

In any case, *everybody is smart about something*. There are certain
questions which you should ask about every character. What is this
person smart about? What does this character find funny? Where is
his pain? How does he play? In what way is he an artist? What does
he most fear? What profession has he chosen or does he aspire to?
Whom does he look up to? What is the biggest thing that has ever
happened to him? How is the character different at the end of the
story (or scene) from the beginning?

You may occasionally come across a character who has no playful
side. This would be very rare, a very bold choice. Most of the time an
important way to bring a character to life is to look for a serious character's sense of humor, and for the serious side of comic characters.

Always ask, what is the character *not* saying? Whenever a character breaks off a speech or is cut off by another person, you need

to ask yourself, what was she going to say? The longer and more thoroughly you work on a script, the more such questions will crop up, which is good. The things that bother you can bring the most creativity, like the grain of sand that becomes a pearl by irritating the oyster. Sometimes when I do this kind of work with writer-directors, and start opening them to the subworld of the story they wrote themselves, instead of congratulating themselves on their good writing, they want to rewrite the script, putting in the subtext! Don't do it! Don't fix! Don't bury! Instead, question, daydream, spin stories. You will enrich the script with layers of association and understanding. And don't forget, the best way to direct actors is by asking questions.

RESEARCH

Questions lead to Research:

Script research - Sometimes a question will be answered, and a fact gleaned, from rereading the script. Or a new question will be generated. When we notice, on a reread, that Stephen does not actually claim to have been called "Red" when he was a kid, the question arises, "When did he start having the notion of being called 'Red'?"

External research - Always find out the meaning of a word or idea you don't understand. I happen to be old enough to remember Raleigh cigarette coupons, but if I didn't know what they were, I'd have to do research. Anything you don't understand you should research. If you don't know where to start, try the dictionary.

Internal research - By this I mean internal to *you* — your experiences, observations, and understandings. Connect your script analysis preparation to *what you know about life*. For example, when you are looking for facts, questions, and choices around the issue of Stephen's name, you should think about your own childhood. Did you have a nickname? Did you wish for one? Was there a hero or storybook character that you identified with and wished you'd been named after? Did you have a friend with a cool nickname?

This is the work that novice filmmakers most frequently neglect to do. But it is the work that must be done if you want to make movies of any insight or originality. How can you ask actors for personal investment unless you make a personal investment yourself? If you approach all your preproduction homework technically, that's the product you will have — a movie technically proficient, without soul.

Two movie-making giants, Federico Fellini and Ingmar Bergman, often made movies that were frankly autobiographical. But Akira Kurosawa, William Wyler, John Huston, John Cassavetes also made every one of their movies personal without necessarily choosing autobiographical scripts.

It always shocks me when people critique Cassavetes solely on the basis of his filmmaking *style*. What to me stands out about his work is that first, his films are always *about* something, and second, he allows *no emotional distance* between the audience and, notably, the main character in "Woman Under the Influence." The prodigious gifts of actor Gena Rowlands make this possible, but the raw intimacy of the performance could not have been realized filmically without the personal identification and commitment of the director.

I am giving you this simple script analysis tool of *internal research* into the facts and images of the script to help you begin making this connection, even if the script seems to have no personal reverberation for you.

IMAGES AND ASSOCIATIONS

The other immutable information from the script is its images. The next script analysis tool is a way to unpack the treasures folded in the images. It's a kind of free association exercise. Your associations come from your own memory and experiences, your observations, your imagination, and from research. These associations stir up and create a soup of unconscious material, and weave a texture of life around the characters and their situation.

200

There are two kinds of images that concern us in script analysis: the writer's thematic images and each character's personal images. These are different from the "actor's personal images" or substitutions which I discussed in the Actors' Choices chapter.

First I'll identify images from the "Red Ryder" scene, listing the images separately for each character. Angel talks about the "schedule" of her "daily fight" with her mother, and about Stephen's "cigarette coupons"; she uses the word "stupid"; she mentions Stephen's nickname "Red" and her own name, "Angel." She talks about Stephen "cleaning your teeth," the "films," the Raleigh coupon "gift book," "the FBI," and "camping." She talks about tattoos: ones that are "out of style," as well as "tattoos that say Love and Peace." She mentions "Lyle," "customers," and the "bypass."

Stephen uses these images: "dump," "Clark," "pencil," "problem," "counts," "Mabel," "medical report," "stool," "crap," "newspaper," "car," "back pack," "home fries in your ears," "Chingado the Chicano," "donut," "hitchhiking," "Turdville," "Elmer's glue," "cold coffee," "my Aunt Fanny's butt," "the clap," "coupla hundred truck drivers," "morons," "sacked out on my rear," "cemetery," and "Born Dead."

The free association technique goes something like the riff I did with the image "rain" in the section on Images from the Actors' Choice chapter. We float around on the image, jotting down whatever pops into our heads in response to it, ranging as freely and widely as possible, without censoring ourselves, not worrying about whether anything we come up with is actually useful. Maybe a tiny amount of what we come up with, say ten percent, will be useful. In order to do a meaningful script analysis, you need to *spend time* on it.

Okay. Let's start with the "schedule" of Angel's "daily fight" with her "mom." "Daily fight schedule" makes me think of daily flight schedule, airplanes, airports, two-seater planes, big jets, air traffic control. "Fight schedule" also makes me think of heavyweight title bouts, Muhammed Ali, George Forman, Mike Tyson (rape, prison, Barbara Walters), and fight gyms; I have never been in a fight gym but I imagine them as dark, with low ceilings, cement walls, noises of punching bags, grunts, sounds of flesh being struck by boxing gloves. Then I think about fights without hitting, verbal fights, family fights. Now we're getting closer. Why did I have to go through "air traffic control" and "fight gyms," which were clearly off the mark of anything useful for this scene, before I got to "family fights," which is apparently what Angel is talking about?

I don't know. I was not censoring myself. I gave my imagination its head; I let it lead me, instead of me trying to lead it. Imagination, by its nature, resists the injunction to be "useful." If I command my imagination to go only to useful areas, it probably won't do anything; it will sit there like a stick. This is what happens when directors sit staring at the page, unable to get started on their script analysis homework.

Back to Angel. To call it a "daily fight" which usually follows a "schedule" makes me think of routine bickering or nagging, perhaps persistently on the same subjects. I have seen affectionate relationships that include bickering or heckling. I have also seen families whose every interaction communicates antipathy and neglect. Which kind is Angel's situation? What do they fight about? Maybe Angel likes to iron her uniform in the morning and her mother thinks the ironing should be done the night before. (When I was a teenager my father and I once had a fight on this very subject.) Maybe Angel serves the toast unbuttered, an act perceived by her mother as brainless, or even as a gesture of disrespect and rejection. Or maybe Mom insists on smoking at the breakfast table and extinguishing her cigarettes in her coffee cup, to the disgust of Angel, who doesn't smoke.

How much do these fights hurt? Here I'll do some "internal research." My own fights with my parents, no matter how infrequent or trivial, always hurt me deeply. At first glance, that experience seems not at all like that of Angel, who seems to trivialize the fight by referring to its "daily schedule." But what if she only pretends to make light of her situation? What if her pain and loneliness go very deep?

The image and association exercise calls attention to what a character talks about rather than what he says about it or claims to feel about it. The theory here is that things people talk about are a good indicator of what is really on their minds, what is important to them, their interests and needs — in other words, what is causing them to do the things they do. It's a peek into the character's emotional storage banks. It gives us questions and ideas that may lead to choices.

It also brings us into the experience that these characters might be having while they say these words. In life people change subjects, make Freudian slips, and forget what they were saying, often without any reason that they are conscious of. Rather, the association they make is *sub*conscious. Angel mentions "tattoos that say Love and Peace." Is this an appealing or an unappealing image to her? How does she feel about the hippies? Does she have dreams of going to San Francisco with flowers in her hair?

When I look at the list I made earlier of Stephen's images, if I free-associate and don't censor myself, a few things jump out. Four of his images have associations with excrement: dump, stool, crap, Turdville, not to mention "my Aunt Fanny's butt" and "sacked out on my rear." Two images of death: his tattoo "Born Dead" and "cemetery." (I am calling "Born Dead" his image even though Angel mentions it because he is the one who wears the tattoo; and since she does mention it, I deduce that it is visible.)

Doesn't this say something about him? Do you see how it is more powerful to invoke his excrement images than to say he has contempt for the town he lives in? Could his two death images mean that someone he cares about has died? Or that ideas of suicide are in his emotional storage banks? This is where my uncensored imagination may pay off. Maybe the "air traffic control" riff off Angel's "daily fight schedule" led nowhere, but linking, via free association, Stephen's death and excrement images may actually end up being useful.

He mentions "the clap" in connection with hitchhiking. Or is the connection with the "tattoos that say Love and Peace"? Does this mean that he believes he can contract a sexually transmitted disease from a car seat? Or that he has sexual fantasies about riding with a carful of hippies? He mentions "medical report" — is anyone in his family ill? "Chingado the Chicano" — is this a racially derogatory epithet? Could it have some other meaning or association? How much Spanish does Stephen know? Does he have Mexican-American friends?

What about the images of the title? When we look at the title, we are looking for thematic images, rather than the characters' personal images, as we have been doing. "Red Ryder" sounds western but has no specific associations for me. However, my husband told me (my external research) that he remembered Red Ryder as a very famous comic book cowboy hero of his youth. Could "heroism" turn out to be a theme of the script? Without the full script we won't be able to make this determination. We can make a note that external research to learn more about the comic book hero Red Ryder is going to be needed.

We can also investigate (internal research) our own associations with heroism. It was a thrilling moment for me, watching the 1996 Academy Awards, when a childhood hero of mine, Miep Gies, was introduced to the audience by the filmmaker accepting his award for the documentary "Anne Frank Remembered." Even though my notions of what constitutes heroism may differ from Stephen's or Angel's — or the author's — I allow my associations with heroism to jumpstart my connection to the script and its characters.

The image and association exercise can even have practical applications. "Tattoos that say Love and Peace" gives us a pretty good idea that the script is set in the early seventies. "Donut" conjures up for me associations around the stale diner donuts I have encountered in my life: the Plexiglas donut display case, which rocks slightly when you open it, the glaze from a glazed donut smeared against the inside of the Plexiglas, the sugar stuck to my fingers when I pick one up; sugar donuts, jelly donuts, chocolate donuts, crullers; the different sensations of breaking open a stale, dry sugar donut as compared to a fresh jelly donut; dunking, my Uncle Andy, who used to love to dunk, the controversy over whether or not dunking was polite. This donut riff could give me some ideas for *activities* for the actors to try in rehearsal.

While you are thinking about images, you might take note of the people, places, and things the characters talk about that are not present: Angel's mother, Clark, Lyle, and truck drivers; the freeway bypass, the back pack Stephen has ordered from the Raleigh coupon book, the coupon book itself. The actors will need to have substitutions, either personal or imaginative, for all these off-camera people and things. If you make a note of them now, when you get to casting you can remember to notice whether the actors, when they speak these words, are talking about something real, or merely saying lines.

Once we know the script's skeleton — its facts and images — we can generate some ideas for choices to flesh out the skeleton. This is also our opportunity to translate ideas into playable direction. The most important thing to remember when looking at possible choices is that we are looking at what might be going on under the lines. Watch for choices that are too "on-the-nose," that come too "dead-on" the surface meaning of the lines. To become more adept at using opposites, consider choices that at first you think are wrong.

IMAGINATIVE CHOICES: CHART 3

1. HISTORY (BACKSTORY)

Actors and writers often write biographies of their characters. These are *facts* that are not in the script. Since they are not in the script, they are only facts if they work, if they stimulate the imaginations of the actors and catapult them into their sense of belief in the moment.

Questions are the tool that gets us to imaginative backstory. For instance, after deducing that Stephen and Angel work in the same diner, we might ask how long they have known each other. They may have met on the job, or they have known each other all their lives. There is nothing in the scene that proves one theory or the other. Even if we read the whole play, there may be no evidence proving one idea or the other.

If they have known each other, are they the same age? Were they in the same grade? Were they good students? Was either of them ever kept back a grade? What kind of friends did each hang out with? Was it the popular crowd? Were their families acquainted? What were their impressions of each other? Is it possible that they ever had anything like a date? If so, what happened?

What if Angel used to let Stephen copy her homework? That would be an example of an imaginative backstory choice. It's not in the script, but there is nothing in the script that makes it impossible, either. It's framed as a "what if?" because it's not an actual fact, it's a choice — the idea is to generate behavior in the actors. It could also be called an adjustment (Column 6). Actors do not have to agree on each other's imaginative backstory. If the actor playing Angel is working with a backstory choice that she used to let Stephen copy her homework in high school (this could be either a suggestion from the director or her own idea), the actor playing Stephen does not have to agree that this ever took place, or even to know that she has made this choice.

IMAGINATIVE CHOICES: CHART 3

1 HISTORY (BACKSTORY)	2 WHAT JUST HAPPENED	3 OBJECTIVE (WHAT THE CHARACTER NEEDS OR WANTS)	4 ISSUES/WHAT IS AT STAKE/ THE PROBLEM/ THE OBSTACLE	5 ACTION VERBS/ INTENTION (WHAT THE CHARACTER IS DOING)	6 ADJUSTMENTS A. "AS IF" B. "WHAT IF" C. "IT'S LIKE WHEN"	7 SUBTEXT	8 PHYSICAL LIFE (BODY, CLOTHING, ENVIRONMENT, OBJECTS, ACTIVITIES)

Now what if they met at their jobs in the diner. Who was there first? Maybe Angel has lived all her life in this town, and Stephen appeared on the scene a year ago. Maybe she befriended him. What if a few months after he arrived, he played some hurtful practical joke on her? Making such an adjustment is different from making the judgment that he is a mean person, and it is more specific. Again, do internal, external and script research on any of these ideas. What practical jokes have you played on people? What jokes have been played on you? Ask other people for their experiences with practical jokes. Keep rereading the script to see if there is evidence to support this idea.

On a reread earlier, we came up with the question, "How long has Stephen had the notion to be called 'Red'?" If it was two weeks ago that he came up with this idea, that would be a different imaginative backstory choice, and would give Angel a different *adjustment* than if he had been calling himself "Red" for a long time. Pay special attention to characters' memories. Memories can never be accepted as full-blown fact; they are always tinted by wish and imagination. But they always contain truth, sometimes a deeper truth than fact. Stephen speaks of having red hair as a kid. How red was it? If he has brown hair now, it is unlikely that he was a "carrot-top." How did he get this idea that he was a redhead? Could he have had a favorite uncle with red hair who was kinder to him than his father, and who he secretly imagined was his real father?

What we are after here are *stories* that may help catapult the actor into his sense of belief in the character's situation. An important purpose of a director's script analysis is to prepare yourself to tell these stories vividly and feelingly.

2. WHAT JUST HAPPENED

This column applies if there is a gap in time between the scene at hand and its previous scene. This is the "off-camera beat," the moment-by-moment life of the characters before the scene started. Firmly rooting a scene thus in the physicality of moment-by-moment life gives it a "texture of life," a sense that the scene is "in the middle of" something.

How long has Stephen been sitting on that stool? What article has he been reading in the newspaper? How many customers were there that night? Who specifically were they? Was it chilly in the empty diner? I have worked graveyard shifts, so I have a place to start imagining the previous eight hours of Stephen's life. If you never have worked a graveyard shift, have you ever been awake all night in a lonely place? Can you imagine it? Do you know anyone who has worked graveyard shifts that you might talk to (research)? As much as possible, create in your imagination the sensory details: the colors of the walls, the broken linoleum tiles, the changing taste of the coffee as the night wears on, crossword puzzles he might try to get interested in, fantasies, naps.

For Angel, how did she arrive at work? Did she drive? Walk? Take the bus? Get dropped off? What is the weather like? Is it warmer or cooler when she walks into the diner (is there air-conditioning?)? Did she wash her hair this morning?

The actor does this kind of work as a sensory preparation for a scene. But it is appropriate to the director's job as well, as part of her investigation of the characters' lives outside the four corners of the movie screen.

3. OBJECTIVE/INTENTION/NEED

During your script analysis, you should come up with as many candidates for each character's objective as you can think of. If you're not sure what a character's objective is, don't anguish over it but make notes anyway. If you don't have good ideas, jot down three bad ideas to at least get you started. If you *are* sure what the objective is, jot down three other possibilities anyway. If you are *so* sure you know what the objective is that you can't think of any others, then at least jot down the opposite of your idea.

While you are learning how to analyze scripts and work with objectives, you should follow this rule: *one* objective per scene per character (unless it's a scene with three or more people in it; then each character may have a different objective for each of the other characters).

What kinds of evidence do we have as to what a character's objective might be? The least useful piece of information is what the character *says* he wants. When characters make a point of declaring the motivations for their behavior, it's usually pertinent to look for the issue or ambivalence underlying their protestations.

Here are some useful ways to go about choosing objectives.

1) Look at the facts, and then ask, "What might a person want in that situation?" Make a list. Don't confine yourself to what you would want if you were in that situation, or to what "the character" would want, or even to what a rational person would want. Don't get stuck in your prejudices. List as many candidates as you can think of.

2) Look at behavior; look at what the character *does* rather than what he says he is doing.

3) Look at the things he talks about, that is, his images. This will give us some clues as to the concerns of the character's subconscious, the things he wants but doesn't know he wants.

4) Look at the emotional event of the scene, what *happens* in the scene, how things end up. Is it possible that the character wanted that to happen? Or wished to prevent it?

5) Look at the things people want out of life: love, freedom, power, control, adventure, comfort, security, family, sex, money, respect, honor. We all want everything, right? But there are certain things we want that we will sacrifice other things for. What is important to the character? What is the thing he will sacrifice for? What does he make the greatest effort to avoid? What interests him?

6) Translate your ideas into playable form. Instead of saying, "He is attracted to her," translate it into the more

playable "He wants her to go to bed with him." Rather than "He is taking out his frustrations," say, "He is picking a fight." Rather than "He wants to talk to someone," say, "He needs a friend."

7) If nothing at all comes to you, take a look at the list of "Sample Simple Objectives" in Appendix C.

8) If you are still feeling blank, ask yourself, "Does he want the other character to feel good or does he want her to feel bad?"

An objective should engage other characters, create its own obstacles, and be something that the actor can personally get behind and commit to. You may find the coolest idea in the world for an objective, but if the actor can't connect to it, another choice must be found. An important thing to remember about objectives is that they don't have to be realistic. People don't always know what they want; what they want is not necessarily something they can have; and they don't always do the right thing to get it.

Let's look at some possible objectives for the "Red Ryder" scene. I'm going to come up with three for each character, and I'll try to make them different from each other. First let's take Stephen.

1) A suggested objective for Stephen is that "He wants to get out of the diner." That is what he says he wants, but what he says he wants is contradicted by what he *does*, which is to sit on the stool and read his newspaper. If he wants to leave, why doesn't he do it? And this idea doesn't connect him to Angel. It will be hard for an audience to stay interested in this scene if Stephen is not connected to Angel via an emotional need of some kind. Let's say we want to make this thinking playable. A playable alternative might be that "he wants *her* to leave." Now this would be irrational, but it would be playable; it might work, and even be funny. We wouldn't know whether it would work unless we tried it.

2) "Stephen wants Angel to take care of him." I'm basing this idea on Stephen's line "...as soon as I get something taken care of." Could this line be evidence that he has

trouble at home? Could he hang out at the diner past his shift so he doesn't have to go home to face the problems there? I'm also basing the idea on events in the scene: she *does* take care of him (cleans up his mess, brings him coffee and donut). Maybe her behavior is a response to his unarticulated need. He even uses the phrase "taken care of." Maybe the presence of that phrase in his emotional storage banks reveals his own need.

　　　3) "Stephen wants Angel to treat him with respect, treat him like a man." Maybe we should take this all the way and say he wants to be a hero. I'm taking this from the image in the title of the piece, "Red Ryder," a cowboy hero. He doesn't seem to do things that might make people treat him with respect or think of him as a hero, but don't forget, people often do the wrong thing to get what they want.

How about Angel? I think it's possible that she wants him to like her, or to make it more specific, wants him to ask her to go to the movies tonight. Another possibility might be that she wants him to respect her intelligence and wit. She could want him to leave. She could want him to stay. She could want him to do his job better, leave the place cleaner after his shift, follow rules, etc. Maybe she needs to be needed.

What I want you to do now is *not* try to figure out intellectually which one of these is right (or why they are all wrong). None of them is right unless it works and none is wrong unless it doesn't work. These are ideas for rehearsal, or ideas to fall back on if the choice you thought would work doesn't work. Above all, they are ways, like the imaginative backstory ideas, to exercise and engage your story imagination.

4. Issues/What's at Stake/The Problem/The Obstacle

One thing you really want to watch out for is any inclination you might have to say that either Stephen or Angel is "just reacting" to the other one, or that either of them doesn't care what the other one thinks. In other words, leaving them with nothing *at stake* in the scene.

A character's *through-line* or *primary engagement* is not always with the other person in the scene. The primary engagement may be with an image or memory, another person who is not present, or even an object. The "Red Ryder" scene could be played with that choice. Say, for instance, that Angel's primary engagement is not with Stephen but with Clark, with staying on Clark's good side, and keeping her job. Maybe she has recently been promoted to manager (that could be why she goes over the receipts every morning). In that case we might say that "her job" is what is at stake for her. Stephen's primary engagement could be with his newspaper; maybe he is struggling to finish an article that genuinely interests him.

Making choices about whether the primary engagement in this scene is between the two of them, or elsewhere, will affect your direc-torial style. One thing that draws me as a director to this scene is its potential for humor, and I suspect that making their relationship the primary engagement of the scene will give me more comedic options. But even though I may want the scene to end up funny, I still look for the characters' pain, which is another way of asking, "what's at stake?" Exploring the idea that Stephen needs to be treated like a man might lead us to say that what's at stake for him is his self-image, or his masculinity. Maybe he has a stepparent who belittles him.

Does Angel's mother have a job? Where is Angel's father? Is Angel her mother's sole support? Why doesn't Angel's mother have a job? Is she sickly? Selfish? It could be that what's at stake for Angel is an unending future of taking care of an ungrateful, demanding mother. This thinking might lead us to say that Angel needs Stephen to stay.

5. *ACTION VERBS*

The action verb is what the character is doing to get what she wants. Sometimes the whole scene will work with one action verb.

This could mean that she is getting what she wants and has no need to change what she is doing to get it; or it could suggest a rigidity to the character's personality. Often the verb changes when the "beat" changes.

If you have in your mind a certain look or sound for a certain line, you might want to translate it into a verb. For example, if in your mind you see the character shouting with a raised fist, perhaps the action verb you want on that line is "to threaten," or it might be "to incite"; it might even be "to beg."

Some directors and teachers say that for preparation you should find an action verb for each line. For a beginner there is danger that this approach will keep you stuck in mechanically translating the preconceived ways you hear the line in your head into a verb. Finding the verb for each line is not a substitute for understanding the scene's central emotional event and the characters' through-lines.

Even though it's on my "Short List," I suggest that you stay away from "to convince." "To convince" is tepid; it is often a way of not doing something else. For example, when I ask my students to play the intention "to accuse," they sometimes take that to mean they must convince the other person to admit that he is wrong. This is what we might do in daily life — it's the more socially acceptable behavior — but probably not as dramatic. (Although it would be preferable to have the actor convince X to admit he is wrong simply and honestly than to have him "accuse" in an overwrought actorish "movie" manner that becomes an attempt to convince us of the truth of the words.)

Actually any of the verbs on the Short List are possible for either Stephen or Angel. It might be hard to imagine Stephen flirting, coaxing, soothing, or encouraging, but you could be surprised. If an actor played his lines with an intention "to soothe," it would be called "playing the opposite" or "playing against the lines." You shouldn't rule it out without seeing an expert actor try it.

6. ADJUSTMENTS

Adjustments are among the most powerful tools a director can have. They are an invitation to "let's pretend." Directors who are able to come up with perceptive and enticing adjustments are rare, and adored by actors.

An adjustment can be an "as if" or an "it's like when" — a metaphor or parallel. Arthur Penn, when interviewed on "Inside the Actors Studio," revealed the adjustment he suggested to Dustin Hoffman for the scene from "Little Big Man" in which Hoffman's character must convince General Custer that he is not a renegade, or be executed. Penn was worried that the scene was coming off merely funny and needed a more powerful undercurrent. He suggested (in lengthier and more vivid terms than this) that an analogous circumstance might be that Hoffman had to deny his Jewishness in a concentration camp in order to eventually be in a position to kill the oppressor. In the filmed scene, Hoffman appears to have the intention "to entertain" Custer. And yet, because of the secret adjustment, there is a second level of danger and threat giving focus to the character's clowning.

Or an adjustment can be a "what if?" — an imaginative backstory choice. In an interview reported in Daily Variety John Travolta spoke about being directed by Robert Altman in Harold Pinter's "The Dumbwaiter": "I had a scene where I was reading a newspaper aloud to someone. I was rattling away. Altman didn't say much at first. Then he came over and whispered in my ear, 'What if your character is really illiterate and can't read a word on the page, is making it all up as he goes along?' Wow. That changed everything, permeated the whole scenario."

What might have been going on in Altman's mind? Perhaps he thought the scene was playing too dead-on and the adjustment would give it more risk. Maybe it was an idea he'd had all along, that it was in this character's personality to pompously pretend to have information on every subject; the adjustment would be a way to create that side of the character without making an unplayable judgment.

Maybe the idea popped suddenly into Altman's head, inspired by something the actor was unconsciously doing, and the director chose to follow that whim. When Travolta says, "That changed everything," he means the new adjustment became his *through-line*.

"What if Angel and Stephen went to high school together and Angel used to let Stephen copy her homework?" "What if Angel has just been promoted to manager of the diner?" "What if Angel and Stephen had sex together once?" These adjustments can be agreed on by both actors (and the director) or they can be private; they can be secrets. Stephen could adjust to the situation as if they have had the conversations about coffee cups and his name a hundred times. Angel, on the other hand, could make the adjustment that the coffee cup issue has never come up before and the name issue only once. Angel could play the scene "as if" she and Stephen had a date once. But Stephen could have the adjustment that the event Angel thinks of as a date was not a date: they happened to be at the movie theater on the same evening and happened to sit (three seats apart) in the same row. In real life people often remember the same event very differently, or at least attach different significance to it.

An "as if" adjustment can be a kind of shape-shifting — a little wrinkle in reality, an interior improvisation. Stephen could take an adjustment that every word Angel says is like a knife through his eardrum, or like fingernails on a blackboard.

There are certain "quick fix" adjustments that can apply to many scenes:

Parent/child. In many real life relationships one person takes the parental role and the other the child role. This can be a way to understand characters' relationships too.

High status/low status. Keith Johnstone's excellent book Impro introduced me to the "high status/low status" game and how useful it is to understanding relationships in scripts as well as in life. A variation I use is asking an actor to think of himself or herself as the "king."

Good news/bad news. Instead of saying the character is happy or the character is depressed, think of the character in these terms: either, "everything she sees and hears is good news," or "everything she sees and hears is bad news."

Bug and suppress. This construct is based on a warm-up exercise that I invented, in which one player does anything he can think of to bother the other player, and the other one discourages or suppresses the first one's behavior. Quite a lot of scenes follow this structure.

As if it's a business deal. As if they are married. There are many more.

7. SUBTEXT

What if in rehearsal the actor playing Stephen becomes so sarcastic and mean that the scene gets heavy-handed, losing its connection and humor, with no obstacle, nothing at stake? You might say to him, "Let's change the adjustment. What if last night a truck driver offered you a ride to Las Vegas on his next trip through plus a promise of a job there with his brother-in-law? So your subtext all through this scene might be this good news that you've decided not to tell anyone." Subtext can help shore up an adjustment or objective and make it work.

Or it might be a way to explain what a certain line means. When Angel says, "Now ya got brown hair," her subtext could be, "You idiot, don't you know brown from red?" Or a different choice could be, "I like brown hair better than red hair anyway. You have nice hair and I think you're handsome and that Stephen is a nice name." The line would come out very differently.

8. PHYSICAL LIFE

Here is where we pay attention to the physical objects and activities of the characters' world. Stephen has his newspaper and cigarettes and coffee. Angel has her coffeepots and donut trays and other paraphernalia of diner counters. These objects almost become characters in the scene. Stephen's newspaper, cigarettes, and coffee are his friends. Angel has her relationships with the glass coffee cups and paper cups; she protects the paper cups from improper usage. The donut is a whole new character who enters in the middle of the scene. Whose side is the donut on? When the objects take on life in your imagination you may start to have ideas for blocking and business. Perhaps Angel is polishing the chrome fittings of the revolving Plexiglas donut case when Stephen gets the idea to ask her for a donut.

It is through their physical life that actors create characters who live in a different time period from their own. The daily use of a manual cash register (as in the early seventies, the time period of this scene) creates a subtly different reality from our present computerized world. Other kinds of physical life to consider are secrets. What if Angel has a headache this morning? What if Stephen has hemorrhoids? How long has it been since Stephen has had a shower?

*   *   *

Now. *You don't need to talk to actors about all these elements of the characterization.* You don't sit them down with the charts and map it all out. The reason for so many columns is to give you flexibility. Very possibly you will end up with a favorite way of analyzing characters and giving direction. You might prefer to use images or adjustments or intentions more than the others. Actors too have favorite ways of looking at things. It's good to have more than one approach. If one doesn't work, you have a backup.

The choice of a tool can illuminate the style of the script. Some scripts are driven by the characters' objectives, some are driven by guiding subtextual images, some will just not work without a wholesale leap of faith into an imagined reality. Choosing to talk to the actors in terms of images instead of verbs, for example, can support the style of the movie.

The choices are completely mutable and playful unlike the facts and images of the script. It doesn't matter what the actor's choice is as long as it works. It doesn't matter if you and the actor agree on the choice, if it works. When an actor comes up with an idea for a choice, the appropriate response is never "that's right" or "that's wrong," but "let's try it." And then after it has been tried, "that works," or "let's keep looking."

EVENTS: CHART 4

Every scene has a central emotional event, something that *happens* between the characters who are interacting. It can be an extremely subtle event, but if *nothing happens* in a scene, that scene doesn't belong in the script. The director is responsible for seeing to it that an emotional event takes place, and for stringing the events of each scene together to make a story.

A helpful way to go about identifying the event of a scene is by breaking it down into its beats. The term "beat" is widely misunderstood to mean changes in mood, or pauses, or something to do with the pace or tempo-rhythm of the scene. The term actually began to be used among actors and directors in this country in the 1920s. The apocryphal story is that one of the great Russian directors had come to New York and was delivering a series of lectures. A student asked the question, "How do you work on a scene?" to which he replied, *"Beet by beet,"* meaning, in his heavily accented English, "bit by bit." Soon, the story goes, the response was introduced into actor-speak as "working with beats."

So really the "beats" are the bits, the little sections of a scene. Stanislavsky called them "units." The simplest, best way to identify them is by *subject* — when the subject changes, that is a new beat. The great thing about this method of determining beats is that it is an objective way of figuring them out. Deciding beats by identifying changes in mood is not a good way for two reasons: First of all, "mood" is very subjective; it will be easy to get into arguments with the producer or writer or actor about where such changes take place. Second, deciding changes in mood brings you perilously close to emotional mapmaking. We don't want to make an emotional map; we want to find a coherent emotional structure to the

EVENTS: CHART 4

1 BEAT	2 SUBJECT	3 WHO BRINGS IT UP	4 TRANSITIONS AND CONNECTIONS	5 WHAT HAPPENS (ISSUES)	6 SCENE EVENT A. DOMESTIC (LITERAL) B. EMOTIONAL (GLOBAL)

scene. We want to find out what the scene is about, and its central emotional event.

The procedure in figuring out beats is first to identify every change of subject, no matter how brief. But eventually we want to identify three major beats: beginning, middle, and end. It isn't always three — sometimes there are two or four major beats — but usually there are three. In addition to their usefulness in understanding the structure of the script, the major beats are useful as rehearsal units. By the way, people often ask whether the beat can change for different characters at different times. The answer is yes.

Column 1 of Chart 4 is a place to identify the beat and key it in some way to the script. You could write "Beat One" and mark the section in the script with a line and a "One" next to it. Or you could write a description, e.g., "page 1, line 1 to page 2, line 6."

Column 2 is the subject of that beat (some people call it the title of the beat); Column 3 is the name of the character who brings that subject up. I always need to go through a scene several times before I discern its structure. On the first pass, I look only for the information in Columns 1 through 3.

Then I go back, linking things up by looking for the information from Columns 4 and 5. The purpose of Column 4 is to start noticing how the beats relate to each other. Often they are connected by small events or issues (Column 5). Going back through the scene noticing these transitions and uncovering these connective events should lead us to ideas about the event of the scene, or what the scene is about (Column 6).

Before reading on, you might want to take a look at the "Red Ryder" scene and break down its beats on your own.

Beat 1: to the line "...in my spare time, ain't it?" Subject: Angel's lateness. Angel brings it up.

Beat 2: from "Stephen, that's a paper cup..." to "...so where's the problem?" Subject: the paper coffee cup. Angel brings it up.

Beat 3: consists of Angel's line, "Stephen. What're ya gonna get with your cigarette coupons, Stephen? Stephen?" Subject: his cigarette coupons. Angel brings it up.

Beat 4: from "How many times..." to "I hate Mabel." Subject: their names. Stephen brings it up. In a way, this is a judgment call. We could say that Beats 3 and 4 are one beat, that Angel brings up the subject of their names by using the name Stephen three times in a row, when she later admits that she knows he doesn't like it.

Beat 5: from "Look, Stephen, if you're in such a big hurry.." to "...will ya look at the waitin' line to get on this stool." Subject: Stephen's continued presence in the diner. Angel brings it up.

Beat 6: films. Angel brings it up.

Beat 7: from "I saw ya circle somethin in the gift book..." through Angel's line "Ya gonna go campin'." Subject: coupon book again. Angel brings it up.

Beat 8: from "No I ain't gonna go campin'." to "...make me some bread." Subject: Stephen's plans. Brought up by Angel.

Beat 9: from "Rye or whole wheat" to "Yeah, yeah." Subject: food. Brought up by Angel.

Beat 10: from "You better let..." to the end of the scene. Subject: hitchhiking. Brought up by Angel.

See? This first step is easy; the more simplemindedly you do it, the better. Now, we go through again, refining our ideas by looking at Columns 4 and 5.

The subject of the first beat is a deficiency of Angel's — her lateness. The subject of the second beat is a deficiency of Stephen's, brought up by Angel. Maybe the event here is that she gets back at him for making a fuss about her lateness. Perhaps she walked in expecting him to welcome her, thank her for her gracious apology, and laugh at her little joke about the daily fight schedule. Instead he punishes her for her tardiness; she retaliates with the coffee cup.

Then, having scored a win, she brings up the subject of the coupon book. He changes the subject to "names" and retaliates for her incorrect use of his name with a put–down inspired by her name. She changes the subject again, pointing out two additional faults: he is not doing what he said he would do (leave), and he is cleaning his teeth at the table. He retaliates once more.

This is one way of defining the first major beat. So far neither one of them has taken a loss. No matter what they are handed, they come right back at the other one. We could call this (up through Small Beat 5) the First Major Beat or section, with the subject or title "a match of wits" or "sparring." Then I would have to call the Second Major Beat (Small Beats 6, 7, and 8) "Stephen's plans." This shift could be seen as Angel taking her "loss" and moving to new subjects (films, the coupon book). The event of this Second Major Beat is that Angel makes the discovery that Stephen is taking concrete steps toward a departure from his life in that town.

In the Third Major Beat (Small Beat 10) the event is that she blocks his escape, and Stephen loses it, threatening to go "to the cemetery" if his proposals are not respected. That's how I thought of it on my second pass. But on my third pass I found that coupon book nagging at me. It actually is first mentioned in what I've called the First Major Beat. Maybe the coupon book marks the beginning of the Second Major Beat. In this construction, the First Major Beat is Small Beats 1 and 2; the Second Major Beat is Small Beats 3 through 8 (subject, "Stephen's plans"), but with a time-out for sparring, instigated by Stephen (in this configuration, the "names" beat is the only beat he introduces), perhaps to deflect the subject of his plans.

Now what about Small Beat 9? I'm starting to feel that the central event of the scene is "a threat of desertion" — i.e., Angel's discovery of Stephen's imminent departure. So perhaps the Third Major Beat consists of Small Beats 9 and 10 — Angel's reaction to the news. First she makes a joke ("rye or whole wheat"), then she blocks his departure. This seems to reveal an ABA structure. The sparring of the first major beat (beginning) could be the foundation of their relationship. The second major beat (middle) contains the event of the scene: a threat of desertion. Then the third major beat (end) returns to the sparring, but with raised stakes.

Under Column 6, I mention the "domestic (or literal) event" and "emotional (or global) event" of the scene. The domestic event is what the characters think is going on. The emotional event is the artistic reason for putting the scene up on a movie screen, what you want to say about life with the scene, and the relationship of this scene to the story arc.

In this scene I have said that the emotional event is a threat of desertion. The domestic event is the changing of shifts in a diner. You — the director — need to know and create the emotional event because the emotional events keep the audience involved in the story. But you mustn't forget the domestic event, because it gives a scene its texture of life. Without a sense of the simple, domestic event the scene can become pretentious. In her interview for the "Inside the Actors Studio" series, Glenn Close said that the thing she needs from a director when she is stuck is to be put on the track of what she called "the simplest, simplest truth." I think she meant that actors can get too much in their heads when they are juggling adjustments and sometimes need to be reminded of the simple, domestic event.

The beats, the tiny events leading up to and resulting from the central event of the scene, must be followable by the audience in order to tell the story. The beat changes may be punctuated with movement of some kind (it can be very subtle movement, even the flicker of an eyelid), or by a change in action verb.

The classic configuration, the "rule," if you will (although it is a rule that is often broken), is that every beat change is punctuated by some physical movement plus a change in each character's action verb. In the "Red Ryder" scene, it might look like this: During Major Beat One Stephen is on his stool, stationary, feet up, newspaper up. Angel is putting away her purse, taking off a sweater, adjusting her uniform, possibly checking makeup. At the end of Beat 1 (Stephen's line, "...so where's the problem?") there would be some change in movement, some blocking or business.

Actually the author has suggested some stage business ("Stephen has taken the last cigarette from a pack, slipped the coupon into his shirt pocket, and crumpled the pack; he basketball-shoots it across the service area") which punctuates the end of the first beat and sets up Major Beat Two, by introducing the cigarette coupons. This is actually a pretty good suggestion. If I had crossed this out when I edited the stage directions, I would probably now go back and erase the cross-out and circle this with a question mark; it's definitely worth trying in rehearsal. If I replace this business with something else, I'd want to make sure that the replacement accomplished the same thing as the author's direction.

The author has Angel change activity as well. The characters' activities create a physical context for their emotional shifts. His ideas are good, but I still would like you to think up alternatives. We're preparing for rehearsal, you see. And whether your rehearsal period is long — say a week or two — or only consists of ten minutes just before actual shooting, the best thing you can do in rehearsal is stay loose. And the best way for the director to stay loose, and focused at the same time, is to have lots of ideas to try, even if you don't try them all.

Stephen is communing with his intimate friends, his newspaper, cigarettes, and coffee. Angel is interacting with objects that are familiar and responsive to her: salt and pepper shakers, wash cloth (when I was a waitress, at the end of each shift, all the chrome fittings were wiped down with a cloth dipped in white vinegar and water, so naturally I would consider adding this detail). These relationships continue throughout the beat. They exert a pull on the characters as strong as whatever pull the characters have on each other.

The food beat (Small Beat 9) occurs right after the central emotional event (the discovery of Stephen's plans, or his threat of desertion). It makes sense that there would be activity around here. Activity around the donut and the coffee refill can help both characters deflect and channel their feelings about the breaking of this news.

Punctuating the beats with movements may lead to a rudimentary blocking plan. Now let's look at how the punctuation might be done by changing action verbs. Here are some suggestions: For Stephen: Beat 1, to scrutinize; Beat 2, to brag; Beat 3, to punish or attack. For Angel: Beat 1, to teach; Beat 2, to charm; Beat 3, to warn or demand. Directing these beat changes into the scene (and making sure that the actors play through each beat) can help the audience follow the story, and can help make a long scene seem less wordy; it can also help you pace the scene. It is always a good idea to learn how to follow the rules before you break them. But sometimes directing the *script* beats into the scene as *playing* beats is not advisable; the scene could come out a little plodding. Whether or not you use the script beats as playing beats, you still need to know what the script beats (structure) are.

We now have an idea for the event of the scene. This leads us to a decision as to what the scene is about. My idea that the event of the scene is a threat of rejection leads me to say (provisionally) that the scene is about a failed love affair. I don't mean by this that I think Angel and Stephen have ever slept together, but, rather, that in directing the scene I think I will want to illuminate the ways that these two could be a good match for each other, as well as the forces in and around them that make a match impossible. This is my vision of the scene.

Now I would go back to Chart 3 and rethink my imaginative choices in light of what I want to see happen in the scene. I'd be looking primarily for through-lines for the characters. But I won't know whether any of my ideas work until I rehearse with the actors.

What I have done here is *not* direct the scene. The scene is not directed until the actors are present. What I have done is *prepare* to direct the scene by investigating its *structure*.

WHAT THE SCRIPT IS ABOUT

At last we come to the fundamental question of script analysis: What is the script about? The *images* and the *events* are the clues to this central question.

"What the movie is about" can be phrased as a theme, an image, a paradox, a question, a spine, or an event.

What the movie is about, when phrased as a *theme*, may be a noun. "The Godfather," for example, is about a family. (Indeed, one of the reasons it is such a great movie is that it is not about shooting a lot of people, but about a family.) A deeper theme of the movie might be "loss" — the loss of an eldest son, the loss of Don Vito's dream for Michael and his heirs, the loss of a father, the loss of the old ways and old values.

It can be phrased as an *image* or *metaphor*. The floating feather at the opening of "Forrest Gump" is an image of surrender to fate. Forrest surrenders to chance (or fate); he accepts whatever life brings him. The most famous line of the movie ("Life is like a box of choco-lates," etc.) is another metaphor for the same theme.

"The Fugitive Kind" contains an image, during the climactic scene of the movie, of a dead fig tree suddenly bearing fruit. This image calls forth associations with fertility, sexuality, perhaps resur-rection. The movie's original title was "Orpheus Descending," another strong image. In the Greek myth, Orpheus was a musician who received permission from the god of the Underworld to enter Hades, claim his dead bride and bring her back to life, on condition that while they walked up from the Underworld, Orpheus would not look at her face. Out of his longing, he broke this rule, and lost her forever. This image of Orpheus, the artist, descending into Hell for the sake of a woman, and losing her anyway, is central to this complex movie, even though the title was changed to exclude that specific image. The director of "The Fugitive Kind," Sidney Lumet, has said that for him the movie was about "the struggle to preserve what is sensitive and vulnerable both in ourselves and the world," a construct that I think encompasses all these images.

When a movie's theme is expressed as a statement, that statement is most often a *paradox*. For example, "Forrest triumphs by surrendering" would be a way to state that movie's theme as a paradox. The hero of "Tootsie," by dressing up as a woman, becomes more of a man. In "Don Juan de Marco," Don Juan, the lover of over a thousand women, teaches the monogamous psychiatrist commitment. You could say that "One Flew Over the Cuckoo's Nest" unparadoxes the paradox that the human spirit is both unbearably fragile and ultimately unconquerable.

The theme of Barbara Loden's remarkable 1971 film "Wanda" is, I think, this: that unconditional love brings healing and redemption to the one who loves, even if not to the one who is the object of love. I think this is also the theme of "Leaving Las Vegas."

What the film is about can be phrased as a *question*. "Will Jake Giddes be able to avoid repeating the terrible mistake he made long ago, in Chinatown?" (The answer, of course, is no.)

It can be phrased as a *spine* or a verb. You might say that the spine of "I Never Sang for My Father" is "to forgive." Or the central or climactic *event* of a movie may tell us what it is about. The climactic event of "Casablanca" is a sacrifice: Rick gives up his claim (the claim of true love, no less) on Ilsa, for the good of the cause. When we look at the rest of the movie, we see the theme of "sacrifice" throughout.

When you are figuring out what the film is about, you must not neglect the domestic event. In other words, even though I said earlier that "The Godfather" is about family, or loss, rather than about the Mafia, it is, of course, about a Mafia family. The filmmaker must make the daily details of such a family specific and real, or else the film will be dismissed as pretentious. "Chinatown," on the "domestic event" level, is about a murder investigation.

SPINE

The spine, at least of the main character, and probably all the characters, will relate somehow to the central theme or themes of the script, but not necessarily in a linear fashion. Even though "Tootsie" is about a man who, by dressing up as a woman, becomes more of a man, that doesn't mean that "to become more of a man" is Michael Dorsey's spine. His spine, both as Michael and as Dorothy, is, I think, "to rock the boat." This spine *does not change*, even though the character undergoes a transformation, from a man whose boat-rocking makes him an oafish know-it-all, to a man who is ready to focus his boat-rocking impulses on the challenges of a committed relationship.

A person's spine (or super-objective, life need, script through-line, or red thread) may change once or twice in a lifetime. Usually in real life it never changes. The thing that drives a person for the rest of her life is often in place by the time that person is eight years old. For some people "family" will be the central force the rest of their lives. Or "to escape from the family," "to win the approval of his mother (or his father)," "to be more successful than his brother."

The once or twice in a lifetime that a person's spine might change are only at the very big life events, such as war or disaster, marriage, the death of a loved one, or giving birth. After one has a child, for example, one's priorities must change to include caring and providing for the child. This could cause a complete change in the person's spine, but not necessarily. If his spine was always "family," then the birth of a child reinforces but does not substantively change that spine. It's also possible that if his spine was always "success," raising children fits into that spine rather than changes it.

Almost the definition of a viable screenplay is that the characters have one spine for the whole movie. It is what the character wants for the whole script. You could almost call it the solution to the character, because once found, you can hang the entire script on it.

Here is my suggestion for determining a character's spine. First, list the facts that are true about the character at the beginning of the script (these can be things that we find out later in the script, but which are true before the story starts). Next make a list of as many *possible* spines as we can think of, as many possible things that a person in that situation might want out of life — the *candidates* for the character's spine. Then go through the events of the script, and by looking at the character's behavior during these events, start ruling out some candidates, and adding others. Sooner or later we will come across the character's transforming event and its consequences. As we look at the character's behavior leading up to, during, and consequent to the transforming event, a viable spine should fall into place.

When we are looking at the character's facts, we should pay special attention to what seems to be the most important thing that has happened to him. In the movie "Smoke" the most important thing that has happened to Paul, the main character, is the death of his wife two years earlier. In one of my classes we analyzed his spine, and it became clear as we looked at his behavior during each event of the movie, that his spine was "to find a way to go on living after his wife's death."

This spine will be more useful to the actor and the director than describing Paul by saying that he is closed off at the beginning of the movie but opens up by the end of the movie (his arc or transformation). Let's look factually at his behavior. At the beginning of the movie 1) he writes every day; 2) he goes to the smoke shop every day (he could buy his cigarettes weekly but instead buys a daily ration); 3) in the first scene, he even tells the smoke shop habitués a story. What I notice from these facts is that even at the beginning of the movie he does work, and he does maintain a (minimal) daily human contact. In the pain of his loss, this is the maximum connection to the world that he can tolerate; it isn't much, but it is something. He might have gone on for years at this minimal level.

His transforming event comes when the young man saves him from being run over by the truck. It's easy to get caught thinking that Paul's walking absently into the traffic indicates a death wish. But what I think is important about this incident is not that Paul walked in front of the truck, but his behavior toward the young man who saves him. He thanks him — the most expressive behavior we have so far seen from him (I'm not critiquing the actor's performance here, but examining the structure of the script). A whole series of events ensue from this incident: Paul reaches out to the world, pulls back, reaches out a bit farther, two steps forward, one step back, but steadily opening up.

Usually a spine is in the form of a verb infinitive ("to revenge himself," "to find love," etc.) but it could be a metaphor, an adjustment, an image, or an intention. We could express the same idea about Paul through a metaphor; perhaps the metaphor of a chick in its shell. The young man, in saving Paul's life, cracks the shell; Paul, awakened, starts pecking from the inside and continues until he is free.

In an interview after the release of "Remains of the Day," Emma Thompson described her central metaphor as a bird beating its wings against the Anthony Hopkins character. When her wings break against this unyielding man, she accepts a marriage proposal (transforming event) from another man who (as we deduce in the last scene; all her relationship with her husband happens off camera) has also never truly joined her in flight. But she has never stopped wanting to fly.

A spine can be simple, and often is simple. But watch out for ideas that are merely glib or obvious. In one of my classes we did an analysis of the spine for the Hugh Grant character in "Four Weddings and a Funeral." We accepted "to get married" and "to stay uncommitted" as candidates, but kept reviewing the facts and events of the script to see if we could come up with something better, since those ideas seemed so obvious. (Of course we rejected the construct "he wants to stay uncommitted until [X] — and then he wants to get married" because that is not a spine at all.)

Someone in this class was British and assured the rest of us that, by reason of the character's behavior and accent, we could accept as a fact that he was upper class. It was then interesting to note that the one woman he could not get out of his heart was an American. Maybe his spine was "to reject his very British background." After some noodling around we noticed the fact that "he has a younger brother with a disability" (the brother is deaf) — a circumstance that we know from life would significantly affect a person, and might even determine his spine. We added to our list of possible spines, "to take care of his brother."

For me, the structure of the movie then fell into place. I could picture a childhood suffused with the duty to put the needs of his younger brother ahead of his own. The older brother could easily fall into a kind of unconscious promise or bond with his childhood family that might prevent him from making an adult commitment. And voilà! It is the brother's action that precipitates the transforming event. The younger brother stops the wedding and gets the main character off the hook from the bad marriage (to which he would never have been committed in his heart), freeing him to commit to the right marriage, to Andie MacDowell. To me it makes perfect emotional sense that the main character must get some extraordinary permission from his brother before he can put anyone else first in his life.

In "Four Weddings" the main character's transforming event was also the climax of the movie, but this need not always be so. The "transforming event" is not necessarily the climax of the movie. It is an event in the personal life of the character, not a plot device. But the important thing about transformations is that they turn on *events*, not realizations. People are what they do (or don't do). In real life a true transformation (a terribly rare thing) may be accompanied by a realization, but usually the realization comes later, if at all. What makes people actually change behavior are things that happen to them, or things they do, not things they realize.

As I have said, a good way to find a character's spine is to look at his response to the deficiencies (or pleasures) of his early nuclear family. Another way to look at spines is to look at the big things we all want: sex, love, success, freedom, survival, power, spiritual attainment, attention, revenge, etc.; then think about which of those things is most important to the character. Yet another way to determine a spine is to translate your (result-oriented) description of the character into a spine. Instead of saying that a person/character is a selfish person, you could say that his spine is his own comfort and convenience. Instead of saying a character is insecure, you could say, "He wants everybody to like him." To be adept at finding spines, you need to be a good observer of human experience and behavior.

SUMMARY

One director I worked with asked me to critique a short film he had directed. When I mentioned a scene that I thought didn't work, he replied that he had never been excited about that scene, because it had nothing visual to shoot. Listen up. *Don't shoot a scene until you have found "something to shoot."* This director's not finding the shootable thing in the scene — what the scene was about — was a failure of script analysis.

Once you know what the script is about, be sure that everyone involved on the project is making the same film. If, for example, the special effects people are not told that the movie is about, say, redemption, they may assume it is about thrills. If you don't tell the costumers what the movie is about, they may assume that it is about costumes. When actors are not connected up to what the script is about, they may start to think it is about their performances.

You don't sit down with the actors and show them your filled-out charts. In fact, when you finish these charts you should probably burn them. The purpose of doing this work is not to fill out charts but to understand the script. The main reason for preparing is to go through your mediocre ideas so you can be ready for the great ideas that can happen when the actors arrive and you begin the collaboration. The reason for preparing is not to "pre-direct" the movie, but to gain confidence that you know the characters and script inside out so you can operate in the moment in rehearsal and on the set. The notes, plans, and charts are a jumping-off place from which to start being creative.

A quick summary of script analysis: Don't be distracted by stage directions — concentrate on relationships. Replace adjectives with verbs, images, facts, events and physical life. Know what the movie is about, who the characters are, and be able to back up your ideas with evidence. Have alternatives, in case your favorite ideas don't work. Keep rereading the script and rethinking and deepening your ideas. The directions that I think most actors respond to best are the ones that show insight.

CASTING

I have some objective criteria and a plan of attack to suggest when auditioning actors. People who cast intuitively, and who are good at it, do these things without thinking about it, without realizing they are taking all these steps. If you've been casting using your intuition and you feel like it works, then you should keep doing that. But in case you're not satisfied with your casting results, here are some objective measures, a checklist, and a set of procedures. Using these methods over time should awaken and train your intuition so that after a while you won't be thinking about rules and procedures.

Let me ask you first: what do you look for in casting sessions? Most directors look for the performance that they have been running in the moviola-of-their-mind. This is a big mistake.

An audition is not a performance. Auditioning and performing are two separate skills. Many actors have both skills, but there are actors who audition well and don't work well. There are also actors who work well and are great in performance, but who don't audition well. Which kind of actor would you rather have in your movie or TV show?

Directors often fall into a "dream lover" approach to casting. This means having an idea/ideal of the character in your head and searching for the actor who matches it. This gets you into a lot of trouble, and it's a drag. The director, producer and entourage sit in a stuffy office, waiting, hoping that an actor will come in and knock them out. They grow more and more anxious as the days go by, their eyes glaze over, everyone starts to look the same, and they can't remember why they ever wanted to film this script in the first place. Waiting to be knocked out by your dream lover is passive.

How can you be active in the auditioning process? If you don't look for a performance, what should you look for?

There are four areas important to casting.

1) The actor's ability.

That is, talent (the cards fate has dealt him, through birth and experience) plus skill (what he has done to develop his talent), including:

    a) intuitive equipment: emotional range and flexibility, sensitivity, intelligence, an ability to listen, to work moment by moment, to be honest, to give himself inner freedom and privacy in public, to make the imaginative leap to a created reality.

    b) acting skills: an ability to play a simple intention, to play against (opposite to) the obvious reading of a line, to create images, to be specific and insightful in his choices, to make transitions cleanly, fully, and believably.

    c) physical abilities: that is, range, flexibility, expressivity, and skills in voice and movement.

    d) artistic sensibility: taste, instincts, sense of humor, sense of proportion.

    e) heart: fearlessness, trust, commitment, emotional and physical stamina, a need to perform.

2) Whether he is right for the part.

I am going to suggest that when you think about whether he is right for the part you put your concern for the actor's "look" and "quality" secondary to whether he has what it takes to play the role. By this I mean, can he connect to the character's spine? Does he comprehend and connect to the character's experience and the transforming event in the character's life? This does not mean that the actor has to have had the same experiences as the character, but it will have something to do with his life experience as well as with his intelligence, sensitivity, range, commitment, and skill.

If you can afford it, it's very helpful to have a good casting director. They know a lot of actors, and may come up with names you haven't thought of, or even fresh casting ideas for some roles. Be sure you are on the same wave length. Before you agree to work together, have a frank, open discussion about your tastes and prejudices, and your ideas about the characters. Arrange to view some of the casting director's past work. Be sure the casting director has already read the script and is excited about the project.

There may be physical requirements for the role. Be clear about this, so you don't waste your time and the actors' time. But I do encourage you to think twice about this choice. Anyone who read Ken Kesey's book One Flew Over the Cuckoo's Nest would know that Nurse Ratchet had to be obese, ugly, and loud; Louise Fletcher, who was slender, attractive and understated, won an Academy Award for the role. Apparently the filmmakers made a creative decision that what was more essential about Nurse Ratchet than her looks was her spine "to control absolutely the men under her care," and that giving her the look and manner of an ordinary bureaucrat made her more effective and frightening in that task.

3) Whether you can work well together.

The bottom line is that you need to cast actors who can take direction from you. By this I don't mean actors who never question your ideas or never counter them with ideas of their own — in fact I mean just the opposite. I mean that you can communicate with each other, that you have a mutual respect, and ideally that you mutually spark and challenge and support each other's creativity; that being in each other's company helps you both to have ideas, that you turn each other on, and that you both like to perform for each other.

There are actors who put the work ahead of their egos, who are truly *open* — open to their resources, their feelings, understandings and impulses, open to the material, open to surprises, open to the contradictions and complexities of the character, open to the actors they work with, open to fresh insights, and willing to find a truthful way to make direction work. These are the ones I want you to find and work with.

4) Casting the relationships as well as the roles.

This means that you understand the relationships of the script, that you know, for instance, what behaviors and experiences make this particular family a family, and that you cast the ensemble, not just the individual roles.

The best way to be conversant with an actor's abilities, and know whether she is right for the part and you work well together is to have worked with her before. There is no real shortcut to this knowledge. Whenever you cast someone you haven't worked with before, you are casting with your fingers crossed. That's why so many great directors — Fellini, Bergman, Cassavetes, Woody Allen, to name only a few — work with the same actors over and over and create an ensemble. There is trust, because a director learns how to work with those actors, knows what he can get, what pushes their buttons, where they can go, and what places they need help going to.

When you're starting out, of course, you have no ensemble, but even if you are making your first movie, why not think in terms of building your ensemble? Instead of looking for the right actor for the role, you'll be looking for the right role for the actor. Instead of thinking, "How can I survive?" think, "How can I build?" Think of casting as farming rather than hunting. Instead of thinking of yourself as getting your sites on the right actor and then scoring the hit, think of yourself as cultivating a crop. Keeping as your priority the building of your ensemble will take some of the burden from casting. It will help you put out energy, and putting out energy will give you more energy.

When preparing for auditions, you need to choose scenes, which are called "sides," for the actors to read with another person. You can have actors read with each other in the first round of readings, although usually in the first round you meet them one at a time. You want to pick scenes that go somewhere, that have some transitions in them. The casting director will have ideas. Usually scenes involving stunts, nudity, or emotional breakdowns are not used for a first reading, but it's up to you. If you are casting a role with no good audition scenes, you might choose a scene from another script, perhaps a play, with a character that reminds you of the one you are casting. By the way, the Screen Actors Guild requires that sides be made available to actors a certain length of time ahead of their audition appointments. Check with your local Guild office. Even if you are shooting a nonunion project, it's good to get in practice abiding by Guild rules.

If you have the actors audition (read) one at a time, I suggest you have them read with someone who is not involved in the casting process. If you have a casting director, usually she or an assistant will offer to read with the actors, but it is helpful to bring in an outside person, preferably an actor. This is because one of the most important things you want to look for when you're casting is actors who listen, so you need to be able to see whether the actor plays off what he is getting from his scene partner. This means the person reading with him has to give him something to play off, which is very hard to do if, at the same time, she is trying to make assessments of the actor's ability and what he has to offer the role. Some very good casting directors have taught themselves to be able to do some giving and taking with the actor at the same time as they are assessing the actor, but it's preferable to bring in an actor to read opposite the auditioners. You can have the same actor for all roles; you don't have to have the right genders and ages, but someone who is giving the auditioners something to work off. It's a good idea to establish ahead of time with this actor that he is not auditioning, but is helping you out.

If you don't feel confident of your ability to tell if an actor can listen or not, you might try this: Make an arrangement ahead of time with the "helper" actor, that if she reads more than once with the same actor, she will read her role a little differently each time. If the "helper" actor plays her part differently and the auditioning actor still reads his lines exactly the same, no matter what he's getting from the other person, then you will have seen that the auditioning actor has locked into a line reading, that he has low flexibility and doesn't listen. You want to cast people with flexibility, whose performance changes when the actor opposite them changes. You can save yourself a lot of hassle if you find that out in casting.

Before the actor starts to read, tell him you'd first like to hear him read the scene the way he prepared it, and then you'll give him a couple of different ways to play around with it. It's helpful to announce this ahead of time, because otherwise if he does it his way and then you tell him to do it another way he'll assume that what he did was wrong and what you are asking now is right. Setting up the idea that there's a right way to play the role is, in my opinion, getting off on the wrong foot. Don't forget that for the people you end up casting, the casting session is your first rehearsal. You can say, "I'd like to work with you a little bit, have you read the scene a few times, some different ways, play around with it. I don't care if you depart from the script. I don't care if you get the words exactly right."

One thing you see the first time is the actor's choices, both the creativeness of the choices and whether they are specific and real, as well as what they respond to about the text. And that's what you should be looking for, not a performance. Noting the creativeness and specificity of the choices will give you information about the actor's ability. Noting what he seems to respond to in the text will start to give you information about whether he's right for the part.

Now what if the actor balks at reading without getting direction from you; in other words, wants you to tell her before she reads the role what the character is like, or how you see the role. This means that she is frightened, that she is used to auditions in which she is expected to "nail it" on one reading, and doesn't want to waste her chance without knowing what is expected of her. This is an opportunity for you to assure her that you are not looking for a performance, that you are open to exploring the characters with the actors, and that she will have the chance to read the scene more than once with different adjustments.

I feel it is important for you to cast actors who have ideas and are willing to take risks; that is why I feel strongly that you should hear what the actors have brought in before giving any direction. And then, even if you hate what he did the first time, you should have him read it again, with some direction, because you said you would. You should make a note of how he was playing the role in the first reading, to be sure that what you ask for next is in fact different. Use objectives or adjustments rather than giving result direction. Instead of "This is how I see the character..." or even "I want you to...," try saying, "What if..." or "Let's try it this way..."

If you ask the actors to do it a few different ways and they read it the same way every time, that's important information. You are finding out if they can follow direction. You are also finding out if they can play an objective or adjustment, and you will also get some idea of their range. You may want to give them some time to work on it; you might want to say, "I don't need you to do it off the top of your head, you can go out and think about it and come back. We'll take you as soon as you are ready." You want to see if they can make this new idea their own and make it real for themselves, but it's not necessary that they be able to do this in ten seconds or less.

You also should be noticing whether they're really talking about something when they come to images. If the line is, "My car is at the shop," do they really seem to be talking about something, or just saying a line? That's what's meant by having images behind everything. You're also watching for transitions: are they quick, clean and full? or forced, telegraphed, or labored? And throughout the process you are always watching for listening and moment-by-moment reality.

You will have been looking, in script analysis, at the behaviors of the character, so you want to find out in casting whether the actor has the capability to create those behaviors believably. If you have some adjustment, intention, or objective that you feel goes to the heart of the character, it would be a good idea to find out in casting whether the actor can handle it believably. This is still not the same as looking for a performance.

I like to use improv in casting to note the actor's freedom and access to subconscious resources. There is a Screen Actors Guild rule now that casting improvs may not be video taped. If you have any questions about this, you should contact the Guild.

It is customary to "call back" the actors you are interested in a second time before you make final casting decisions. At callbacks it is a good idea to pair them up with other auditioning actors, and observe different combinations to see how they communicate with each other. This is known as chemistry; what people call chemistry is communication. You are casting a relationship, not two performances. You can say exactly that: "I'm looking for a relationship."

There are unusual things you can do in casting: You can read with the actors yourself. This goes against what I said earlier about having the actors read with someone not involved in the decision-making. But if you read with actors — as long as you don't do any performing — you may be able to find actors you have a special affinity with. You would need to have a high tolerance for eye contact and connection.

In one audition, the director asked me in what ways I identified with the character and in what ways I didn't. An actor friend of mine told me of an audition where she was asked to do an improv in which she would count to ten — but take as long as she needed. She reported that she took ten minutes, and ended up going many places, laughing, even crying. Although she didn't get that role, the producers later cast her in something else. You may feel bad about not casting actors after you have asked them to put out a lot, but actors feel less bad about not getting a role if they know they have had a chance to give their all.

As you know I love opposites so it won't surprise you that I love to cast against type. Successful casting against type is a hunch about the actor's secret soul. When it works you are liberating the actor's hidden real self. When I am assigning my students their first monologue, I have just met them and only exchanged brief introductions around the room. I have the luxury of finding the right part for the actor rather than the right actor for the part. I look for something in which I do *not* hear their voice; in other words, I cast against type, but I make a hunch as to what might *interest* them. A student will often tell me later that the piece I chose for her was very meaningful. That's what I think works in figuring out whether the actor is right for the role — whether there will be something about the character or his experience that *captures the imaginative resources* of the actor.

Incidentally, I don't believe it is possible to cast well from videotapes. The tapes may be useful to jog your memory about some decision or idea you had during the audition, but you won't be able to see any of the subtleties I've been talking about. You will be forced to look for a performance. If producers or studio executives want input into casting, rather than sending them the tapes, encourage them to come to a callback.

You can reference-check an actor with other directors he has worked with, just as you would with any employee, but be sure to talk to the director, not to crew members. Crew members may have different criteria for judging actors, and many film sets are rife with mean gossip. Use what you know already about hiring people. A student of mine who had been a studio executive told me that at the studio she would always take an hour to interview every job candidate. Her peers questioned this procedure, but her department always had high productivity and low turnover. When she began directing she allowed herself to be pressured by her producer during auditions to choose before she really was ready — and she regretted it.

If you want to have some social conversation with actors, don't start by saying, "Tell me about yourself." "Tell me about yourself" is perceived by actors as a stress interview. Most actors are really quite shy. Managing to look comfortable in a stress interview has very little to do with acting ability. If what you are hoping to gain from social conversation is a more open and frank connection with the actor, remember that the best way to encourage another person to be frank and open is to be frank and open yourself. Put energy out.

When actors get to a certain level in their profession, they don't audition for roles. Most of the time, a film needs one or more stars of this level of prestige in order to get the financing. The stars must be presented with a firm offer before they will even read the script. This offer is made "subject to a meeting," so both sides can get out of it if the first meeting between actor and director goes badly. Unless this offer meets the actor's "price" which has been set by his agent, the agent will not forward the offer or the script to the actor, or, usually, even inform the actor of the offer.

There are, however, established stars who will consider doing a role for less than their usual price if the script is very good and the project interests them. If you have a low-budget project that you think fits this description, you can try to find some way of getting the script to the actor other than through his agent. This means meeting someone who knows his brother, or his hairdresser — or whatever.

Sometimes once one star is attached to the project you can ask him to read with other actors in line for other roles. This is a good idea if it can be worked out because, after all, you are casting relationships.

But maybe the best way to get a star in your movie will be to discover her yourself. What about Martin Scorcese and Harvey Keitel? They met when Scorcese was shooting his first film as a student at NYU. He advertised in a newspaper for an actor; Harvey Keitel, who had never acted before, answered the ad on a whim. They have made each other famous. You won't be able to be good at casting unless you are interested in actors. Go to plays, go to independent films, look for newcomers, find out who you like and what you like about them.

The thing to understand about casting is that you are going to make casting mistakes. To be a successful director you will have to learn how to work with them. Correcting your casting mistakes depends on your ability to recognize actors' strengths and work with their weaknesses. Actors are not perfect; they all have weaknesses. You are not looking for a perfect actor, someone you don't have to direct, but one whose plusses are exhilarating enough that you can live with his weaknesses.

Rehearsal

"When I met Marty [Scorsese], I was keenly aware of my meeting a part of myself. With Marty, I was getting to know myself better. The work between us was never a case of 'you walk over there and then turn around.' It was about finding what we were searching for in my own being." — **Harvey Keitel**

"I want to thank our director Tony Richardson for...giving us actors permission to play." — **Jessica Lange, accepting her Academy Award for "Blue Sky."**

"I'd go through the fire for you, man; any time, any place, any project." — **Don Cheadle, speaking to director Carl Franklin, as Cheadle accepted his Los Angeles Film Critics best supporting actor award for "Devil in a Blue Dress."**

There is an area of deep permission that some directors are able to bring actors to, at which the actors' work achieves lucidity, and choices of intelligence and power are made without effort or strain. It's the kind of permission Quentin Tarrantino gave John Travolta, which I talked about in the Moment by Moment chapter. I believe Harvey Keitel, Jessica Lange and Don Cheadle, in the quotes above, are speaking of this same deep permission and its rewards. Director Sidney Lumet is, I think, referring to this phenomenon when he says that at a certain point, watching dailies halfway through the filming of "Dog Day Afternoon," he began to feel that the movie had taken on its own life and was virtually shooting itself. Of course the script has to be good, the director has to know how to shoot the movie, the actors must be skilled, talented, and right for the parts, and the preparation must be done. This chapter is about the preparation the actors and director do together — the rehearsal.

Some directors don't rehearse at all, which means they are rehearsing with the camera rolling. Tom Hanks has described Penny Marshall's shooting technique for "Big" as "filmmaking by attrition," because she shot so many takes of every scene. William Wyler in effect rehearsed with cameras rolling, exposing often a million feet of film for one movie; the Wyler legend is that the only direction he ever gave actors was, "Do it again."

If you have a way of rehearsing and shooting that works for you, you should keep using it. Some people may find the rehearsal ideas of this chapter radical, even controversial. Like the script analysis techniques, they are designed to defeat whatever inclination you may have to do it "right," so you can work lucidly, in the moment.

Directors refer to the lack of time for rehearsal in movies and television as a given. In fact, there is plenty of time for rehearsal. Actors spend hours on sets with nothing to do. Directors certainly have other responsibilities besides their responsibilities to the actors, but out of a working day of ten hours, how much of the time is spent in actual shooting of film? Very little, right? The rest of the time is preparation. Why is all the preparation time on a set devoted to technical requirements and none to the acting? Of course, if you don't want to squeeze rehearsal into the hustle and bustle of shooting days, you can rehearse off the set before the technicians arrive.

Some actors and directors fear rehearsal or say they don't believe in it. They say that rehearsal kills the freshness and spontaneity of performances. This is a misunderstanding of the function of rehearsal, which is not to set out a connect-the-dots schema for the actors to follow by rote, but to open up the possibilities of the script, find its emotional and physical structure, and give the actors permission to play. What I think many directors (and actors) mean when they say they don't have time to rehearse or they don't believe in rehearsal is that they don't know how to rehearse. And if you don't know how to rehearse, then you shouldn't. Cast well, make sure the actors are listening to each other, and then back off. The harsh reality is that rehearsal can be a disappointing and frustrating experience. If all that is done is to set line readings and try for results, whatever was good about the audition or first reading will be lost and the work will only get worse.

Rehearsal is not performance. The purpose of rehearsal is not to "nail it" but to get ideas about what will work in front of the camera. In rehearsal we are looking for information, not performance. The goal of rehearsal is not perfection. The only way the rehearsal can be productive is if it is understood and treated as a *process.*

And even process-oriented rehearsal gets worse before it gets better. Often what worked instinctually in the audition or first reading must be dismantled or even discarded in order to create, with technique, a playable structure that will reliably work again. This can be a frightening experience. A director may feel he wants to hang on to whatever was fresh and good in the first reading while the scene is repeated over and over, but that's not going to happen. If the actors do a great audition or a great first reading, that means they *can* do it, not that they *have done* it. That brilliant first reading is over, it's gone. It's like a one-night stand. If you decide to take the risk of a committed relationship, there are going to be bad times as well as good. Two steps forward, one step back.

But here's the good news. Creativity is bountiful, self-replenishing, inexhaustible. The more you use it the more you will have. That's why rehearsal can lead to performances of extraordinary range and freedom, such as those of Stockard Channing in "Six Degrees of Separation," or Judy Holiday in "Born Yesterday," or Marlon Brando in "A Streetcar Named Desire," each of which had, in effect, long rehearsal periods, since each played many months on Broadway before being made into films. The proper purpose of rehearsal is to limber up the actors' emotional and imaginative "muscles" so they can do their job without strain or tension. When the actor is working *without any tension*, scene rehearsal, even hours of it, keeps yielding new emotional and imaginative information; the constant influx of new feelings and insights keeps the actor in the moment and, paradoxically, freshens the performance. This is why the "filmmaking by attrition" methods of Wyler and Marshall can work. Repetition *ad nauseam* can tire the actor to the point that he stops tensing himself to do it "right," lets down his defenses, quits checking and controlling his performance, ceases to "act with a capital A," and is finally simple, instinctual, and in the moment. Tom Hanks, describing Penny Marshall's "film-making by attrition," said that at one point he finally begged her to stop, declaring he could no longer "see the words in front of me." This kind of surrender is probably what she wanted!

If your budget does not include an unlimited supply of film stock, it would be a good idea to learn how to rehearse before the camera is rolling. If you do know how to rehearse, you won't have to leave all your decisions as to timing, pace, and dramatic moments for the editing room. You won't have to panic when an actor makes a weird choice, challenges your authority, or develops a resistance to the role. You won't have to worry about whether the actors are "peaking" too soon, because you will know how to work.

REHEARSAL PLAN

Whether you have a week or a day or half an hour to rehearse, you need to know what you want to accomplish in the time allowed, then set a schedule for it, and plan tasks. Some directors — Rob Reiner, Sidney Lumet, Roman Polanski, for example — set up a rehearsal period of a week or more before the technicians arrive. This way of working can save a lot of time, money, and heartache on the set and in the editing room. Other directors prefer to rehearse each day of shooting; Mel Gibson, when directing, holds rehearsals during the last part of the day for the next day's scene. Other directors rehearse each morning for the day's scenes. Or, on the fly, snag a half-hour here or there during the shooting day.

Organize the scenes for rehearsal purposes during script analysis. Decide which scenes you wish to rehearse together. Locate scenes that are continuous action and therefore really one scene, even if they include more than one setup. For instance, a scene that starts in a restaurant and continues on the street should be rehearsed as one scene even though it is two setups; then when you get to shooting it, the actors will have a sense of through-line to the scene. Since movies are almost always shot out of chronological sequence, you may wish to rehearse in chronological sequence in order to locate and create the script's arc. Or you may wish to rehearse all the scenes of one relationship together on the same day, to concentrate on the arc of that relationship.

Write out a rehearsal plan. Include these areas:

1) your ideas of what the film is about, what it means to you personally;

2) the spines and transformations of all the characters;

3) for each particular scene, its facts, its images, the questions it raises;

4) what the scene is about, its emotional event, and how the scene fits in the arc, or story, of the script;

5) possible through-lines, including candidates for each character's objective, and ideas for imaginative backstory adjustments;

6) the beats of the scenes (beginning, middle, and end), each beat's subject and event, and ideas (action verbs, adjustments) of how you might work on each beat;

7) the scene's physical life and its "domestic" event;

8) research you have done, and research you have left to do;

9) your plan of attack, what you wish to accomplish in the rehearsal, and what procedures you have in mind to follow;

10) a blocking diagram.

The rehearsal plan is not a blueprint to be slavishly followed. It is a digest of the script analysis tools outlined in the Script Analysis chapter, a way of reminding yourself to prepare. Once prepared, you can throw away your preparation and step into the moment. I strongly recommend against even bringing the rehearsal plan to rehearsal.

FULL CAST READ-THROUGH

Many directors like to have a read-through of a full-length script with the full cast. The purpose is to generate excitement about the project, to allow the actors to begin bonding with each other and the material, and to hear the words spoken.

You need to introduce people (or ask them to introduce themselves) and you should speak a few words. It's an opportunity to tell the cast what the script means to you, reveal your commitment and trustworthiness, and talk about what kind of acting you like. Tell them your priorities. Tell them how you plan to work in rehearsal. Let them know that you want to hear all their ideas and problems, and specifically, that if they have any ideas or problems related to another actor's performance, you want them to tell you personally. By all means, tell them you feel lucky to have this cast!

Give them the ground rules for this reading. Tell them it is not a performance, that they can do anything they want, move around, or not, as they wish. You could say, "I want you to have some fun, meet each other and hear the script read. I'm not looking for a performance."

Decide ahead of time what stage directions you want read (as few as possible) and find someone to read them. You might want to say something like this: "[So and so] will read some of the stage directions but it doesn't mean that we are married to them. As we go deeper into rehearsals, we'll be aiming to create relationships rather than execute stage directions."

The director has the opportunity, which she should begin to avail herself of at this first reading, to create a sacred atmosphere, the sense that this is not just a job. I recommend that the first reading (sometimes called a "table reading") take place in an open circle *without* any tables, since the table can function as a barrier. In order to have meaningful rehearsals of individual scenes, you must convey to the cast your own dedication to the rehearsal process and instill in them a seriousness of purpose.

Scene Rehearsal

The good news about rehearsal is that nothing can go wrong because it's not the real thing. Beware of perfection. Don't try to be inspired. Keep the focus on believability. Don't expect the actors to have their lines learned before scene rehearsals. Some do and some don't. It would ordinarily not be appropriate to demand that actors have lines learned for rehearsal unless you have worked with them before and established that procedure.

The goals of rehearsal are first, to make sure the actors listen and work honestly, use themselves, and find some authentic connection to the material; second, investigate the text: that is, explore questions, problems and possible meanings of individual lines, and solve the structure of the scene (events, through-lines, and beats); third, block the scene and find the physical life; fourth, establish the actor-director relationship, set up your system of communication, hear and try the actors' ideas, and smoke out their resistances.

Opening Remarks

At the beginning of a scene rehearsal, you can take five minutes to talk about the scene, and ask the actors if they have questions or ideas. Listen to the questions, and take note of the actors' concerns. If there is a quick answer, give it, but usually such questions are not meant to be answered in one sentence; they are areas to explore in rehearsal. You might say, "That's a good question. I have some ideas," or, "I wondered that myself. We'll have to figure that out."

If you wish you can speak briefly about the theme of the script. Even better, make simple, relaxed references to your own connection to the material. For example, "My mom works in a state psychiatric institute like the one in this script," or, "The relationship between these characters reminds me of my grandfather and grandmother," or, "Something like this happened to me once." Steven Spielberg speaks very openly in interviews about his personal connection, because of his parents' divorce, to his movie "E.T." I am sure he must have spoken as openly to the actors when he was directing.

Set up the framework and goal of the rehearsal. Perhaps it is to connect with the characters and relationships; perhaps it is to get at what is unspoken in the scene; or perhaps it is to work out physical activities. Tell the actors your policy about stage directions. Make sure there is a clearly understood rule preventing any hitting or other violence that is not agreed on and choreographed. Very soon do a reading of the scene. Here's a rule of thumb: Don't ever talk for more than five minutes before having the actors do something.

What about warm-up exercises? Sometimes they help, sometimes not. According to Emma Thompson's published diary, Ang Lee had the "Sense and Sensibility" cast do warmup exercises, even though some of the actors grumbled. If you do them, be sure they are inventive and engaging, and that they further the goals of the rehearsal.

FIRST READING OF SCENE

Start out with a simple, free, conversational reading of the scene with no acting and no blocking — talking and listening only. It's a kind of ground zero from which to work. Some people call this "reading it flat," which I find a confusing way of putting it. You don't really want the actors to speak in a monotone or keep glued to the page. You want them to engage with each other — talk and listen — without big emotional stakes, especially without any attitude. In a way you want them to read the scene as if they are talking about the weather or what they had for lunch, rather than as if they are talking about whether their mother has started taking drugs again.

Sometimes people talk about rehearsal as a time for the actors to get "comfortable" with the script and with each other. What is meant by this is making sure that the actors are talking and listening, rather than giving performances. Although you can't hang on to the freshness of the first reading, you can insist that the actors listen and affect each other throughout rehearsal.

Sometimes if the actors listen and respond to each other and are aware of the physical environment, that is enough to make the scene come alive, and it's better not to mess with it any further. The director's final responsibility is to the events of the script, and sometimes the best way to realize the events is if the actors get out of the way of the lines, that is, if they listen, and stay very simple. That way the audience can at least hear the lines. If you only have a few minutes to rehearse, make sure the actors are relating (listening) to each other. This includes making eye contact unless there is a good reason not to. Then add some simple physical life, and voilà! The scene is directed.

Now you have a choice. Do you want to go further into the structure and shaping of the scene? If you do, I'm afraid you are asking for trouble. As soon as you start giving substantive direction, you are engaged with the actors, and you bear a responsibility. If things go wrong, you can't go back to the way it was. The gears are engaged. Read further at your own risk.

THROUGH-LINES

Looking for the characters' through-lines is the first step toward solving the structure of the scene. When I say "solve the structure" of the scene, I mean find the way to make it tell the story of the script. When an actor has confidence in the structure of a scene, he is not shackled, but *freed* to fill it with spontaneous, moment-by-moment life.

Find out the actors' ideas about what is going on the scene for their character. If an actor has an idea, that's good, even if it's different from your idea. It gives her honesty and energy, a connection. Don't make her wrong but, rather, build on what she gives you. For example, if she says, "I think this happens all the time in this relationship," you can say, "Yes, I was wondering about that. What have their previous arguments been like? Or could this be the first time this particular issue has come up?" Rehearsal is a place to try out ideas, so try out the actors' ideas, too. Try it both ways: run through it one time *as if* there have been many other discussions on the same topic; and a second time *as if* this is the first time it has come up. Or improvise the last conversation of this topic (I'll speak more about improv a little later). You may be surprised and delighted by the new information brought to light by an improv. You have to let go of fears about your status or ego. Your purpose in having prepared thoroughly (via script analysis) for rehearsal was not to get rigid about your ideas, but to feel relaxed and open, to give you the natural authority of knowledge and preparedness. Then the actors' ideas will not feel like a threat but will feed and strengthen your authority.

Asking questions is a good directing technique, even if you have some ideas about what you think the answer might be. We want the actors to make the direction their own, even feel it was their own idea. The reason this procedure is not patronizing to the actor is that the director does not in fact know if his idea is good *until* the actor makes it her own. It is not necessary or even desirable to spell everything out for the actors, even if they want you to. John Cassavetes would never answer *any* of the actors' questions. This made Peter Falk furious! Falk knew that Cassavetes knew what he wanted in the performance, but was refusing to tell him what to do or how to do it! Cassavetes' dedication to the rehearsal process and to honest acting was absolute. He also had huge personal charisma and didn't care if his films were commercially successful.

You may not find yourself in Cassavetes' position or see yourself in his methods. In that case, be ready to jump in with an answer to your own questions if the actor seems not to have any ideas. The actor may be embarrassed to reply to a question, because she is afraid she will look stupid; this can be just as true of stars as of inexperienced actors. Actors hate it when the director has no ideas himself.

Your script analysis should have given you an understanding of your vision in terms of *event*. To create the event, structure the scene, and deepen the actors' connection to the material and each other — find through-lines. You have already gotten ideas for through-lines from your script analysis; now you try them out. Although sometimes it is useful to address the through-line toward the end of rehearsal, the rule of thumb is to find the through-line first and then add layers and beats.

The basis for a character's through-line is his given circumstances, that is, his facts or his situation. A simple reminder of the characters' facts, or backstory ("You're seeing your ex-lover for the first time in ten years, and he is now married with two children") may create the through-line and be adequate direction for some actors in some scenes. Learn how to do this storytelling well. Don't put the actors to sleep with your descriptions of characters' backstory. If your ideas about the script are merely clever or intellectual, you won't be a good storyteller. Allow yourself to connect to the story on a feeling level. *But don't tell the actors how to feel.* Use the storyteller's tools: facts, images, events, verbs, physical detail. Put yourself imaginatively in the character's shoes, and the actor's shoes, and make your own substitution while you tell the story by (in this example) letting yourself recall your own experiences with ex-lovers. You can even speak of such experiences to the actor, since this lets the actor know your connection to the material, and invites her to make her own connection.

Another way to get at through-line is via the character's objective or need. That is, instead of discussing what the character is like, look at his behavior — what he wants, and what he is doing to get what he wants. Every character (every person) always has an objective, and the objective (in real life as well as movies) doesn't change very often. In terms of dramatic structure, every well-written scene has one objective per character. These are the reasons why the "objective" can be a useful way to create through-line and begin a discussion with an actor about the character. If an actor is talking about the character in an intellectualizing or judgmental way, you can (gently) interrupt with, "What does the character want?"

The objective, however, is not necessarily the best tool for every actor. Some actors have not trained with objectives and don't like to work with them, since they find objectives and action verbs too intellectual. That's why I want you to have other directing options (discussed in earlier chapters), such as adjustments, metaphors, images, or issues. Or the concept of the character's "primary focus" or task, his problem; or his subtext; or his physical life.

Use only one of these tools at a time. The reason for coming up, during script analysis, with ideas for all these different directing tools is so you will have several to choose from, and so you will have another idea if the first one doesn't work. Whatever you do, don't give the actor a laundry list all at once, of backstory *and* objective *and* adjustment *and* action verb *and* images *and* physical life, etc. Work on one thing at a time.

LAYERS

Directors commonly tell actors too much at once. Work in layers and in sections (beats). If you tell the actor, "You love your husband and want to cheer him up, but you also still have feeling for your ex-boyfriend," you have given her an impossible direction to follow. The two contradictory elements cancel each other out. The actor may simply think that you don't know what you want, or she may only hear and follow one of the two directions anyway. At worst she may try to do both; the two ideas will cancel each other out and the work will become either forced or flat. If, on the other hand, you establish a through-line for an actor that she "wants to cheer her husband up," on the next run-through of the scene you can add the adjustment that on a certain line she is recalling the image of dancing with her ex-boyfriend.

If the actors are listening and you don't like the way it comes out, you might add a layer. Some people use the term "colors" or "levels" for what I am calling choices or adjustments or layers, as in, "Let's see if we can add another color here." Or you might try a different through-line choice, say, "get her to take care of you" instead of "get her to feel sorry for you." But you don't need to give a specific suggestion as to the choice to try next; it's okay to say, "I'm wondering if we need a stronger choice here."

Look for a light in the actor's eyes when discussing choices. Whenever you ask a question or give a direction and get a blank or frightened look in response, quickly say, "Or...it could be this..." And come up with another idea or another question. The actor must make a choice he can get behind. The hope is that the choice that captures the actor's imagination will be the same as the choice that goes to the heart of the material. When good actors are working organically on a good script with a well-prepared director in a free, creative atmosphere, this will usually be the case.

WORKING IN BEATS

You recall that in the chapter on script analysis I said the major beats could function as rehearsal units. It is hardly ever a good idea to rehearse a whole scene all the way through over and over. After you have run it through once or twice or so, to establish listening and connect with through-lines, break it down into beats; that is, work in sections. Each scene has either two or three (sometimes four) major beats; an extremely short scene may have only one.

Don't describe the content and transitions of all the beats and then run the whole scene. Work on one beat, perhaps after some brief discussion or direction; then work on the next beat. When you work on the second beat, don't rerun the scene from the top; isolate that one beat and put your attention to it.

This is the heart of rehearsal. This is where you can investigate troublesome lines, cultivate images, unpack subtext, create events, set up transitions, deal with objects, and find activities and movement. You are structuring the scene, anchoring the emotional life to the blocking and the pacing.

In the meanwhile, you are creating a soup of association, subtext, image, and circumstance around the lines and activities of the script. You are asking questions, using imaginative connections, personal memories and images of your own, anecdotes of behavior you have observed in life, and comments about what you see going on in the actors' faces and bodies during rehearsal. You are directing.

REHEARSAL GUIDELINES

It may not be necessary for actors to make a full emotional investment in rehearsal. In rehearsal we are looking for a choice that brings to life the scene's structure and engages the actor's interest. We're not looking for performance, but for the routes that may take us to performance, and usually some investment is needed to see if the choice will work. Rehearsal is a place where actors experiment with different ways of getting to what they will need on the set. It's better, you see, for them to try out these different emotional routes with the actor they will be working opposite, because the "how" of the emotional journey must come out of their interaction with that particular actor.

The amount of emotional investment needed in rehearsal may depend on the material. When the material is rich and layered, the actors, in order to open their imaginative and emotional gates to the deeper layers, will probably have to work at full emotional tilt all through rehearsal. Lightweight material needs a light touch in rehearsal; the sense of imaginative *play* needs to be maintained. In any case, just as there should always be listening in rehearsal, there should always be enough endowment that the actors never fall into indicating or setting line readings.

If you feel they are not endowing their images and given circumstances, you can try telling better stories, using questions, images, and your own personal associations with the material. For instance, you might say, "Have you ever been stranded in a hurricane? I was once." Or you can say something like "I understand you're not making a full investment now in rehearsal. I know you will keep working on that." You might ask while discussing choices, "Is that something you can connect with?" Or, "Is that something you can make real for yourself?" You can always ask questions about how they like to work.

Rehearsal rhythm is slower than performance rhythm. During rehearsal the actors need to explore, to let themselves live between the lines, to find colors and transitions, and to build connection (communion) with the other actor. If they don't take that time, they may start rushing or fall into attitudes. So it's okay if actors don't have the pace you want in early rehearsal. You can mention, "Later [or "soon"] we'll be picking up the pace, but for now it's fine to take your time."

But don't let them work at low volume. Often when actors are not speaking loud enough it means they are worried about doing it "right" and are afraid to take a chance on committing to a choice. Or they haven't found a choice they can commit to, and more work needs to be done to find it. Sometimes they are holding on to an emotion and not giving it to the other actor. If you have not yet acquired the skill to feel confident talking about the problem, it's all right simply to say, "We need more volume."

Notice whether you are repeating the same direction over and over. That means it isn't working or the actor doesn't understand it or is resisting it. When an actor says, "Tell me again what we're doing here" or, "I'm trying to take this all in," those are clues that your direction is confusing or too elaborate.

If an idea or direction doesn't work, take it on yourself. Say, "I think we're on to something, but I don't think that idea of mine was enough to get us where we need to go." Or, "I'm not sure I explained that right. Let's try it again, only this time..." Every communication you have with an actor, including social chit-chat and body language, is part of your actor-director relationship; in other words, everything you say or do in the actors' presence is de facto direction of the script.

Learn to give direction in the language of permission, rather than the language of enforcement: "It's okay to slow down," instead of "You're going too fast." Good direction often comes indirectly, and offhandedly. If the director gets too excited about an idea, the actors can feel pressured to do it right, frightened of failing to execute it properly.

Good ways to phrase direction are: "What if...?" or "Let's try..." or "I wonder..." or "Let's see if this works," or "Maybe..." or "I had an idea about this section..." or "But here's another interesting thing." My own personal favorite (I'm giving away my best secret here) is "This might not work." It takes off the pressure. The reason "It might not work" always works is because I always mean it. The reason I want to try something is *to see* if it will work. I have an idea in my mind and until the actors make it work, that's all it is — an idea. I also favor, "I thought you had an impulse," or, "Something you did gave me an idea." These are always true, if you put full attention on the acting. Rehearsal is collaborative. The actors' contributions, when they are working well, are more instinctual. The director can capitalize on the actors' instincts to build the structure.

More effective than asking actors to "underplay" would be to suggest "going against the lines," i.e., an opposite. If you want the performance "heightened," try using language that suggests digging deeper rather than pushing harder. Instead of asking for "more tension" or "more build," ask for a stronger choice and more listening. Instead of "bigger" you probably mean "more free." Instead of "take it down" you probably mean "Stay honest. Keep it simple."

Don't say to actors, "Put stress on this word." Instead suggest an image or fact that might be behind it. If an actor asks you how to say a line, you might reply, "You mean, what does it mean? Let's take a look." If an actor suggests an attitude or emotion for his character, you can say, "Let's find the verb of it," or "I don't care how it comes out looking." When praising actors, it's good to say things like "The work is going well," "We're on the right track," "Let's keep going in that direction," "We're in sync," rather than "That was perfect," or "You have nailed it," or "When we shoot, do it just like that."

These are all suggestions to get you off the track of result direction. You will want to find your own ways of putting things. The better you get with this the more you will feel you are communicating rather than using jargon.

In one Rehearsal Techniques class I was teaching, the actor's first line had to do with asking the other character to give her some privacy.

The director signaled, "When you're ready..." The other actor walked in and the first actor said, "Would you do me a favor and give me more time before we start?" It was classic, really, because the actor's impulse toward her scene partner mirrored exactly the character's interaction with the other character, but she didn't use it. Indeed when the rehearsal continued, her line asking her partner to leave her alone a minute never had the truth of the accident. A director who is alert can capitalize on such accidents. It's legitimate to say to an actor, "Earlier I overheard you complaining to the A.D. about the muffins. That's what I want in this scene." You mirror back to the actors behavior of theirs that was spontaneous and make it useful to them as a playable choice.

Don't let the actors direct each other. As soon as you notice an actor coming forth with opinions about how someone else's character could be played, take steps tactfully but firmly to discourage it. You can use the language of permission, something like "You don't need to worry about that. I can take care of it." Let the actors know that you welcome all their ideas but that their ideas should be imparted privately to you, not to the other actors, the producer, the writer, or anyone else. Keep the actors from making bargains with each other. Don't confuse "getting comfortable," which is a proper purpose of rehearsal, with an actor retreating to his "comfort zone," which is never a good thing. The purpose of maintaining an atmosphere in which actors can be deeply relaxed, open and free, is to encourage them to be receptive to obstacles. Don't let them take out the obstacles. You may wish to talk to the actors separately about their work and their choices. I talk to actors separately in the early part of rehearsal; if rehearsal is going well, soon the actors are spontaneously working with privacy in public and don't even hear what I am saying to the other actor.

Sometimes when one actor is very strong and you work with the other actor for a while, to bring him up to his level, he gets better and then the other actor gets weak! You need to keep at it, going back and forth. Sometimes you can get a scene to work by working with only one of the actors. It may be best to work with the one who is strongest, who may then be able to carry the weaker actor. If you work with the weaker actor, concentrate on getting him to be as simple as possible.

Be inventive. You may give a good direction and the actor doesn't follow it or it doesn't work. First use alternative ways of asking for it — that's the purpose of the detailed script analysis. If nothing works, there may be a resistance, or there may be a better way of solving the scene. You can enlist the actors' help in finding the solution. Your yardstick should be the truth of the scene, rather than a need to impose your own will.

Stay relaxed. Be yourself in your body. Stand and move around to keep your energy flowing. If you are tense, your tension will be communicated to the actors; you won't be able to listen, or to hear the dead spot, the false moment, the line that doesn't work. Whenever a dead spot occurs, there is work to do; there is an event that is yet to be realized, lines not yet understood, facts behind the lines to justify, images to explore, more specific choices to make, and transitions to deal with.

While you are learning how to rehearse, I strongly suggest taking time to do it (both the through-lines and each beat) three different ways, including at least one way that you feel sure is "wrong." It is a way to learn how to explore, how to use opposites. Eventually the use of opposites and juxtaposition will become second nature. It's also an extremely useful technique if the actors are inexperienced or don't know how to work, to keep them from falling into set line-readings.

If the rehearsal starts to get boring, try making it more physical. Have the actors throw a pillow back and forth, or even have a pillow fight. Let them speak the subtext. Ask them to say "I don't believe you" if they feel the other actor is not in the moment. If they are familiar with the Meisner Repeat Exercise, invite them to incorporate it into rehearsal. This means that any time an actor feels stuck, or feels that she is saying lines with no connection, she can say how she feels or make an observation about the other actor, or repeat what the other actor has said.

If the actors resist such exercises, you might say, "It's too dead-on, I want to do something wrong to shake this up, to get the relationship more fresh." Or, "You guys seem stiff. I have an idea about something that might loosen up the situation. Are you willing to try it?" If they say no, you can say, "Well, we have a problem; you tell me how we're going to solve it. The acting has gotten a bit stiff here and I want to get back to the ping-pong, the give and take. How do you work? Tell me what I can do for you."

IMPROV

Although improv is sometimes used to change or add lines of dialogue during rehearsal (see John Schlesinger's comments in the Criterion laser disc version of "Midnight Cowboy," or accounts of improvisational methods director Mike Leigh uses when writing scripts), I am more interested for this book in improv as a rehearsal technique. John Cassavetes used improv this way, and the acting in his movies always had such immediacy that people often thought that the actors were improvising as the cameras rolled. Improv as a rehearsal tool can help the actors find themselves in the roles and inhabit the world of the characters, but it can do even more than that. One of the most central, and difficult, tasks of the actor is to say lines he has read, memorized, and rehearsed *as if he is saying them for the first time*. To do this, his *moment-by-moment emotional life* or *subtext* must be improvised. Going so far in rehearsal as to improvise, not only the emotional life, but even the words and movement, can help create that deep permission to live in the moment even when memorized lines and blocking and emotional structure (through-lines and beats) have been added to the scene.

Using improv doesn't mean you don't prepare. A director who is well prepared will get much more out of improv as a rehearsal tool. He will get the most out of improv if he can "mirror back" to the actors, in playable terms, the useful insights gleaned from a good improv.

Some actors don't like improv. They may be afraid it's not really improv, that the director is expecting a certain result and not telling them what it is. There must be freedom and trust for improv to work. Improv is not a frivolous undertaking; it is a sacred tool, a door to the subconscious. Whatever unconscious material is brought to light in improv must be respected. There is no such thing as an improv that is "wrong."

Here are some kinds of improv that can be useful in rehearsal:

1) Paraphrasing

You can invite the actors to put the lines of the scene in their own words. This can take them off the effort to prove to us that the lines are true, and allow them to make the images, impulses, and activities of the character their own.

2) Improv based on the facts

This is a favorite of mine. I love to pick out the bare facts of the scene and have the actors improvise around those facts with total freedom, restricted only by the two rules of improv: "no denial" and "no obligation" (and, as I mentioned earlier, the understanding that no one is to get hurt). I tell them to allow the facts to be true, but not to use any of the lines and not to follow the plot of the script. This is an unstructured, exploratory approach. It can give you information and insight into the characters' objectives, their primary relationships, their subtext, and their issues. It can create opportunities for layers.

For instance, let's say the two actors rehearsing the "Red Ryder" scene had voiced in discussion their belief that the two characters didn't like each other or get along at all; then let's say they had done a read-through of the scene with objectives "to pick a fight," which had gone fairly well. Next, you, as director, could suggest an improv on the facts of the scene, which are simple: Angel and Stephen work at the same diner; Angel lives (or speaks daily) with her mother; her shift follows his; the diner has very few customers; there has been a previous conversation between the two of them on the subject of his name. The actors, given total freedom to follow impulses, and having already had the chance to try out their ideas, will very often come up with an improvised scene that is not hostile at all! A new layer, perhaps of affection, even longing, has surfaced. If you can point it out to them in a playable form — for example, "You almost seemed like brother and sister" (an adjustment) — it can be usable. You don't need to point it out to them right then. You can make a note of it to mention during shooting, to whisper to one (or both) of them before a take.

3) Improv to create backstory

You can improvise scenes from the characters' past. For instance, for the "Red Ryder" scene, the director could ask the actors to improvise Stephen and Angel changing shifts, not on the morning of the script, but on some other morning, say two months ago. Or, to explore the possibility that Angel did Stephen's homework for him in high school, a scene from that era could be improvised. This is more helpful, I think, than discussing intellectually the characters' pasts.

John Cassavetes used to write whole scenes that he had no intention of putting in the final movie, and have the actors improvise around them. Al Pacino, when asked, in a 1989 Vanity Fair interview, whether he continues to use the Method technique of affective memory, said he prefers "off-script" improvisations.

4) The pre-scene beat

It's very useful to improvise what might have taken place just before the scene began, specifically physical life, so the scene can be "in the middle of something." If you were rehearsing "The Graduate," for instance, you could have the actors improvise the car ride home from the party that Benjamin gives Mrs. Robinson. At some point you can say, "Go into the words of the scene."

5) A parallel event or relationship

An improv is an elaborate "as if." It is an "as if" acted out. Instead of saying, "Let's try it as if..." you actually improvise the reality of the "as if."

Let's say in your script analysis you have thought of a metaphor for the central event of the scene, such as "The thing that happens in this scene with you and the truck driver is like what happens when a clerk at the post office tells you he has no twenty-cent stamps." In rehearsal you could improvise the post office scenario, and then go into the truck driver scene. Or for a scene about a lawyer you could propose an improv about "not that lawyer, but one like her."

It can be very useful, especially for a scene of high emotion, to start with a "lower stakes" improv, a situation that parallels the event of the scene, but is less dramatic. For example, if we take a scene taking place on a space station in which one of the characters is about to push the lever that will jettison the other character into space, I think we can safely say that this is a situation neither of the actors will have encountered in life. We might begin rehearsal with a "lower stakes" improv, say that one character has to fire the other one from a job.

"Higher stakes" improvs can work really well too. Strangely, even if the improv/metaphor is more far-fetched than the situation in the scene to be played (e.g., the *scene* is about a firing, and the *improv* is about the space station ejection), the actors may find the connection and sense of belief more effortlessly, simply because they are off the lines, off the sense of obligation.

"Parallel event" improvs can be constructed to create a sense of intention. You may have decided that the character's intention is to punish the other character. But perhaps the actor is falling into a stagy, overdramatic idea of punishing. You might say, "I want you to punish the way that *you* punish.

266

Let's say that [the other actor] agreed with you to learn lines before rehearsal, then didn't learn them. Punish him for it." Then go into the lines of the scene.

6) Silent improvs

Silent improvs give a texture of life to the relationships and physical world of the characters. You set up the physical world and let the actors live in it without any talking. Again, you can go right from the improv into the scene. Silent improvs are very useful when shooting, as a way for the actors to start working and connecting with each other before the director says "Action." If you are going to suggest them during shooting, it's a good idea to get comfortable with them in rehearsal.

7) "Third character" improvs

You can ask the actors to play the scene as if the "third character" about whom they are speaking or thinking is actually in the room. I have seen this technique bring a scene to life in extraordinary ways.

Or have the actors switch roles. Or do a high status/low status improv. Or...

8) Improvise!

Design your own improvs. Try to keep your setups for improv physical and factual rather than abstract and psychological.

Improvs are often longer than the scene. The actors are spontaneously speaking the subtext of the scene. Sometimes they become so excited about their inventions that they then want to add some of the lines that they have improvised to the script. If you don't want to do that, you can say, "Yes, definitely, let's add it, but let's add it as subtext!"

Improvs are not performances. They give information for possible playable choices — imaginative backstory, objectives, adjustments, subtext. That's what you should be looking for, so that later during shooting you can say, "You know in that great improv we did yesterday, it seemed that your intention was to control him. Let's try the scene that way." That is, you *mirror back* to the actor in playable terms the insight released by the improv.

BLOCKING: PHYSICAL OBJECTS AND PHYSICAL ACTIVITY

Think of "blocking" as the characters' relationship to the environment, and "stage business" as their relationship to objects. Blocking and business physicalize the inner life of the characters, illuminate the events of the scene, and add the texture of life. If you don't know how to block a scene, your master shots will be a waste of time and film stock.

One of the great things about usable master shots is that they can allow the actors to overlap dialogue. It has become a given that actors must always make a tiny pause before they speak, so there will be unlimited options in the editing room. This tiny pause is something that almost never happens in real life conversations; it is a great barrier to listening. Although actors can overcome this barrier by playing intentions, when actors are allowed to overlap the dialogue and freely *play* with each other, the chances for fresh, free, alive performances are hugely increased.

In any case, at some point in rehearsal you begin to add some movement. Try to work as organically as possible. You can say, "Let's start to add some sense of the physical environment." Add a chair, an object, a little at a time. Create the objects' histories; make friends with them. Or paint an imaginary picture of the physical environment, thus inviting the actors to imagine it; allow them time to see it, believe in it.

When actors are working well and organically, they are likely to move spontaneously in ways that physicalize the emotional events of the scene. You can build on such impulses. You can say, "Let's keep that hand movement you made on line X." Then you should make a note of it. You need also, if you can, to make a note of the intention or adjustment that seemed to create the movement. The movement ideas that capture your attention will be things that happened accidentally. The actor probably won't remember, because she was working in the moment.

Your script analysis will have given you ideas for activities for the actors. Rehearsal is the place where you find out whether these ideas work, adjust them if they don't, and give actors the chance to make these ideas their own. An insightful gesture can create all the inner life that is needed for a scene. For example, you may be certain that in a particular scene you want one actor to touch the other actor's face. It is all right to give that direction and let the actor find the way to get there believably. It can help if you say something like "I want you to touch his face here. I don't expect you to get there emotionally right now. You can take whatever time you need." By the way, pay attention to actors touching each other — make sure it counts.

Knowing when to ask the actor to move and when to ask him not to move can make the scene work, but it can also help the actor find his energy and his center. Sometimes actors dissipate their energy with aimless movement; sometimes they get stuck emotionally because they are stuck physically.

Bring objects to rehearsal. Objects are a powerful tool of the actor. Finding the right object, offering it to the actor at the right place in the script, at the right point in the rehearsal process, can completely turn around the actor's performance. Some actors love to find objects — physical business — to add to their characterizations. In rehearsal actors who are uncomfortable with physical business have time to practice and make it their own. Perhaps an actor is given eye glasses in the hope that some humor can result if she searches for them, forgetting they are perched on top of her head. She will need time to work with the prop and make it her own, especially if she doesn't wear glasses in real life. Otherwise it will pull her performance down rather than add to it.

If you love a piece of business, set it free. A divine piece of business is only divine if it is working. If the life goes out of it, you must let it go, and find something new. You have to trust that if you were smart and inventive enough to come up with it, you'll be able to come up with something else too. This principle is true for *all* the ideas you came up with in script analysis. They are a jumping-off place, not a blueprint.

If you give a blocking direction and the actor forgets it or can't make it work, you should investigate. It means either the blocking is wrong and you need to change it, or there is something the actor doesn't understand about the scene. You may need to discuss choices with the actor and rework the character's emotional life.

You can create a through-line to the blocking — an activity the actor is engaged in throughout the scene. Then, as you work beat by beat, you find specific places to do this or that. A character can have a territory, which is respected or invaded, circled, approached, etc. Obstacles can be created physically. There can be objects which separate the characters, function as allies to one of the characters, or provide a lightning rod for the relationship; that is, instead of punishing the other character, the actor punishes the pie crust she is rolling out. But objects must have the texture of life, even if they also have stylistic or thematic or storytelling purposes. For instance, if you want a confrontation to take place across a table, pay attention to how you introduce the table to the actors. If you introduce it as a prop on which to lean during the confrontation, you are calling attention to the effect you want to produce. It is better to allow the actors' primary connection to the table be as the table on which they ate dinner last night, to call attention to its place in the physical texture of their lives.

Even though I favor blocking organically off the actors' impulses, I recommend that you create a blocking diagram ahead of time. Make a floor plan or model of the set. Get doll house furniture (or make furniture out of cardboard) and a set of toy soldiers. Move the toy soldiers around while you say the lines of the scene. Next make an aerial view floor plan of the pattern of movement you have come up with. Then do it again. Come up with at least three possible ways to have the actors move in the scene. Don't make your shot list or do any storyboarding until after you have done this work. Some directors don't storyboard until after they rehearse with the actors (if at all), so that the blocking can be arrived at collaboratively with the actors. I recommend to you the book <u>Film Directing Shot by Shot</u> by Steven Katz, which contains information on the physical staging and composing of dialogue scenes.

You will rarely be rehearsing on an actual location or set. Sets are often being lit — or built — during rehearsal. To use a rehearsal space, measure and mark off with tape the dimensions of the set, and bring in furniture and objects (props) of roughly the same size as those you expect to have on the shoot. It can be useful to work on the emotional dynamic of a scene outside the context of its location: for example a scene that takes place in a car; no one has to rehearse being in a car. If you find the emotional solution in a rehearsal room, when you get to the set and the actors must contain the emotional event in a car, that will add an obstacle that may help the scene. On the other hand, for a scene in which there is loud music, or especially dancing to music, rehearsal is an opportunity to practice with the music, even though during shooting there may be no music.

Actors should always be in the moment during rehearsal. The exception to that is if you are "marking through" the blocking. Sometimes you need to practice complicated blocking like a dance choreography; that is, go through the steps of it mechanically so it becomes second nature before filling it with any emotional life. This is often essential to directing scenes with lots of people. It is called "marking it through" or "walking it through." When actors are marking through a staging, they should not try to act at the same time, because if they do a half-job of acting they will probably fall into a sing-song, setting line readings. Rehearsal on the set, that is, setting the blocking for the lighting crew and camera operator, is marked through by the actors without any investment.

Violence and sex in a scene should never be improvised, but should always be choreographed and marked through without invest- ment; the emotional life should be filled in after the physical life is set and the actors' safety assured.

Often each beat change is punctuated with movement, or a change of action verb, or a new pace. Physicalizing the beat changes helps the audience follow the story. Experienced directors develop a sense of when to "play through" a beat change, or when to create a kind of syncopation by "going against" the rhythms that are written into the script. It is part of a director's talent and artistry to know when to allow a "moment" or beat change, and when it is more effec- tive to "play through." You can work on beats out of sequence. Especially if time is short, I often find it useful to work first on the meatiest beat, the one containing the central event of the scene.

A director needs to develop a sense of when to let the actors run the scene, and when to stop and work a moment. Even if you have told them you were going to run the scene, you can stop it if you see something you need to work on.

RESISTANCES

Actors can have resistances to choices which in fact tap into their deepest soul. Once an actor I was working with, who was playing a character named "Celia," was having a terrible time with a scene, refusing to engage with the other actor, whose character name was "Johnny." Finally she burst out: "But I hate Johnny! He's lazy and selfish and treats Celia very badly."

Underneath her judgment of Johnny was an implied judgment of her own character, Celia, as a woman who was weak because she put up with this unsuitable man. I asked her to think of Johnny as a man Celia had once loved and was still attracted to even though she wanted him out of her life now. Then I said, "I think that's something that's happened at one time to everyone." I wanted her to allow the obstacle to be personal, and I wanted to not make her wrong. If I had told her that her anger was wrong for the role, I don't think I would have gotten the performance I did finally get from her.

Even though what the actor is resisting may be a part of her own personality that she doesn't want to face, there is no need for the director to take it on himself to analyze her neurosis or character defects, discuss her acting problems, accuse her of laziness, or inform her that she has a problem with authority. The best way to approach resistances is by smoking out the judgments the actor is unconsciously making.

Another thing you can say (privately) to an actor who is resisting is, "You seem to have some resistance here, but I believe you can do it. Do you want me to leave you alone to work on it or do you want me to work on it with you?" Or, "Is there something on your mind?" "Is something bothering you?" "Am I doing something that you don't agree with?" When in doubt, *ask*. Ask them to go farther. Ask them what they need from you to get there. Ask them how they work, and what is bothering them, but respect the actors' privacy. If you need to discuss a choice, you might add, "if you don't mind sharing it with me." This advice is based on artistic even more than ethical considerations. It may dissipate the energy of the choice to talk about it.

There is a difference between a director who is respectful of actors' privacy and their different ways of working and a director who is timid. Respectful is good. Timid is bad. As a director you must learn the difference.

There are some actors who are ornery, who question every direction, who, no matter what you suggest, find a reason why it won't work or why they can't do it. The funny thing about actors like this is that, often, once they have complained and argued and threatened over a direction, they go ahead and do it anyway! I have sometimes been this kind of actor myself. All I can say in our defense is: Would you rather have an actor who says no and then does it, or an actor who says yes and then doesn't do it? Since resistances are often unconscious, they can be covert. That is, the actor may try to be cooperative when he doesn't feel it. He may say "yes" when every fiber of his being is resisting. Covert resistance is actually more subversive of the rehearsal process than overt resistance. Covert resistance has to be smoked out before it can be dealt with.

Sometimes it works to give a resistant actor permission not to do it, but have as your own unspoken subtext, "yet." In other words, "Okay, let's forget that idea [for now]." The actor may need time. He may register the direction without executing it immediately. Reassure him there is no need to nail the direction right now. Instead of thinking of someone being a difficult actor, think of him as an actor having difficulty. Treat all problems with actors as artistic problems; that way you won't get sucked into anyone's neurosis. But don't retreat from the relationship. Anytime you are having trouble with an actor, increase your commitment to the solution. You can even say this: "I am committed to solving this problem." That way you let your energy be committed to something higher than insecurity. Don't let the actor's insecurity (which is always at the base of actors' bad behavior) cause you to get involved with your own insecurity.

Whenever you get overt resistance from an actor, or smoke out a covert one, I want you to say, "I'm glad that happened!" Or, "I'm glad you brought this up." Many directors know so little about actors that they think that the purpose of casting is to find actors with whom there won't be any problems. There is no such animal! When an actor keeps forgetting a line, for example, it may be because of a resistance. Even actors who are truly *open* — the kind I want you to work with — have resistances, but they are more likely to know and admit them. They might say, when something isn't working, "I must be resisting something here." If an actor says this in your presence, this is not an occasion for alarm; it means he is trusting you, letting you in on the process.

Actors can panic if they feel they are miscast. There can be a very fine line between a risky role that provides a thrilling stretch for the actor, and a role that he is just not right for and in which he is likely to look inept and foolish. A director needs to take responsibility for the casting even if it wasn't your idea, but was insisted upon by the producers or studio. Don't project anxieties of your own about a possible casting mistake. If you don't recast, you need to proceed *as if* the actor is the best person for the role, you need to communicate to him that what you want for this role is whatever he can honestly bring to it, and you need to support him in exploring the script, so he can keep digging and making the role his own. You need to always communicate this to *all* the actors. This is the deep permission.

Sometimes actors judge the director and resist direction because they don't respect his ability. You mustn't take this personally. You must focus always on the work, not egos or personalities. Keep your concentration on bringing the script to life. Listen between the lines to the communications you are receiving from the actors. Maybe they need proof that you know what you are doing. Most actors arrive on set prepared to direct themselves. If you are an untried director and you want to have a significant rehearsal period, you may need to convince the actors that rehearsal with you will be a productive rather than a painful experience. Good actors would much rather be left alone than suffer pedestrian, unenlightening, intrusive direction.

Stars need direction as much as any actor, maybe even more, since they have a lot at stake. And they are surrounded by people who don't tell them the truth, who are currying favor by telling them everything they do is wonderful. Stars need a director they can trust. They need to know you will tell them the truth.

Don't be intimidated by good actors. Director Betty Thomas, on the first day of shooting an HBO movie with Kathy Bates, saw that Bates seemed to be holding back. After watching dailies, the producer confirmed that the scene should be reshot and encouraged Thomas to take charge. The next day Thomas said to Bates, "I never got to say anything to you or give you any direction yesterday, but I know you're a thousand times better than that, so we have to do it again." This is exactly the right way to approach the situation of a good actor who is not delivering what you hoped, and it doesn't mean you are shining them on — it is the truth. When you are working with actors think of yourself not as manipulating them to your vision, but as making it safe for them to take the risks needed to meet the material. Let them know they are safe. Tell them, "I won't let you overact." Or, "If it's too much I'll let you know." Then make sure you do.

Rehearsal is useless unless you can listen to what the actors are doing, what they are giving you, what they are resisting. A good director works differently with each actor. Sometimes it is best to leave an actor completely alone to work at his own pace. The way to develop the intuition needed to tell you when to push, and when to leave actors alone to find their own way, is by connecting deeply with the material and listening to the actors. If you ask a question of an actor, listen to the answer, and listen between the lines. When an actor asks you questions, it is more important to hear the questions than to answer them. What is the subtext? What is on his mind?

Once a student who was playing the mother in a mother/son scene said out of the blue to me: "There can't be any sexual feeling between these two." So I of course said, "Hmmm. Let's look into that." Her statement doesn't mean that she has a rigid opinion on the subject, or that she will fight you if you suggest an adjustment "as if" the other character were her lover. On the contrary it means that the idea has occurred to her; it is floating around in her emotional storage banks. Perhaps it is the aspect of the scene she is resisting, but she is letting you know she is getting ready to give up her resistance.

Some actors work at a level of image and intuition that is more like a child's than an adult's. Encourage the actors to play. Their job is to find the honest behavior, not to control the effect. You are the safety net. Actors need constant reassurance. If an actor is not getting constant reassurance and astute, honest feedback — direction she can hear, understand, and *follow* — from her director, she will look elsewhere for it, to members of her entourage, her publicist, hairdresser, or other equally unfortunate sources. Don't kid yourself about this — when an actor seems self-sufficient and unneedful of your attention, this is more likely to be a danger signal than an occasion to relax.

Don't let an actor shut down. Sometimes you need to grapple with actors, challenge them, even confront them if they are faking or bullshitting. But don't argue, because you can't win an argument with an actor. She may give in but there is likely to be some shutting down, and shrinking. Learn the difference between arguing and grappling. Arguing originates in a more pessimistic perception of the relationship. So don't argue with anybody.

Whatever actors do, love them anyway, the way a mother loves her children, even the difficult ones. Give them unconditional love. When there is a problem, let them understand that you are ready to reach into your own chest and hold out your heart.

EPISODIC TELEVISION

Actors in episodic television have the opportunity to rehearse their characters' spine and physical life sometimes for five or more years. This frees them, on the good shows, to have true ensemble work. On some long-running shows, actors fall into playing attitude, but on the good ones, they really play off each other.

A "hired gun" episodic director needs to have figured out from watching other episodes of the show what the characters' spines are. Then, if you know how to make a good script analysis and have enough practice at it that you can do it fast (you may get the script only a few days before shooting), and can focus on the events of the script, you may be able to give actors suggestions that will help make the dramatic moments more startling and real, and the comedy sharper and funnier.

Don't forget the guest artists and day players. In order to bring the guest actors into the ensemble, they need attention from the director and an opportunity to rehearse with the regulars. You can be inventive. An actor friend of mine who, as a guest artist on "Roseanne," was playing a poker-playing buddy of the John Goodman character, reported to me that the director had the actors in the poker scene spend a morning playing poker together.

Summary

A documentary director told me that when she is pre-interviewing documentary subjects, sometimes within a few minutes she can see what it is that the subject has to give. She doesn't ask them the important questions in the pre-interview; she waits for the camera. At other times she has to dig, spend a long time talking with the person, and ferret out the material that she wants to get on camera. This process is completely analogous to fiction rehearsal. It's not a formula or recipe. Sometimes you need a cup, sometimes a pinch.

Don't read off your script analysis notes while you are directing rehearsal. Your script analysis was preparation. In rehearsal you should work in the moment. The best thing that can happen in rehearsal is that *your ideas may change*. You may, with the actors, find richness and complexity or simplicity that you didn't see when you were working all alone on the script. You may adopt wholesale some good idea of an actor's.

So take chances. Make choices. You can always change your mind. If something doesn't work, don't think of the occasion as a failure. Think of it as an opportunity to move forward. Be yourself. Keep your sense of humor. Don't forget in rehearsal that there is nothing wrong with having fun. Don't talk just because you think you're supposed to. If you don't have something useful to say, don't say anything.

Rehearsal should end with questions, with things for the actors to work on while they are waiting to shoot the scene. If you end rehearsal with a performance, the actors may spend the time until the scene is shot (whether it is two weeks or fifteen minutes) trying to hold on to that performance. We don't want them to approach shooting trying to hold on to their rehearsal. We want them to approach shooting *ready to work*.

A summary of what to do if you have five days or more of rehearsal for a full-length script: Read each scene at ground zero, with no adjustments. Improvise on the facts of the scene, backstory, pre-scene beats, objectives, etc. Try the scene with several different through-lines, including at least one that you all agree is wrong. Work beat by beat to find movement and objects and create events. Watch for unrealized moments and solve them. Connect with the imagery of the script.

A summary of what to do if you have twenty to thirty minutes to rehearse a scene: After reading the lines together, seated, and relaxed so actors can connect, find some simple movement and objects. Look for false moments; solve them.

Shooting

"Once they're in that starting-gate position and ready to go, it's really a case of nurturing, and trusting, and letting them have a good time. I don't even necessarily mean, by a good time, laughing on the set — although we have a lot of that at times. But what I mean is being allowed to make mistakes, being allowed to try things. The key is that you all agree that you're making the same film." — **Martin Scorsese**

Shooting should be seen as an extension of rehearsal — that is, unpressured, exploratory, free — and better than rehearsal, a treat and an adventure. We want everybody's best energy and concentration. We want fresh, simple, honest, emotionally alive, moment-by-moment work. We don't want an actor who was great in rehearsal to start "acting with a capital A" as soon as the camera rolls. The big question is how to maintain a creative atmosphere in the midst of all the technical and financial pressures of shooting.

One thing you can do is find time with the actors that is not social time, and not exactly work time either, but magic time, where you recreate the magic circle that you had in rehearsal, and reestablish your relationship with them as a primary factor in their work. I can't tell you how to do this; each director's method is unique to his or her personality. Some are playful, some are parental; some are almost military in their concentration and authority, while some are so low-key that they seem almost "not there." Some take the "rope-a-dope" route, that is, affecting to have no control over the proceedings (when really they are on top of everything). Some are business-like;

some are sexually magnetic; some radiate a deeply intuitive, even spiritual sensibility.

Marlon Brando, in his autobiography, described an afternoon he spent on the set of "A Streetcar Named Desire," watching Elia Kazan direct a scene which he, Brando, was not in. Kazan was seated on the moving camera dolly, completely emotionally involved in the scene, mouthing the lines, moving his hands, mirroring the actors' expressions in his face. Kazan's *total immersion* gave him the information he needed to make changes for the next take.

Here are some thoughts on how to develop and maintain the attention and connection needed to recognize and guide actors to the spark, the sizzle, the sense of "something happening" — the *life* of a scene.

1) Say something to each actor before and after every take.

During shooting the actors are (we hope) at their most raw. Everything that comes in affects them. Let them feel your attention by speaking to them before and after every take. If possible, give them something new to work on.

Sidney Lumet, when asked in a 1993 interview for <u>Premier</u> how much he sets out to accomplish in rehearsal, said, "75%. I leave about 25% for the camera, for us to work on. Usually it's just enough for me to be able to give them fresh emotional approaches. One of the enemies of creating emotion is repetition, and if I can find something new that amounts to the same thing, that's a preferable way to work. That's what I save for camera. I don't use up all my variations."

What he means by his "variations" are all the ideas he has come up with in script analysis. This is why a full script analysis in which you come up with a number of different ideas and a number of different ways to express your ideas is so useful. You will have fresh ways to stimulate the structure you and the actors worked out in rehearsal, or ideas for ways to completely change the structure if it suddenly ceases to work. You will have a store of playable tidbits to give the actors after each take, to keep their attention forward, because if an actor's work on a scene is not getting better it is getting worse. It's like the love affair that the Woody Allen character in "Annie Hall" compares to a shark: if it doesn't move forward it dies.

Direction at this juncture has to do either with focusing the actors on some playable task (such as "I want you to keep track of every time you get her to smile"), offering them more freedom, or getting them to relax and simplify if their work has become intellectual or actorish. You may wish to talk to each actor separately. There needs to be a privacy to all communications between actor and director. It can be a "privacy in public": in other words, you create a privacy between the two of you even if other people, e.g., the crew or other actors, are within earshot; "privacy in public" is, in fact, an important skill for a director to develop. In some situations, it is preferable to speak to the actors together. You need to make such decisions thoughtfully.

If there is really nothing productive to say — if, for instance, there must be multiple takes unrelated to this actor's performance, or if a good actor is unaccountably struggling and you know he already knows there's a problem — then don't try to say something profound. But say or do something anyway — make eye contact at least — to keep things loose or focused or, in any case, connected. Let the actor know he is supported. Tell a joke, even, or a secret.

Whatever you do, when you communicate with the actors, don't communicate anxiety. Keep your attention forward. If there is a problem, get excited about finding the solution.

2) Don't ask for a re-performance.

If you love the take or rehearsal that just happened but need to go again, don't say, "Do it again just like that." Instead say things like: "We're starting to cook"; "It's working well, let's stay on this track"; "You're coming up with new things, it's getting richer." Keep the attention *forward*.

3) Don't let them be bad.

Watch for actors lapsing into set line readings. Watch for tension in actors' faces. Watch for overacting. Make sure the actors understand that you will protect their moment-by-moment reality. If you are relaxed and alert and if you put your total concentration on the actors, you will be able to detect false notes because they will cause your own attention to wander. Anytime an actor hits a false note, it needs to be addressed by his director.

Sometimes a layer can be added. Sometimes the whole structure of a scene will need to be reworked. Even on the set, with the minutes and dollars ticking away, it is important to approach these problems without tension or pressure, or else you won't be able to come up with creative solutions.

When you need a quick fix, consider an opposite. Even if it is patently "wrong," it can sometimes work on a dime because it has shock value. It can impart freshness because it liberates the actor from his line readings and from a sense of obligation.

If all else fails, ask them to let go of their preparation and be simpler, "just talk and listen."

4) Use the language of permission.

"It's okay to pick up that knife a little earlier," rather than "You didn't pick up the knife on the right line." Make all your direction and feedback to actors as positive as you can. Imagine yourself in the actors' shoes. Tell them what you like as well as what still needs work. If an actor is struggling, offer him time, even if there isn't any. Tension and strain are the enemies of our work. All problems must be embraced as creative obstacles.

5) Be honest.

Actors want to know if it's not good enough. If your relationship with the actors and your own personal charisma are strong enough, you can say things like "You seemed a little off"; "We're not quite there yet"; "It's in and out"; "Let's try something new, I'm not sure this is working anymore"; "It's gotten surface-y, the inner life is missing"; "The give-and-take is missing, I want you to play off each other." Or, "Tell me what I can do to help. Are you stuck? Tell me what's bothering you." "I'm afraid my direction was not very clear, but I know you can do better and I want more." Sometimes the shock value of plainly telling an actor, "It's not real enough" is exactly what's needed. By the way, "It's not real enough" is a better direction than "It's not angry enough."

6) Don't use result direction.

In rehearsal the actor has a chance to ponder a result direction and translate it into something playable, but on the set he doesn't have that time. In fact, you may not *want* the actors to mull over the direction. You may want to catch them off-guard and catapult them into the scene. This is best managed with verbs, facts, images, events, and physical life; that is, playable direction.

Result direction is inaccurate direction. Say an actor on the first take wrinkles her forehead in a way that you like, and the take must be repeated. If you ask her to repeat the wrinkle you're not actually asking for what you liked. What you liked was the listening, the interaction, or the emotional event resulting from her concentration on a verb, fact, image, etc.

If you must give result direction, you should say, "I know I'm giving you a result direction," or, "I know I'm giving you a result and you'll need to translate it into something playable." If you are reduced to line readings, say something like "Don't follow this as a line reading — I'm doing this badly." Having said all this, I need to admit that result direction sometimes works, but usually only once. Letting the actors in on the effect you want to produce may give you the take you need. But if it turns out there was dust on the camera lens, you will probably need to come up with a new, playable idea for the next take.

7) Make sure that the actors receive feedback from one source only.

Any complaints (or even compliments) that the writer, the producers, the editor, director of photography, script supervisor, crew, or other actors have about an actor should be told privately to you. Thank the person for their communication. Then determine what, if anything, should be done about it.

Make sure that you are the one who says "Cut." Explain to actors that even if they make a mistake you want them to keep going until you cut the scene. Don't let the D.P. or the technicians cut the scene. If your budget requires you to be conservative in your use of film stock, to the point that you want the camera crew to let you know before the end of the scene if in their opinion the take is no good, then arrange a signal with them ahead of time so they can discreetly let you know, and you can say, "Cut."

8) Just before the camera rolls...

When you say "Action," try not to have an unconscious subtext of "On your mark, get set...GO!" This unconscious "starting gun" subtext creates tension for actors and a feeling that "now it's time to start acting," which is not conducive to good moment-by-moment work. Say "Action" with a sense of allowing, letting go, permission, and connection.

A scene should always happen in the middle of something. You need to watch for an actor "winding up" to start a scene; it can be as simple to spot as an actor taking a deliberate breath when he hears "Action." There needs to be something going on before the scene starts: an awareness of the physical life of the scene; a relaxed freedom and presence in his own body; and a connection to the other actor(s).

You can allow or encourage actors to play their intentions silently, to improvise out loud the pre-scene beat, or to speak out loud the anchoring subtext of their intentions, even to say "hello" to each other just before the camera rolls. Shelley Winters reported in the May 1996 Interview that director Jane Campion, on the set of

"Portrait of a Lady," asked the actors to say out loud whatever they were thinking before every scene started. This works best if you encourage them to speak without censoring or deciding if their impulse is appropriate.

9) Stand next to the camera.

In order to see the tiny differences between a good performance and a mediocre performance, you need to watch the actors, not from the video monitor, but from next to the camera. Some directors can tell if the actors are listening without watching or without even hearing well: Akira Kurosawa has been nearly blind for some years; William Wyler lost most of his hearing during his World War II military service. It's the director's concentration that I am speaking about. The director cannot give his full concentration to the actors from behind the video monitor. The actors can feel your connection and concentration when you stand next to the camera; it feels very strange to an actor not to have the director there.

10) Give actors permission to fail.

"This won't be the last take. I'll definitely do another, no matter how this goes." "This might not work." Freedom to fail is one of the most powerful tools a director can use in relation to actors. Tension is the biggest enemy on the set. When either you or the actors are tense you (they) won't be able to see and hear, to think and choose in the moment. When an actor blows a take because he got the lines wrong, tell him you don't care if the lines are right. I have seen this work like a charm.

It can be very useful to shoot a scene two different ways. It takes the pressure off both ways. Two different endings were going to be shot of "Casablanca." After watching the first take, which happened to be the one in which Ilsa goes off with her husband, the filmmakers didn't bother to shoot the second ending in which she goes off with Rick. I think it's indisputable that the ending chosen was the right one for story reasons, but it also seems possible that the performances are enhanced by the freedom afforded the actors because they were not thinking of that take as "the end of the movie."

If you get pressure from an actor or a producer to shoot a scene his way instead of yours, think of the idea of shooting it both ways as an opportunity, not a burden. If you have not gotten what you want from an actor after many takes, you might try saying, "I'm printing that last one; I've got what I need. Let's do one more, just for fun. Let's do it different. Let's do it wrong."

11) Learn to match energies.

Communication can be difficult if your energy is much higher or much lower than that of the person you are trying to communicate with. Actors, especially on set, can be very volatile. If you feel an actor's energy is low, allow your energy to be just a little bit higher than his; that way he will be able to hear you, and, as a bonus, you may be able slowly to coax his energy up. If his energy is unnaturally high, allow yours to be high too, only just a little bit lower than his; it may calm him.

The worst thing about shooting for actors is all the waiting; it can be a terrible energy drain. Physical warm-ups that engage actors with each other — such as tossing a ball, playing tag, pillow-fighting, air-boxing, air-fencing — can enliven the actors and guide their concentration toward each other.

If the actors get upset with anything — a problem on the set or with a costar, a disagreement with your direction, even personal problems — gently encourage them to use these feelings as energy. All feelings are energy, and energy is a good thing. Turn problems into opportunities, not failures.

12) Marks, matching, overlapping.

The director's priority should be to have the scene go somewhere, to move, to take the audience somewhere, to create that shimmer that gives the sense of something happening. The actor's priority should be to be real in the moment, to connect to the emotional life of the script in the moment. The worst thing that can happen to an actor's performance is that he buys into a set way of saying his lines. Actors who stay alive and dynamic on every take and seem not to change the performance are actually moving, each time, a little deeper into the meaning of the script and into their own resources. This creative priority of *forward movement* (remember the word "emotion" has as its root the word "motion") should be honored.

When actors make technical considerations of matching shots and hitting marks their priority, their performance can become slick and technical. I think it is possible for directors and technicians to approach the problems of hitting marks, matching performances, and overlapping, more creatively than the conventional wisdom. Woody Allen, for example, practically never shoots coverage, and relies almost exclusively on long masters. One reason he does this is so the actors can be free to overlap dialogue. Sidney Lumet says that it is possible to cut dialogue even if the actors do overlap and don't make that little pause between each line — it's just harder.

13) Sex and Violence.

Talk about your plans for blocking and shooting a nude scene separately with each actor, then together with both actors. Walk through the choreography of the movements with clothes on, without emotional commitment. After that, a nude scene should be approached like any other scene in which emotional nakedness is required by the actors, in which the actors are required to create solitude in public. Not all nude scenes are alike. The characters still have backstory, problems, intention, a physical environment, etc.

All violence and stunts should be supervised by a professional in that field.

14) Know when to say "Print."

Sometimes (but not necessarily) an actor can give you help deciding whether a take is good enough to go with by letting you know whether it "feels" solid. An actor needs to not watch, not check and control his performance in order to connect with the subconscious. He may sometimes give a marvelous, unaffected, in-the-moment, unguarded performance and think the take was bad. He may feel destablized by unguarded moments or by direction that leads him to unguarded moments. Sometimes an actor will say "I don't feel it," or "I have to feel it." But when acting is really good, when it has simplicity and truth, it often doesn't feel like anything. When you find (through script analysis and rehearsal) the objective structure, a scene can work and the story get told, even if the actor is not "feeling it."

15) Concentrate.

I've said this already, but I'll say it again. The actors need your full concentration if you are going to be able to tell whether the emotional event of the scene was achieved. This does not mean that I think shot composition and framing are unimportant; but if you want the actors to fill up the screen, you need to put out energy toward that goal.

16) Be inventive.

If you are following your notes like a blueprint on the set because you are too frazzled and stressed out to make decisions and come up with new ideas in the moment, or if you are answering questions just to have something to say, without an idea you really believe in, or if you are trying to use the right jargon and not make a mistake, I can just about promise you that your movie will not come out the way you hoped.

Even if you become very adept at working with actors, there will still be times when you make mistakes and say the wrong thing to an actor. Your talent will lie in how you are able to recover from these mistakes and turn them into adventures and opportunities.

You don't have to shoot a scene the way you rehearsed it. You don't have to follow your script analysis notes. Preparation and rehearsal is not wasted, even if you don't follow it. A writer wouldn't think of publishing a first draft. Script analysis is a director's first draft. Rehearsal is the second draft. Take One is the third draft. Etc.

Prepare exhaustively. Concentrate. Then let it go. Don't aim. Have fun, even. It's the greatest job in the world.

EPILOGUE

"But to dig deeply into the way things are through people is what I like, and what the people who work with me like also. To find out the delicate balance between living and dying. I mean, I think that's the only subject there is." — **John Cassavetes**

There are daily exercises directors can do to keep developing their craft. Read. Go to museums. Watch documentaries. Daydream. Eavesdrop. Interview your friends and find out their life stories. Tell stories to children. Give good street directions. Become a person to whom people tell their secrets. Learn about the human heart and what makes people tick. Embrace your own memories.

Many directors need to listen more to actors. Directors who are shy need to get in there and grapple with actors. Most need to talk more cogently, stick to facts and images, and stay away from explanations. Study and prepare, then practice with actors, and trust that if you follow the rules you will start to have intuitions about what to do in new situations. Allow your imagination to flourish. Let the characters take on a life of their own, not just a movie life, but a life outside the borders of the camera, and be unafraid to involve your own feelings and insights about life.

You can't learn to direct from a book, so it's important to practice rehearsing with actors. If you cannot take a class in rehearsal techniques, then meet actors, find scripts, and work out on your own. Or direct theater; it's cheaper than film, and in some ways harder than directing film actors, so it's good preparation. Take chances, make mistakes, pick yourself up and try again!

All learning, like all rehearsal, is two steps forward, one step back (the only alternative scenario is *one* step forward, *two* steps back). I know I am taking a big chance when I give you my secrets in a book, where I can't respond to your questions and can't watch and monitor your use of them. Any of these ideas can misfire. Once a student reported to me that her first attempts to use the techniques from the Acting for Directors workshop were distressing. She said, "The tools you gave us were power tools; they were like a sharp-edged sword. When we used them incorrectly we cut ourselves." Find a way to practice the use of these tools in a safe situation. Make them your own.

Don't operate out of fear. Don't say, "I had no choice."

Most actors in their scene study classes, even if they don't ever perform on stage, work on scenes from plays. A director who has not read any plays seems virtually illiterate to a trained actor. Film has been around for a hundred years; before that the people who were producing plays would have been producing films if they'd had the technology. Even if you're not interested in theater, you should read plays and study the history of theater, especially Shakespeare. Shakespeare is extraordinarily cinematic. A serious filmmaker has a lot to learn from the study of Shakespeare, regardless of whether you have any interest in directing films based on Shakespearean plays.

Many directors direct one gender more effectively than the other. The gender many, though by no means all, directors have more trouble directing is the one that is not their own. Make a special effort to get inside the experience of the other gender. A useful book on this subject is Deborah Tannen's You Just Don't Understand.

All the actors' tools are useful for you: listening, choosing an objective, taking adjustments. In meetings you can use the actor's technique of putting all your concentration on the other person, in order to feel less self-conscious. It's also useful in meetings to be able to tell the difference between what someone is saying, and what they are actually doing (their subtext).

Think about your own objective. There may not be a right or wrong one, but be honest and specific with yourself about what it is; on some days a perfectly valid objective might be to get through the morning without collapsing. Directors can fall into unproductive unconscious objectives, such as "to not make a mistake," or "to protect my ego." Always put the work first.

What is your objective toward the audience? If you want them to see how smart you are, how sensitive, or to be a witness to your pain, if you want to indoctrinate them or punish them or ingratiate yourself slavishly to them, then you could be headed for trouble.

Think of your film as a story that you are telling to one person. Pick a specific person from your own life that you are telling this story for, and keep an empathic sense of that person's interest and connection to the story uppermost in every decision you make. By keeping your story personal and specific you will paradoxically stand the best chance of telling a story with universal appeal. But by keeping your focus on the specific person you are telling the story to, rather than on your own need to tell it, you can avoid self-indulgence.

Your creativity is not a bowl with a finite amount in it, which can be emptied, but a natural spring from an unseen, unknowable source. When you give of everything you have, you are priming the pump. If you're not sure what you're doing, don't hold back, be expressive anyway. A breakthrough is then possible. If you play it close to the vest, then you might not get into trouble, but you won't get anywhere else either.

You cannot decide what your vision is, or even to have one, but you can trust that you have a vision, and you can find it. The path to finding it is your search for the truest truth in every detail of your work. Challenge yourself. Aim high, because we are human and are going to fall short. If your aim is to "get by," then you won't. If your aim is to give your all and hold out for the truest truth, then, with a little luck, you might get by.

APPENDIX A
DIRECTING THE "NATURAL" ACTOR: CHILDREN AND NONPROFESSIONAL ACTORS

"Natural" actors are free, uninhibited, unafraid of what people think. They have something to offer; that is, they have some experience or understanding of life that fits them for the role. They open up when they are being looked at rather than shut down like most people who are not professional actors.

Whether or not they have had acting training, you want to find children whose imaginations are susceptible, who are bright and sensitive and free with their emotions. Audition the mothers as carefully as you audition the kids. Parents may drill the kids on their lines in the wrong way, making them learn line readings. Children learn lines very quickly, so often you don't need to give them the lines in any case until the last minute.

Improv is very useful when casting children, to find out if they can get to the places you need them to go via imaginative suggestions. Improv is useful in rehearsal, too. You want to tap into their imaginations, because that is their strength. You don't have to trick them; you don't have to say, "Your mother is sick." You can say, "Your mother is fine, but can you imagine what it would be like if your mother was sick?"

You need to go to where they are. You need to be able to match energies with them. If your energy is much higher or much lower than theirs is, you won't be able to communicate. You can talk to them more freely about feelings than you can talk to adult actors, because they haven't intellectualized their feelings yet (unless they are taking acting lessons!).

Jafar Panahi, director of "The White Balloon," described in an interview how he worked with seven-year-old Aida Mohammakhani: "I knew immediately Aida could play this character, yet on the second day of shooting I decided to test her. I forbade her to do something and made it impossible for her not to do it; then I scolded her and she started to cry. I said to her, 'See how easy it is for me to make you cry? But I don't want to do it that way because it makes you unhappy, and I want us to have another kind of relationship. I suggest we look into each other's eyes every time you have to cry in the film, and when I start to cry, you cry.' She didn't believe it would work, but the first few times we looked at each other we cried together, and then she cried alone."

I can't imagine a better method than that for directing a child.

Preteens and teenagers are on the borderline between childhood and adulthood. Their free imaginations can still be captured, but they can also get self-conscious and mannered. A director needs to obtain their trust and respect on a personal level in order to get their most simple and truthful performance.

To get the best from non-professional actors, make sure that what you ask them to do is close to who they are and that it is simple. Tell them to talk to the other person the way they would in real life. You can use a few simple action verbs and adjustments: "Scold her the way you would scold your own kids." "Tease him the way you tease your husband when he falls asleep in front of the TV." "Really look at his face and in your mind decide whether you would take a check from this man." Don't forget, non-professionals don't know about hitting marks or not overlapping or finding their light.

APPENDIX B
COMEDY

What a person finds funny is of course a very personal thing, but there are some principles of comedy that I think you will find useful. These principles apply to the four ways that a movie or show can be funny: the situation, the lines, the characters, and/or the physical business may be funny.

ALWAYS PLAY COMEDY FOR REAL

Comedy, like drama, is best achieved when actors concern themselves with moment-by-moment reality rather than the effect. If the situation is funny, playing it straight, connecting with it as simply and honestly as possible, makes it funnier. Under the best humor is often real pain. The problems of Ralph Kramden (Jackie Gleason on "The Honeymooners") were always desperately serious.

If the lines are funny, they come out funnier when the intention is more important than the lines. If the actor's subtext is "look how funny this line is," the fun is gone.

Sometimes after a bit of physical business gets a laugh, the actor is tempted to milk it to get the laugh next time, to do the business *for its own sake*. This means it is no longer coming out of the situation. It has become schtick. It now takes the audience out of the story, and is, finally, not as funny. If, in rehearsal, a funny bit comes out of a character using toilet paper to blow her nose, when the actor has to repeat the activity for the camera, she has to be sure that the reason she is using the toilet paper is *to blow her nose*, not to make the audience laugh.

Many actors train in "comedy improv" classes or "sketch comedy" classes, where they develop a number of "characters" that they can "do" in many different imaginary situations. Actors who "do characters" should never *play character*. What makes the good character actors good is that they can create the physical and behavioral adjustments of a wacky character, and still put their attention on playing the reality.

It can happen that a director has to step in to let an actor know he has crossed the line into shtick. Paul Newman recalled getting this direction from Martin Scorsese during rehearsal for "The Color of Money": "Don't try to be funny."

LISTENING

When actors listen, they are getting out of the way of the lines. Then, if the lines are funny, the audience can hear them and get the joke. Comedy works best when there is ensemble playing. The actors play off each other — a ping-pong effect. I think it is no accident that in the better written comedies, there is more listening. First of all, superior actors are drawn to superior writing. And second, the actors trust the writing and know that if they play off each other and don't push, they will get their laughs.

James Burrows said in a <u>Los Angeles Times</u> interview of his years of directing the television show "Taxi" that his role was "more of a wrangler than anything else. There were a lot of egos on that show. I was really a wrangler to get the ensemble nature. That was my job — check your ego at the door." What this means is that he got the actors to listen to each other. I believe that his ability to get actors to behave as an ensemble, to listen, to give the scene to each other instead of trying to prove how funny they are, is central to his phenomenal success in directing television comedy.

SENSORY LIFE

Physical comedy needs to be rooted sensorially, not indicated. This means that the actor doesn't demonstrate his wide-eyed wonder; he creates an image that really affects him, or he surrenders to the physical sensations in his eyes; perhaps both.

FREEDOM, RISK, AND IMAGINATIVE PLAY

True comic invention is a risky business, requiring headlong, uncensored access to the subconscious — with a light touch. Clowning is in my opinion a very noble profession. Great comedic actors expose the most chaotic reaches of their imaginations and in some small way make the world safe for the rest of us. The comedic actor must not be watching himself, or paying attention to the effect he is having on the audience. Watching to make sure the right effect is created is the director's job. The comedic director must be a safety net for the actors, able to tell whether the work is good and give them permission to risk, to fail, to commit.

It can also help if the director knows a few comic techniques.

SETTING UP GAGS

Every joke must be set up. A "straight line" sets up the situation; the punch line or "payoff" delivers the twist. In vaudeville the roles of "straight man" and "funny man" were very clearly defined. When George Burns first teamed up with Gracie Allen, he thought of himself as the funny man and gave her the straight lines; soon he noticed that she was getting more laughs than he, so they switched roles and, with his simple questions ("What did you do today, Gracie?") he became the best known "straight man" in the business. Dan Ackroyd, in a Daily Variety interview for the issue commemorating George Burns's hundredth birthday, described himself as the "straight man" to John Belushi and Bill Murray on the early days of "Saturday Night Live." The character played by Jessica Lange was the "straight man" of the movie "Tootsie." Playing "straight" does not make an actor subsidiary to the "funny" actors, or mean that he never gets laughs. The early years of "Seinfeld" positioned Jerry as the "straight" center of the show, as was Mary Tyler Moore of her show; the zanier "second banana" characters bounced the gags off the more "normal" lead characters. Sometimes a single character performs both duties: paying off one gag and setting up the next one with the same line.

Some jokes are wordless. For example, a scene in "Ace Ventura: Pet Detective" depicts Ace's clandestine search for medical records in a dark storeroom. This gag is set up in two stages. Stage one of the setup (the serious situation) is that we know Ace needs to be very, very quiet. In stage two, the camera watches his stealthy entrance into the storeroom from low inside the room — behind a length of bubble wrap piled on the floor. The loud popping that issues from his accidental step on the bubble wrap is the punch line — the first punch line, that is. The popping becomes the setup for the next gag: Ace, alerted to danger, struggles to keep his feet in the air to prevent further popping. Gravity, of course, defeats him, and more and more popping ensues. This is an elaborate gag that continues to "pay off" until the last bubble is popped. But even a "cheaper" gag such as a character unexpectedly banging his head on a rafter needs to be set up by establishing his reason to leave the room.

TIMING

Timing simply means knowing how long to wait before delivering a line. Sometimes it is funnier to pause; sometimes it is funnier not to pause. Timing involves a relationship to the audience, and good instincts for timing are rarely perfected without exposure to live audiences, either through theater training or through experience in a live comedy troupe or as a stand-up comedian.

LOUDER, FASTER, FUNNIER

Comedy needs comic energy. This doesn't mean every line must be shouted, but often comedy depends on the actors "topping" each other. On the other hand, sometimes the punch line is delivered with a sudden drop in energy — the actor "comes in under."

GIVING THE AUDIENCE PERMISSION TO LAUGH

This is a subtle, mysterious thing that comic actors have to feel in their bones. It has something to do with timing, comic energy, and risk, and it means that the actors *let the audience in*, allowing them to laugh. It's a very fine line, because the actor has to let the audience in without playing the effect.

OPPOSITES

Surprise and juxtaposition are the heart and soul of comedy. Playing an intention that is opposite to the apparent meaning of a line is a common comic technique.

COMIC ADJUSTMENTS

If a character is carrying on about losing his pack of chewing gum *as if* he has lost an envelope containing a thousand dollars, the inappropriate adjustment might be funny.

ACTION VERBS

Playing a simple verb (intention) full out for as long as it will hold and making crisp, full transitions can aid in setting up or delivering gags.

RISING OR FALLING INFLECTIONS

This technique is better phrased as an adjustment. Using the rising inflection technique, for instance, means that every line is spoken *as if* it is a question.

It's hard for actors to deeply trust a comedy director unless she knows how to give actors feedback and advice on matters of comedy technique: for example, whether it is likely that there will be a bigger laugh if the actor holds a microsecond longer before giving the punch line; when it might be better to come in "under" instead of topping; when a rising inflection might just polish a gag. You also need a good imagination to see opposites and think up comic adjustments.

But the techniques and gadgetry of comedy should always be in service of the central situation of the *story*. The comedic director's primary tasks are to put the story ahead of the cheap trick, to turn the actors into an ensemble that keeps hitting the ball back to each other, and to maintain a light touch and a free atmosphere where imaginative play is respected. And finally...

Everything Is Everything

The director is the guardian of the integrity of a film or television show. I recommend that as you develop your aesthetic judgment, you look always for the humor in a dramatic script, and the pain that is underneath comedy.

APPENDIX C

I. SHORT LIST OF ACTION VERBS
(WITH ANCHORING SUBTEXTS)

demand	"I demand it."
convince	"I think you should..."
persuade	"Look at it this way..."
encourage	"I know you can do it."
incite	"To the barricades." "I have a dream."
brag	something you are sincerely proud of
complain	"It's not fair."
beg/plead	"Please help me."
cajole	"Come on, sweetie..."
coax	"Are you sure you wouldn't like to..."
charm/flatter/compliment	"You're wonderful." "You'd be very good at..."
soothe	"Everything will be all right, nothing to worry about."
tease/tickle	"I think you're cute."
flirt	"Come over here and sit next to me."

seduce	"I'm very attracted to you."
dazzle	"Wait til you see…"
challenge	"Are you man enough?" "I dare you." "I bet you can't."
accuse	"You lied to me." "I saw you do it."
nail	"I know your game." "I see right through you."
goad	"You wanna fight?"
warn	"I'm warning you."
punish	"You're a bad person." "I'm sick of you."
ridicule	make fun of clothing, etc.
belittle	"You are worthless, nothing, not important."
knife	"You hurt me." "I want you to suffer."
scrutinize	count wrinkles, notice details of dress and person
pry	ask questions which are none of your business, especially re: money, sex
stalk	"I'm watching you."

II. Sample Simple Objectives

I want you to laugh.

I want you to cry.

I want you to put your arms around me.

I want you to take care of me.

I want you to wait on me.

I want you to feel sorry for me.

I want you to kneel down in front of me.

I want you to hit me.

I want you to leave the room.

I want you to kiss me (make love to me).

I want you to play with me.

Find out how much you know about me.

Find out if you are telling the truth.

III. More Action Verbs

accuse	belittle	guide
blame	discourage	maneuver
punish	deflate	massage
shame	dampen	cajole
scold	demean	coax
reprimand	deny	sell
condemn	disparage	nag
berate	sneer at	pout at
attack	vilify	complain to
menace	undermine	gripe at
badger	discourage	whine at
browbeat	reprove	wheedle
bully	criticize	steer
intimidate	taunt	goad
knife	jeer at	bait
coerce	stalk	prod
pressure	nail	provoke
persecute	pounce on	dare
rag on	confront	get his goat
crush	test	engage
rape	demand	one-up
castrate	order	pester
destroy	summon	pry
hammer	direct	quiz
suppress	instruct	interrogate
torment	lecture	insinuate
confine	teach	inspect
weigh down	preach	calculate
poison	brag	diagnose
warn	upstage	categorize
admonish	bluff	encourage
threaten	plead	empower
harangue	beg	boost
remind	entreat	bolster
ridicule	convince	build up
mock	persuade	crown

accept	string along	battle
approve	beguile	grapple with
affirm	wean from	startle
flatter	guard against	shake up
compliment	shut out	expose
salute	defend against	interfere with
applaud	revolt against	repulse
praise	renounce	tease
greet	challenge	tickle
bless	defy	needle
surrender to	incite	play with
forgive	exhort	please
rescue	kindle	cheer
heal	galvanize	dote upon
confide in	enflame	relish
attend to	infuse	savor
entrust	inform	nuzzle
soothe	explain to	entertain
caress	clarify for	clown
cherish	justify self to	dandle
hold	expound to	amuse
touch	reason with	divert
grieve	negotiate with	lighten
lull	accommodate	humor
pamper	concede to	jolly
pacify	capitulate to	celebrate
appease	tolerate	dazzle
placate	overwhelm	electrify
subdue	take care of	arouse
enfold	reassure	awaken
smother	appreciate	shock
suffocate	apologize	ogle
push away	pick a fight with	hypnotize
dodge	fuss at	lure
deflect	quibble with	tantalize
fence	contradict	seduce
fake out	negate	flirt

entice
woo
fondle
spoil
undress
reach for
make love
reminisce
dream
speculate

FILMOGRAPHY

Films listed by title, director, and year of release, in the order mentioned in the book.

Batman Returns, Tim Burton, 1992
Never Say Never Again, Irvin Kershner, 1983
Unforgiven, Clint Eastwood, 1992
Blue Sky, Tony Richardson, 1994
Deception, Irving Rapper, 1946
When Harry Met Sally, Rob Reiner, 1989
On the Waterfront, Elia Kazan, 1954
The Fugitive Kind, Sidney Lumet, 1959
Patch of Blue, Guy Green, 1965
The Last Picture Show, Peter Bogdanovich, 1971
Leaving Las Vegas, Mike Figgis, 1995
Red, Krzysztof Kieslowski, 1995
Get Shorty, Barry Sonnenfeld, 1995
Pretty Woman, Garry Marshall, 1990
Dead Man Walking, Tim Robbins, 1995
Father of the Bride, Vincente Minnelli, 1950
Network, Sidney Lumet, 1976
Colors, Dennis Hopper, 1988
Rudy, David Anspaugh, 1993
Schindler's List, Steven Spielberg, 1993
The Godfather, Francis Ford Coppola, 1972
Godfather II, Francis Ford Coppola, 1974
Last Tango in Paris, Bernardo Bertolucci, 1973
Last of the Mohicans, Michael Mann, 1992
Hamlet, Franco Zeffirelli, 1990
Cry, the Beloved Country, Darrell Roodt, 1995

Howards End, James Ivory, 1992
Driving Miss Daisy, Bruce Beresford, 1989
The Postman, Michael Radford, 1995
Toy Story, John Lasseter, 1995
An Affair to Remember, Leo McCarey, 1957
A Steetcar Named Desire, Elia Kazan, 1951
Wings of Desire, Wim Wenders, 1988
Crimes of the Heart, Bruce Beresford, 1986
Shawshank Redemption, Frank Darabont, 1994
Little Big Man, Arthur Penn, 1970
Ed Wood, Tim Burton, 1994
My Left Foot, Jim Sheridan, 1989
Starman, John Carpenter, 1984
The Days of Wine and Roses, Blake Edwards, 1962
Kramer vs. Kramer, Robert Benton, 1979
The Autobiography of Miss Jane Pitman, John Korty, 1974
Lolita, Stanley Kubrick, 1962
The Waterdance, Neal Jimenez and Michael Steinberg, 1992
Platoon, Oliver Stone, 1986
Copycat, Jon Amiel, 1995
Marathon Man, John Schlesinger, 1976
Nixon, Oliver Stone, 1995
The Silence of the Lambs, Jonathan Demme, 1991
Remains of the Day, James Ivory, 1993
Autumn Sonata, Ingmar Bergman, 1978
Fatal Attraction, Adrian Lyne, 1987
Bridges of Madison County, Clint Eastwood, 1995
Forrest Gump, Robert Zemekis, 1994
The Dumbwaiter, Robert Altman, 1987
Woman Under the Influence, John Cassavetes, 1974
Smoke, Wayne Wang, 1995
Four Weddings and a Funeral, Mike Newell, 1994
Tootsie, Sydney Pollack, 1982
Don Juan De Marco, Jeremy Leven, 1995
One Flew Over the Cuckoo's Nest, Milos Foreman, 1975
Wanda, Barbara Loden, 1971
Chinatown, Roman Polanski, 1974
I Never Sang for My Father, Gilbert Cates, 1970

Dog Day Afternoon, Sidney Lumet, 1975
Six Degrees of Separation, Fred Schepisi, 1993
Born Yesterday, George Cukor, 1950
E.T., Steven Spielberg, 1982
Sense and Sensibility, Ang Lee, 1995
Casablanca, Michael Curtiz, 1942
Midnight Cowboy, John Schlesinger, 1969
The Graduate, Mike Nichols, 1967
Annie Hall, Woody Allen, 1977
The White Balloon, Jafar Panahi, 1995
The Color of Money, Martin Scorsese, 1986
Ace Ventura: Pet Detective, Tom Shadyac, 1994
Twister, Jan De Bont, 1996
Devil in a Blue Dress, Carl Franklin, 1995

BIBLIOGRAPHY

Adler, Stella, <u>The Technique of Acting</u>, Bantam Books, 1988

Ball, William, <u>A Sense of Direction</u>, Drama Book Publishers, 1984

Bates, Brian, <u>The Way of the Actor</u>, Shambhala Publications, Inc., 1987

Bergman, Ingmar, <u>Images</u> , Arcade Publishing, 1994

Brando, Marlon, with Robert Lindsey, <u>Brando: Songs My Mother Taught Me</u>, Random House, 1994

Broadley, Margaret, <u>Your Natural Gifts</u>, EPM Publications, 1972

Clurman, Harold, <u>On Directing</u>, Macmillan Publishing, 1972

Clurman, Harold, <u>The Fervent Years: The Group Theatre and the Thirties</u>, Da Capo Press, 1975

Cole, Toby, and Helen Krich Chinoy, eds., <u>Actors on Acting</u>, Crown Publishers, 1970

Cole, Toby, and Helen Krich Chinoy, eds., <u>Directors on Directing: A Source Book of the Modern Theater</u>, Bobbs-Merrill Educational Publishing, 1976

Funke, Lewis, and John E. Booth, eds., <u>Actors Talk About Acting</u>, Avon Books, 1961

Grandin, Temple, <u>Thinking in Pictures: and Other Reports from My Life with Autism</u>, Doubleday, 1995

Hagen, Uta, <u>Respect for Acting</u>, MacMillan Publishing Co., Inc. New York, 1973

Johnstone, Keith, <u>Impro</u>, Routledge/Theatre Arts Books, 1979

Katz, Steven D., <u>Film Directing Shot by Shot: Visualizing from Concept to Screen</u>, Michael Wiese Productions, 1991

Kazan, Elia, <u>Kazan: A Life</u>, Alfred A. Knopf, 1988

Leonard, George Burr, <u>Mastery: The Keys to Long Term Success and Fulfillment</u>, Dutton, 1991

Lumet, Sidney, <u>Making Movies</u>, Alfred A. Knopf, 1995

Mamet, David, <u>On Directing Film</u>, Penguin Books, 1991

Meisner, Sanford, and Dennis Longwell, <u>Sanford Meisner on Acting</u>, Vintage Books, 1987

Redgrave, Vanessa, <u>An Autobiography</u>, Random House, 1991

Reich, Wilhelm, <u>Character Analysis</u>, Touchstone, 1945

Ross, Lillian, <u>Player</u>, Simon, 1962

Ross, Lillian, <u>Picture</u>, Doubleday, 1993

Shepard, Sam, <u>Cruising Paradise</u>, Knopf, 1996

Sherman, Eric, <u>Directing the Film: Film Directors on their Art</u>, Acrobat Books, 1976

Shurtleff, Michael, <u>Audition</u>, Walker Publishing Company, 1978

Stanislavski, Constantin, <u>An Actor Prepares</u>, Theatre Arts Books, 1936

Stanislavski, Constantin, <u>My Life in Art</u>, Theatre Arts Books, 1948

Stanislavski, Constantin, <u>Building a Character</u>, Methuen/Theatre Arts Books, 1949

Stanislavski, Constantin, <u>Creating a Role</u>, Routledge/Theatre Arts Books, 1961

Strasberg, Lee, <u>A Dream of Passion: The Development of The Method</u>, Plume, 1987

Tannen, Deborah, <u>You Just Don't Understand</u>, Morrow, 1990

Thompson, Emma, <u>The Sense and Sensibility Screenplay and Diaries</u>, Newmarket Press, 1995

Ueland, Brenda, <u>If You Want to Write</u>, Graywolf Press, 1987

FURTHER ACKNOWLEDGMENTS

The Paul Mazursky and Ralph Nelson quotes from Chapter II, the Jean Renoir and Jack Nicholson quotes from Chapter IV, and the John Cassavetes quote in the Epilogue were all found in <u>Directing the Film: Film Directors on Their Art</u>, by Eric Sherman for the American Film Institute. The Adrian Lyne quote from Chapter II is from <u>Film Directors on Directing</u>, by John Andrew Gallagher. The Elia Kazan quote that begins Chapter II is from a pamphlet which was given to me by Paul Gray.

The following quotes were all found in articles in the <u>Los Angeles Times</u>: Helen Mirren, Diane Keaton in Chapter II; Dennis Franz, Joan Allen, Garry Marshall in Chapter III; Bryan Singer in Chapter IV; Emma Thompson in Chapter VII; Jafar Panahi in Appendix A; James Burrows in Appendix B.

The Ralph Fiennes quotes in Chapters II and IV were from a 1995 <u>Vanity Fair</u> article. The Morgan Freeman quote in Chapter II is from <u>Los Angeles View</u>.

The Vanessa Redgrave quotes in Chapters III and VI are from her <u>Autobiography</u>. The Liv Ullman quote in Chapter VI was found in <u>The Way of the Actor</u>, by Brian Bates.

The Harvey Keitel quote in Chapter IX is from <u>Daily Variety</u>, as are the Anthony Hopkins quote in Chapter VII, the Martin Scorsese quote in Chapter X, and the Don Cheadle quote in Chapter IX.

Information about how Anthony Hopkins worked on "Nixon" is from the Orange County Register and The New Yorker.

All the anecdotes and quotes attributed to Sally Field, Paul Newman, Glenn Close, Sydney Pollack and Holly Hunter are from their appearances on the Bravo Channel series, "Inside the Actors Studio," except for the "Hamlet" anecdote from Chapter IV, which I found in the Los Angeles Times. The Betty Thomas anecdote in Chapter IX is from DGA Magazine.

The play with the ironed shirts images from Chapter IV was "Mrs. Cage," which was written and directed by Nancy Barr, and produced by Mado Most in 1990.

ABOUT THE AUTHOR

Judith Weston lives in Los Angeles, where she conducts classes and workshops in the studio she runs with her husband, John Hoskins. For directors, her workshops include Acting for Directors, and advanced workshops in Script Analysis and Rehearsal Techniques. For actors, she teaches ongoing classes in scene study, technique, improvisation, cold reading, and Shakespeare. For actors and directors together, she teaches the Actor-Director Laboratory.

Photo by Susan Schader

She consults privately for directors in pre-production, for projects including studio and independent films as well as television, to help them clarify their directing choices and prepare for casting and rehearsal.

In addition to her Los Angeles workshops for directors and actors, she travels with these workshops, and has taught them in Europe, Canada, and other cities of the US, including New York, San Francisco, and Seattle.

Her first book, *Directing Actors: Creating Memorable Performances for Film and Television*, is widely read by directors, writers, and actors. It has been translated into German, Japanese, Finnish, Korean, and Spanish.

If you wish to study or consult with Judith, or to arrange an on-site workshop, please consult the website, or call or write for more information:

Judith Weston Acting Studio
310 392-2444
www.judithweston.com
judyweston@aol.com

THE WRITER'S JOURNEY – 3RD EDITION
MYTHIC STRUCTURE FOR WRITERS

CHRISTOPHER VOGLER

BEST SELLER
OVER 180,000 COPIES SOLD!

See why this book has become an international best seller and a true classic. *The Writer's Journey* explores the powerful relationship between mythology and storytelling in a clear, concise style that's made it required reading for movie executives, screenwriters, playwrights, scholars, and fans of pop culture all over the world.

Both fiction and nonfiction writers will discover a set of useful myth-inspired storytelling paradigms (i.e., "The Hero's Journey") and step-by-step guidelines to plot and character development. Based on the work of Joseph Campbell, *The Writer's Journey* is a must for all writers interested in further developing their craft.

The updated and revised third edition provides new insights and observations from Vogler's ongoing work on mythology's influence on stories, movies, and man himself.

"This book is like having the smartest person in the story meeting come home with you and whisper what to do in your ear as you write a screenplay. Insight for insight, step for step, Chris Vogler takes us through the process of connecting theme to story and making a script come alive."
> – Lynda Obst, Producer, *Sleepless in Seattle*, *How to Lose a Guy in 10 Days*;
>   Author, *Hello, He Lied*

"This is a book about the stories we write, and perhaps more importantly, the stories we live. It is the most influential work I have yet encountered on the art, nature, and the very purpose of storytelling."
> – Bruce Joel Rubin, Screenwriter, *Stuart Little 2*, *Deep Impact*,
>   *Ghost*, *Jacob's Ladder*

CHRISTOPHER VOGLER is a veteran story consultant for major Hollywood film companies and a respected teacher of filmmakers and writers around the globe. He has influenced the stories of movies from *The Lion King* to *Fight Club* to *The Thin Red Line* and most recently wrote the first installment of *Ravenskull*, a Japanese-style manga or graphic novel. He is the executive producer of the feature film *P.S. Your Cat is Dead* and writer of the animated feature *Jester Till*.

$26.95 · 448 PAGES · ORDER NUMBER 76RLS · ISBN: 9781932907360

SETTING UP YOUR SHOTS, SECOND EDITION

GREAT CAMERA MOVES EVERY FILMMAKER SHOULD KNOW

JEREMY VINEYARD

This is the 2nd edition of one of the most successful filmmaking books in history, with sales of over 50,000 copies. Using examples from over 300 popular films, Vineyard provides detailed examples of more than 150 camera setups, angles, and moves which every filmmaker must know — presented in an easy-to-use "wide screen format." This book is the "Swiss Army Knife" that belongs in every filmmakers tool kit.

This new and revised 2nd edition of *Setting Up Your Shots* references over 200 new films and 25 additional filmmaking techniques.

This book gives the filmmaker a quick and easy "shot list" that he or she can use on the set to communicate with their crew.

The Shot List includes: Whip Pan, Reverse, Tilt, Helicopter Shot, Rack Focus, and much more.

"This is a film school in its own right and a valuable and worthy contribution to every filmmaker's shelf. Well done, Vineyard and Cruz!"
— Darrelyn Gunzburg, "For The Love Of It" Panel, *www.ForTheLoveOfIt.com*

"Perfect for any film enthusiast looking for the secrets behind creating film... It is a great addition to any collection for students and film pros alike....." Because of its simplicity of design and straight forward storyboards, this book is destined to be mandatory reading at films schools throughout the world."
— Ross Otterman, *Directed By* Magazine

"Setting Up Your Shots is a great book for defining the shots of today. The storyboard examples on every page make it an valuable reference book for directors and DP's alike! Great learning tool. Should be a boon for writers who want to choose the most effective shot and clearly show it in their boards for the maximum impact."
— Paul Clatworthy, Creator, StoryBoard Artist and StoryBoard Quick Software

JEREMY VINEYARD is currently developing an independent feature entitled "Concrete Road" with Keith David (*The Thing, Platoon*) and is working on his first novel, a modern epic.

$22.95 · 160 PAGES · ORDER NUMBER 84RLS · ISBN: 9781932907421

FROM WORD TO IMAGE
STORYBOARDING AND THE FILMMAKING PROCESS

MARCIE BEGLEITER

BEST SELLER

For over a decade, Marcie Begleiter's acclaimed seminars and workshops have made visual communication accessible to filmmakers and all artists involved in visual storytelling. Whether you're a director, screenwriter, producer, editor, or storyboard artist, the ability to tell stories with images is essential to your craft. In this comprehensive book, Begleiter offers the tools to help both word- and image-oriented artists learn how to develop and sharpen their visual storytelling skills via storyboarding.

Readers are taken on a step-by-step journey into the pre-visualization process, including breaking down the script, using overhead diagrams to block out shots, and creating usable drawings for film frames that collaborators can easily understand. The book also includes discussions of compositional strategies, perspective, and figure notation as well as practical information on getting gigs, working on location, collaborating with other crew members, and much more.

"From Word to Image *examines the how-to's of storyboard art, and is full of rich film history. It demystifies an aspect of filmmaking that benefits everyone involved — from directors, to cinematographers, to production designers.*"
— Joe Petricca, Vice Dean, American Film Institute

"*Begleiter's process is a visual and organizational assist to any filmmaker trying to shift from story in words to story in moving image.*"
— Joan Tewkesbury, Screenwriter, Nashville; Director, Felicity

"From Word to Image *delivers a clear explanation of the tools available to help a director tell his story visually, effectively, and efficiently — it could be subtitled 'A Director Prepares.'*"
— Bruce Bilson, Emmy Award-Winning Director
of over 350 television episodes

MARCIE BEGLEITER is a filmmaker and educator who specializes in pre-visualization. She is the owner of Filmboards, whose clients include Paramount, New Line, HBO, ABC, and Lightspan Interactive.

$26.95 | 224 PAGES | ORDER # 45RLS | ISBN: 0-941188-28-0

THE MYTH OF MWP

In a dark time, a light bringer came along, leading the curious and the frustrated to clarity and empowerment. It took the well-guarded secrets out of the hands of the few and made them available to all. It spread a spirit of openness and creative freedom, and built a storehouse of knowledge dedicated to the betterment of the arts.

The essence of the Michael Wiese Productions (MWP) is empowering people who have the burning desire to express themselves creatively. We help them realize their dreams by putting the tools in their hands. We demystify the sometimes secretive worlds of screenwriting, directing, acting, producing, film financing, and other media crafts.

By doing so, we hope to bring forth a realization of 'conscious media' which we define as being positively charged, emphasizing hope and affirming positive values like trust, cooperation, self-empowerment, freedom, and love. Grounded in the deep roots of myth, it aims to be healing both for those who make the art and those who encounter it. It hopes to be transformative for people, opening doors to new possibilities and pulling back veils to reveal hidden worlds.

MWP has built a storehouse of knowledge unequaled in the world, for no other publisher has so many titles on the media arts. Please visit www.mwp.com where you will find many free resources and a 25% discount on our books. Sign up and become part of the wider creative community!

Onward and upward,

Michael Wiese
Publisher/Filmmaker